The Hillary Factor

The Hillary Factor

The Story of America's First Lady

by Rex Nelson
with Philip Martin

Gallen Publishing Group
New York

First Gallen Publishing Group edition 1993

Richard Gallen & Company, Inc.
260 Fifth Avenue
New York, NY 10001

To Melissa and Austin for putting up with my long absences during the completion of this project. May we have more time to spend together in the years to come.
—Rex Nelson

For Karen, Bork, Coal and Tsingtao.
—Philip Martin

ACKNOWLEDGMENTS

Thanks first to David Gallen for seeking me out prior to the 1992 election to do this project.

It would not have been possible without the support of *Arkansas Democrat-Gazette* Executive Editor Griffin Smith jr, Managing Editor Bob Lutgen and City Editor Ray Hobbs. They allowed me use of the newspaper's files, offices and computer system to work on this book. They also had confidence that I could both complete the book on time and carry out my duties at the newspaper. for that confidence I always will be indebted to them.

My thanks also go to the library staff at the *Democrat-Gazette* who gave me full use of the library twenty-four hours per day. Without their cooperation the project would have been impossible to complete.

Credit is especially due to the many fine reporters currently at the *Democrat-Gazette,* the former reporters at the *Arkansas Democrat* and the former reporters at the *Arkansas Gazette.* They chronicled Hillary Rodham Clinton's activities in Arkansas for almost two decades, a period when most Americans did not know who she was.

Additional thanks go to the fine reporters nationally who followed her during the 1992 presidential campaign and have reported on her activities since she became first lady on January 20, 1993. I read thousands of inches of their copy, and it provided important fodder for this book.

Thanks also to those in Arkansas, Washington, D.C., and elsewhere who consented to interviews. They are too numerous to mention, but all were gracious in providing their time and their insights.

—Rex Nelson

Philip Martin would like to thank Karen Knutson, Bill Jones, Ed Gray, Matt Jones, Griffin Smith jr, and the staff of the *Arkansas Democrat-Gazette.*

CONTENTS

Introduction
An Unconventional Woman

"A woman preaching is like a dog walking on his hind legs. It is not done well; but you are surprised to find it done at all."
—Samuel Johnson

"When a man gets up to speak, people listen, then look. When a woman gets up, people look; then if they like what they see, they listen."

—Pauline Frederick

In the last days of September 1993, Hillary Rodham Clinton carried a small briefcase into the high-ceilinged Senate Caucus room, from which both John and Robert Kennedy had launched their presidential campaigns and where the Watergate hearings were held, and became, as the press was forever pointing out, only the third first lady in history to testify before Congress, after Eleanor Roosevelt and Rosalynn Carter.

Hillary sat alone at the witness table, a teapot at her elbow, as members of various congressional committees asked complex and intricate questions about the Clinton administration's health-care proposal. Some members of the media seemed unduly impressed that a first lady could command detailed information and answer questions by the hour from senators, with poise and—the stories stressed this—without notes. A comparable performance from, say, a Robert Reich or an Ira Magaziner might hardly have been deemed newsworthy, but Hillary's display of competence was met with a kind of fawning admiration on the part of reporters who seemed to be just discovering the woman's remarkable faculties.

Women have often found occasional advantages in the sexism of male-dominated institutions; surely Hillary did not mind when the headlines gushed that she had, with her display of intelligence and preparedness, "captivated" lawmakers. She smiled, but did not protest when Illinois Representative Dan Rostenkowski suggested Bill Clinton might soon be known chiefly as "Hillary's husband." Throughout the hearings, serious men turned giddy in Hillary's presence; the first lady heard herself compared to Martha Washington, Eleanor Roosevelt and Abraham Lincoln. She even got the best of an exchange with Texas Representative Richard K. "Dick" Armey, a Republican who had proved himself a formidable and serious critic of the Clinton health-care proposals.

In June, Armey had, during a speech in Plano, Texas, voiced his fears about the Clinton administration in general and Hillary Clinton in particular. "Hillary Clinton," he said, "bothers me a lot. . . . Her thoughts sound a lot like Karl Marx. She hangs around a lot of Marxists. All her friends are Marxists."

Armey, a former professor of economics, is, as chair of the House Republican Conference, charged with heading up a GOP alternative to the Clinton scheme. Unlike some of the more illiberal members of the House, he apparently has no personal distaste for the Clintons; he even has been quoted as saying it's impossible to spend an hour with Bill Clinton and not like him.

But Armey also has called the administration's health-care package a "Kevorkian" plan (after the notorious Jack Kevorkian, the retired Michigan pathologist who has assisted with or been present for the suicides of eighteen patients) because employer mandates would kill many jobs.

During the first lady's testimony before the House Education and Labor Committee, Armey opened his remarks by telling Hillary he intended "to make the debate as exciting as possible."

"I'm sure you will do that, you and Dr. Kevorkian," Hillary answered, invoking first gasps and then nervous laughter.

"I have been told about your charm and wit," the red-faced and visibly flustered Armey said. "The reports of your charm are overstated, and the reports of your wit are understated."

Armey laughed to himself and shook his head. Then he left the room. The next Republican to question Clinton, Representative Harris W. Fawell of Illinois, began his inquiry: "After seeing how you impaled my colleague—"

"I couldn't resist after his most recent comment," she interrupted.

"I'll proceed with caution," he continued.

"Nobody's quoted to me anything you've said," she assured him.

"Good," he sighed.

Hillary's performance on Capitol Hill effectively demolished any lingering doubts about her intellectual fitness for the role she'd undertaken for the Clinton administration. With that distraction gone, the merits of the health reform she helped devise can be debated.

Of course, we here in Arkansas were not surprised by Hillary's competence, her flashy brilliance or even what might pass for a mean streak. We've seen it all before, wondered at it and finally reconciled ourselves to Hillary Rodham Clinton's special powers of concentration and persuasion. She is an effective complement to her husband, with strengths and vulnerabilities that shore up his public persona. Many people like Bill Clinton more because they trust Hillary's instincts—if she married him, he can't be all bad.

They are no ordinary couple. Instead, they seem more like business partners, coconspirators who aren't above applying Machiavellian techniques to—and one hopes this is their ultimate goal—do good for their country and its people. They are much smarter than most of us, yet both manage to appeal to the masses.

As we write this, Hillary Rodham Clinton's popularity remains greater than her husband's, and the public thinks her more intelligent. An impressive seventy-six percent call her a role model for girls.

Former Clinton campaign aide James L. "Skip" Rutherford of Little Rock travels to Washington regularly in his job as senior vice president for one of the South's largest advertising agencies.

"When I come home, my twelve-year-old daughter doesn't ever ask me if I got to meet with the President," he says. "The first thing she says to me is, 'Dad, did you get to see Hillary?' I don't think we've seen anything like this since Eleanor Roosevelt.

"I was on a flight to Washington with some college students from Louisiana, and I asked one of them what she hoped to accomplish while visiting Washington. She looked at me and said, 'I would give anything to meet Hillary.' When I tell people who sit beside me on planes that I am from Little Rock, men ask, 'Do you know the president?' But women ask, 'Do you know Hillary?' Even those who disagree with her politically tend to respect her ability.

"Americans feel like they know her. Notice the fact that most people simply refer to her by her first name.

People rarely say 'Mrs. Clinton.' It's just Hillary. It's an interesting phenomenon."

Hillary's popularity will increase if she accomplishes what she says she intends to. She wants to "be able to look every American in the eye and say that they are guaranteed health security," and provide "psychological security" to families who "feel the future is closing in on them."

If that seems a Pollyannaish wish, then one needs to consider how Hillary and Bill Clinton got to where they are, and how they came so far so fast. Whatever one thinks of the Clintons's politics, it is hard to deny that they are able and clever people who have, at times, displayed a capacity for transcending partisan politics, and for adopting contrarian positions. The critics who think Hillary Clinton a liberal shrew need only to examine some of the remarks attributed to her during her campaign for education reform in Arkansas—at times, she sounds more like the conservative Republican Methodist she was reared as than any kind of progressive. Hillary Clinton was talking about family values before it became a catch phrase, and her commitment to children's issues belies any attempt to paint her as "antifamily."

"What does Hillary believe?" Pat Buchanan thundered from the Astrodome podium. "Well, Hillary believes that twelve-year-olds should have a right to sue their parents, and she has compared marriage as an institution to slavery and life on an Indian reservation."

To say the least, that is an extraordinarily simplified version of what is, in fact, a complex and humane worldview, informed in nearly equal parts by Hillary's conservative upbringing, the liberal education she received at Wellesley College, the social activism she was exposed to at Yale and her experiences as a children's rights advocate, a crusader for education reform, a private attorney and a well-paid member of corporate boards.

All that, extruded through her Arkansas experience (which is the prime focus of this book) has resulted in Hillary's strength, character and uniqueness.

Hillary came to Arkansas because she fell in love with Bill Clinton while at Yale. She remained at Yale an extra year so they could graduate together in 1973. Upon graduation, however, they went their separate ways for a short while. Bill headed South to teach law at the University of Arkansas at Fayetteville and plot his political future. Hillary went to work as a staff attorney for the Children's Defense Fund, and in January 1974, landed a plum job as a member of the special impeachment investigation staff of the House Judiciary Committee. That job ended abruptly on August 8, 1974, when President Richard Nixon resigned.

As legend has it, an exhausted Hillary, needing a break and missing Bill, decided to visit him in Fayetteville. He talked her into moving there and joining the staff of the law school. Of course, Hillary quickly fell in love with the state. She brought order to Bill's chaotic—and unsuccessful—1974 campaign for Congress.

Woody Bassett, now a prominent northwest Arkansas lawyer, had both Bill and Hillary as professors. "I'll never forget that first day of class," he says. "As we sat in the room waiting for our criminal law class to begin, many of us wondered what Professor Rodham would be like. We had heard a little bit about her, namely that she was Bill Clinton's girlfriend and had come to Arkansas to join him in his effort to get elected to Congress. We knew that she had just successfully completed her work with the House Judiciary Committee.

"All of a sudden she strode into the room, and it was clear from the very beginning that she was a confident, aggressive, take-charge woman. There would be no southern drawl or midwestern twang from this lady.

Instead, her northern accent and eastern background resonated through the room. . . . She was tough, intelligent and highly articulate. Some of her students were intimidated by her brilliance and others downright resented it. Back then, as now, people were never indifferent about Hillary. You either liked her or you didn't. But no matter what, you grew to respect her. That's the way it has been for Hillary since then, in her life and in her political endeavors.''

Bassett says everyone at the law school knew of Hillary and had an opinion about the way she dressed, the way she talked, the things in which she believed.

''She dressed like a throwback to the 1960s and never really spent much time worrying about her appearance,'' he said. ''This was in stark contrast to the sorority girls who lived on the other side of Maple Street. Hillary was not much older than most of us and, in fact, a lot younger than some.

''Her youthful vigor and overwhelming intelligence were not everyone's cup of tea, at least at first. Bluntly put, some of the guys were not used to being taught and led by a woman with an aggressive personality who seemed to be in complete control of the classroom environment. However, as time went on, the students, including the men, warmed up to (her). By the end of the year, most of us who were her students looked at her not as a woman who was a law professor, but instead as a law professor who happened to be a woman. Female students looked to her as a role model and often sought her out for guidance and inspiration. . . . To me, it was in Fayetteville where her rise to leadership really began.''

It is, in a way, ironic that America met this unconventional woman while she was playing that most conventional role—the political wife biting her lip and standing by her man. The defining moment of Bill Clinton's drive for the presidency came on January 26, 1992 when a supermarket tabloid, the *Star*, reported a former Arkansas state employee, Gennifer Flowers, was claiming she had conducted a twelve-year affair with Bill Clinton.

Although Flowers's well-recompensed allegations were hardly credible—at the very least, it is difficult to believe that Bill Clinton sustained an extramarital affair with Flowers for a period of *years*—it does seem that had Hillary Clinton not acted as she did, the Clinton campaign could have died in the snows of New Hampshire.

The Clintons agreed to appear on a special edition of the CBS television program *60 Minutes* that would air immediately following the network's telecast of the Super Bowl. During the previous decade, an average of 113 million viewers had tuned into each Super Bowl, which meant the *60 Minutes* spot was a grand, bold stroke that offered tremendous opportunity for disaster.

More than two million residents of Arkansas knew Hillary as an outspoken, politically astute individual. We knew she was not the typical candidate's wife, someone who would stand beside her husband, smile benignly and say nothing. So did those who had grown up with her in the Chicago suburb of Park Ridge, who had attended college with her at Wellesley, who had attended law school with her at Yale University and who had worked with her at the Children's Defense Fund—all of us knew Hillary would speak her mind. Still, the vast majority of Americans would be introduced to her via *60 Minutes*.

On Super Bowl Sunday, the Clintons taped an interview with CBS correspondent Steve Kroft at Boston's Ritz-Carlton Hotel. Clinton staffers worked frantically that morning to prepare the couple, peppering them with possible questions. Despite the preparations, things did not go well.

At one point during the taping, a bank of lights fell and bounced off Hillary's shoulder. Unhurt, she kept going. Even now, she thinks the best parts of the interview were left on the cutting room floor, snipped out by editors who wanted only to emphasize the inherent drama of the couple struggling for their public life.

That day, Hillary Clinton came across as the more forceful and eloquent partner.

"I think it's really dangerous in this country if we don't have some zone of privacy for everybody," she said. "People can ask us one hundred different ways and in one hundred different directions, and we're just going to leave the ultimate decision up to the American people."

She glared at Kroft, the interloper, as she continued: "I'm not sitting here because I'm some little woman standing by my man like Tammy Wynette. I'm sitting here because I love him and I respect him and I honor what he's been through and what we've been through together, and you know, if that's not enough for the people, then heck, don't vote for him."

With that statement, Hillary Clinton saved her husband's campaign. Whatever infidelities Bill Clinton might have committed, whatever pain he might have caused, all that fell within the zone of privacy Hillary Clinton insisted on for every American. In effect, she told us all it was none of our business, and that she wouldn't subject her marriage to that kind of inappropriate scrutiny.

Because she loved him, or because she needed him, which is not always the same thing or even a good approximation, but all the same, some things ought not to be the subject of speculation in the newspapers or a flash biography.

Of course, it's not that simple. Character matters, and many people who agree with Bill Clinton politically are bothered by what appears to be a rather cavalier attitude toward the truth. Some of us, in fact, are encouraged by Hillary's seemingly more ideological nature, imagining it may yet prove to be an effective restraint on Bill's cheery pragmatism. Bill Clinton knows that to do good, one must first be elected. Hillary Clinton, we suspect, sees little use in being elected if not to do good.

That is our judgment. History may confer another on Hillary and her husband, but at this relatively early stage in her career and her public life, we would at least like to imagine that a few more of her dreams might come true. She may already be the most powerful woman in the brief history of the Republic, and it is hard to imagine that she will retire after her husband's term in the White House has run its course.

At the very least, Hillary Rodham Clinton is a revolutionary figure. In a culture that fears unadulterated and original thinking, she fearlessly offers her agenda of progressive, substantive, and unbowdlerized ideas. Demonized by the right, and widely condescended to by the popular media, she may be a radical of the most dangerous sort—the sort that refuses to accept the standard and long-held assumptions of our intellectual and political culture simply because they are standard and long-held. Hillary Rodham Clinton has always displayed a healthy impatience with convention.

She is a fascinating woman, who frightens many men (and women too) because of her undeniable power. She is the sort of woman who is whispered about, because she threatens the self-esteem of the small minded; Hillary Rodham Clinton is an unconventional woman of some steel—and the country is divided between those who love and loathe her.

Although this book is intended as an "objective" summation of Hillary Rodham Clinton's record so far, we would be amiss if we did not confess some affection for our subject. Like all good citizens, we wish the first lady of the United States well, and hope "the Hillary Factor" continues to draw the national discussion about how we ought to live into the realm of practical virtue.

Philip Martin
Rex Nelson
Little Rock, Arkansas
October 2, 1993

I

CHAPTER ONE
Stand By Your Man

Hillary Rodham Clinton broke into the American consciousness in January 1992 amid the klieg-lit glare of one of the strangest presidential contests in United States history. She was the she-tiger, ferociously defending her sheepish—and possibly unfaithful—husband on *60 Minutes* in front of a nationwide audience.

With that appearance, Hillary probably saved Bill Clinton's political life. Within a year, she would be one of the most famous women in the world, the first lady of the United States of America. But she would be not just the wife of the President; Hillary would assume a significant role in his administration as one of his most influential advisors, and more importantly, serve as a font of substantial and undiluted progressive ideas.

Bill Clinton's greatest gift may be for artful compromise, but Hillary is a fearlessly liberal idealist, a former Goldwater Girl gone feminist, reinvented as a visionary Saint Hillary (as *The New York Times Magazine* styled her) struggling with Niebuhr and Paul Tillich as she gropes toward "a unified field theory" of existence.

She is among the country's most loved and loathed pop culture figures, grist for Camille Paglia's mill as well as Rush Limbaugh's. Her bearing and confidence threaten some of those who espouse "traditional family values." Hillary has replaced the Soviet Union in the minds of a few people who demand physical manifestations of Evil, whereas many other Americans— especially young women—feel stronger and more connected to this country because a woman like Hillary cohabits the White House. People are scared of this efficient woman, with her blonded, sensible hair and her lawerly suits.

So impressive is Hillary that even were she not the wife of the President, her voice would likely contribute to the national discussion about how Americans ought to live. And so it is ironic that the first glimpse many people had of Hillary Clinton was on *60 Minutes*, ferociously defending her man.

To understand why Hillary had the impact that she did, we have to realize that every presidential campaign is in some part a reaction and reflection of campaigns past. The race that ended with Bill Clinton's election was in no small measure shaped by the sustained nastiness and purposeful frivolity practiced during George Bush's 1988 pursuit of the presidency.

In 1988, Bush strategists, chief among them the late Lee Atwater, were able to convert the election into a referendum on patriotism, employing such hot-button "issues" as Willie Horton and the Pledge of Allegiance. This led the race into strange and uncharted depths, perhaps reaching a nadir during a televised presidential debate when Cable News Network anchor Bernard Shaw probed for Democratic nominee Michael Dukakis's reaction to the hypothetical rape and murder of his wife, Kitty.

Bush and his team exploited the Massachusetts Democrat's clinical, measured nature as well as his Robespierre-ian reluctance to deal with issues he considered tangential or irrelevant. By engaging and embracing images of national comfort and pride, and by converting everything into the truncated grammar of television, Bush made members of the press accessories in his landslide, as he dragged their cameras to flag factories and Boston Harbor.

Bush and his people took their cue from Reagan, who discovered that no matter how critical a correspondent voice-over, what really mattered was the pretty pictures flashing on the nightly news. Even as reporters covering the campaign railed against the polities of the sound bite and the photo op, they were powerless so long as they were locked into the traditional styles of covering politics. They followed the candidates, who repeated the same, simplistic message at every stop.

Arkansas Governor Bill Clinton was determined not to repeat the mistakes of Michael Dukakis. Under the political strategist James Carville, the Clinton campaign organization became a supple, simple organism designed to massage and manipulate the media. Every night the campaign staff studied newspaper, television and news-agency coverage in order to plan the next day's media hit.

Although such spin control tactics have perhaps always been part of politics, the 1992 campaign saw the media environment expand, as cutbacks in network coverage, combined with the growing influence of local television stations, changed how most Americans received their news. The rise of local talk radio shows focusing on politics pointed out that the mainstream press had lost touch with their subscribers because journalists were too focused on strategy and minutiae rather than on the policy basics that move voters. Pop culture outlets such as MTV and television and radio talk programs hosted by the likes of Larry King, Arsenio Hall and Phil Donahue were used increasingly by politicians seeking to circumvent both parties and the press and deliver their message directly to the people. These techniques both democratized and lowered the standards of the media.

Rumors, innuendo and gossip all became stories—
fair game for the mainstream media—after they gained
momentum in the least responsible press. And so, in
1992, the *Star*, a supermarket tabloid, achieved a kind
of awkward parity with *The New York Times* and *The
Washington Post*.

This was an especially problematic environment for
an attractive young couple like Bill and Hillary Clinton.
Whatever his foibles, Clinton is a stunning man,
equipped with the semiotic potential of a demagogue,
tempered with the thoughtfulness of a professor. In Arkansas, he was at times criticized for being overly reflective and less decisive than Hillary, who often
seemed the more dynamic of the duo.

Attractive and at times a shameless flirt, at forty-
five, Bill had yet to outgrow his boyishness, which led
many to suspect he had done foolish things with his
clothes off. Bill and Hillary were attractive young people who had grown up in the '60s. For some, that was
enough to make them morally suspect. Bill Clinton
chose to run for the highest office in the country at
precisely the time American journalism was reaching a
nadir of taste. Given the circumstances, the "bimbo
eruptions" of the winter of 1992 might have been
inevitable.

Bill Clinton delivered a standard-issue campaign
speech, nothing out of the ordinary, before about four
hundred people that Saturday night in Bedford, New
Hampshire. At that point he seemed the destiny-kissed
front-runner, the Democrat with the best chance of de-
throning the amiable but faltering George Bush.

Adultery—the petty vice that had overexcited the
American imagination since before Hawthorne invented
Hester Prynne—was, of course, the sin for which this
presidential candidate would sooner or later have to
seek absolution. Whatever the facts, the rumors surrounding Bill Clinton were too thick to be ignored.

During his years as governor of Arkansas he had

been compared to both John Kennedy and Benito Mussolini, and more than one journalist had been initially charmed by Bill Clinton, only to later discover the scent of sulphur in the air. Though little, if any, concrete evidence of extramarital misbehavior had ever been detected by Arkansas reporters who had covered Clinton for years, it sometimes seemed as though everyone in the state had heard stories. Some Arkansans believed the stories, some didn't, and a surprising number thought them immaterial to Clinton's job performance.

This night in Bedford the Clintons were no doubt prepared to face the question sooner rather than later—a few days before, the *Star*, a supermarket tabloid based in Lantana, Florida, had published an "exclusive story" alleging Clinton had conducted a twelve-year affair with an Arkansas state employee and sometimes lounge singer named Gennifer (nee Eura Jean) Flowers.

Under the terms of her contract with the *Star*, Flowers was barred from talking to other media until the paper deemed it appropriate. In other words, until the *Star* had milked the episode for everything it was worth, Flowers would speak only through its less-than-credible pages. But while the mainstream media couldn't interview Flowers, they could report what the *Star* was saying.

All hell was about to break loose.

Even before he announced his candidacy, Clinton had acknowledged to select members of the national press that his marriage had not been "perfect." Even so, he stressed that he and Hillary had weathered the worst of it and intended to stay together. If his wife—obviously no sycophant or timid housewife but a respected attorney and formidable intellect in her own right—could understand and forgive the governor's indiscretions, why should these unspecified mistakes disqualify him from serving as President?

Why indeed? Some reporters and columnists in Arkansas thought Clinton's decision not to seek the Democratic presidential nomination in 1988 was in part driven by the crack-up of Colorado Senator Gary Hart. Hart, overcome by hubris, had answered the adultery question by daring the press to shadow him. They did, and wrecked his chances of becoming President.

Though, at the time, Clinton said his decision not to run was based on his reluctance to subject the couple's then eight-year-old daughter Chelsea to the upsets of campaigning, in the wake of Hart's monkey business, an emboldened press seemed certain to examine the rumors surrounding Clinton if the Arkansas Democrat entered the race.

To some, who discerned in Bill Clinton a reflexive instinct for maintaining politic viability, Flowers's allegations seemed dubious. Even if Clinton had strayed in the past, most who observed him thought the governor too shrewd to get caught up in an ongoing affair with the chance of exposure so great and the costs so dear.

More cynical observers of the couple privately thought that the Clintons had an "arrangement," that theirs was more a working partnership than a traditional marriage, yet many friends and intimates of the Clintons maintain that they are a close couple, best friends who had grown even closer after Bill's decision not to enter the 1988 presidential race.

But the most curious, and in retrospect most opportune, aspect of the adultery question was that it was directed not to the rakish candidate but to his impressive wife. When Hillary Clinton was tested, she was ready.

"From my perspective and the perspective of my husband, that's an issue we are very comfortable with in our own marriage,'' she began. ''We had very much expected we would be hit with all kinds of accusations when we decided to make this run for the presidency. . . . Our marriage is a strong marriage. We love each other, support each other and we have a lot of strong and important experiences together that have meant a lot to us. In any marriage, there are issues that come up between two people who are married that I think is their business.''

Hillary spoke with a confidence and clarity that seemed to shame the question. And it was apparent that the crowd felt her response was mature and appropriate, exactly the sort of thing a presidential candidate—or candidate's wife—should say. They applauded for nearly a minute.

''I guess I have to tell you that it is important to me that what I care about in this world—my family and what we mean to each other and what we have done together—has some realm of protection from public life,'' Hillary said that night in Bedford. ''I know there will be voters who disagree with that, and I respect that disagreement if that's how they choose to decide.''

Hillary concluded by reversing a bit of coded Republican rhetoric; she said she was proud of her family and what should be important to New Hampshire residents was how well or poorly their own families were doing. Again, the crowd responded with applause.

In the afterglow, her husband took the podium.

''We all know that we now live in a world where all people have to do is make third-party accusations, and if everybody says it's not so, it's still news,'' he said. ''I'll tell you this: That story wasn't true.''

As always, Clinton was careful with language. He was careful to say ''that story'' wasn't true, meaning, perhaps, that other stories were true. Like most politicians, Clinton was capable of dissembling; campaigning occasionally required that the truth be selected, parceled out in self-serving sound bites.

"Slick Willie" was not entirely a term of derision—
something akin to admiration was folded in. Clinton
was a pro, a campaign-tested veteran who wasn't likely
to self-destruct.

Still many of the reporters covering the Clinton campaign were unconvinced the candidate was telling the
whole truth about Gennifer Flowers. Had it not been
for the support of his wife, his presidential campaign
surely would have collapsed in the snows of New
Hampshire. Yet for a time during those confusing days
of early 1992—when new Clinton rumors were break-
ing every day—it seemed that Hillary's outspokenness
might be a factor in her husband's defeat.

First, the campaign had to act to control the damage.
Mindful of what the politics of passivity had done for
Michael Dukakis's 1988 campaign, Bill, relying on his
own political instincts, quickly counterpunched. So
did Hillary.

Prior to Flowers's allegations, Hillary had spent
much of her time campaigning separately from her husband. For instance, she spent the second week of January in Maine in order to pick up commitments from a
number of high-profile Democrats during a four-city
campaign swing. She also took time to answer media
requests, such as posing for photographs for *Vogue*.

After the allegations against her husband, Hillary seldom wandered far from his side. She was quite literally
standing by him.

"It's not true," she said about the allegations during
a visit to Atlanta. "I just don't believe any of that. It's
really unfortunate that political opponents of Bill
started in 1990 to make charges against him. The people of Arkansas didn't believe them. All of these people, including that woman, have denied this many,
many times. I am not going to speculate on her motive.
We know she was paid."

Flowers had, in fact, previously denied having had

an affair with Clinton. In 1990, she was among five women named in a lawsuit filed by Larry Nichols, a former state employee who had been fired for using state telephones to try to raise money for the Contra rebels in Nicaragua. When he was fired Nichols filed the lawsuit, which gave information about Clinton's misconduct with Flowers and the other women. Nichols's allegations were never substantiated, and his suit was eventually dismissed.

But when a caller to a Little Rock radio talk show with a minuscule audience mentioned Flowers in connection with the suit, she, through her attorney, threatened to sue the station. (After Flowers made her allegations in the *Star*, KBIS talk show host Bill Powell would wonder if the governor had "orchestrated the whole thing" as a kind of preemptive strike designed to deter political opponents from spreading rumors.)

Of course, Flowers's allegation was all many people needed to revise their opinion of Bill Clinton. Many thought he was glib and facile, definitely a philanderer. No amount of damage control could salve the initial injury—there was no way to prove he didn't sleep with her.

"The sad thing is that we've tried to be very straightforward and talk to people about what we think is important," Hillary said.

Would the allegations cripple the Clinton campaign?

"I think my husband has a very strong public record," she said at the time. "We have a very strong marriage, and we're committed to each other. We're very much involved with each other's lives. We're just going to let the American people make their own decisions about these accusations. They're going to judge us and make their judgments over the course of this campaign, and that is what we're going to rely on."

Despite this straight-on engagement of the problem, the judgments of the American people seemed decidedly negative in the early days of the campaign—

toward both the governor and his wife. Hordes of reporters dogged the Clintons through the snow, and virtually all their questions revolved around Flowers's claims.

Hillary agreed to a one-on-one interview with *Newsweek* in which she portrayed Bill as a good husband and a good father to their daughter, Chelsea. She said that any previous marital problems were between the two of them.

"We don't talk about this kind of stuff in our marriage with family and friends," she said. "It's the way we are and how we live. And I think it's the way most people live."

When asked how she felt about being first in line to defend her husband against sexual allegations, Hillary said, "I'm bewildered by the kind of press attention that they've generated. But I recognize that we don't set the rules, and that is the way the whole situation has developed in the last couple of years. I feel very comfortable about my husband and about our marriage."

If the couple were to make it to the White House, they would have to learn to play by the rules set by the media, which increasingly was taking its cues from pop culture magazine shows and trashy tabloids. No one seemed interested in hearing about substantive public policy issues while there was all this juicy flesh to tend to.

Paradoxically, if the couple were divorced, she said, no one would be making a big deal about Bill's personal life. But they weren't divorced, so the questions continued to come.

Hillary consistently refused to answer specific questions about problems she and her husband had faced within the context of their marriage and how they had worked out those problems.

"I really don't want to open that up," she told *Newsweek*. "I don't think that is anybody else's concern.

What is important to us is that we have always dealt with each other. We haven't run away or walked away. We've been willing to work through all kinds of problems. I'm talking about all kinds of things that happen in a marriage. . . . And I think it is inappropriate to talk about that.''

Her marriage, she contended, was like thousands of others across America—marriages that had problems. The clear implication was that the governor had not always been faithful to her.

''We're like a lot of couples in America right now,'' she told the magazine. ''We've tried to keep our marriage together.''

It seemed her way of saying that, yes, there had been infidelities. And if she could forgive her husband, then the American people ought to accept that. It was a strong, nearly defiant, stance. Hillary Clinton didn't seem like a victim or a woman wronged by a cad. She seemed clear-eyed and resolute, somewhat tougher than her beleaguered husband.

January 26 brought the most important moment in Hillary Clinton's public life.

After days of backchannel negotiations that had the Clintons weighing an offer from ABC's Ted Koppel to appear on his late-night *Nightline* program, they accepted an offer to appear on a special edition of the CBS program *60 Minutes*, which would air immediately following the Super Bowl. Desperate to put the Flowers issue behind them, the Clintons selected the highly rated CBS program over a host of other proposed joint interviews because of the potential immediacy of its impact. It was a big risk.

During the previous decade, an average of 113 million viewers had tuned into each Super Bowl broadcast. It was almost always the most-watched program of the year.

''It's an opportunity to reach a very large audience,''

campaign press secretary Dee Dee Myers explained to anxious reporters the day before the taping. "It could reach one hundred million people. It's a rare opportunity to address the issue in detail as opposed to a thirty-second sound bite."

"The stakes are the highest I've ever seen in my twenty years of presidential politics," Democratic political analyst Bob Beckel said during an appearance on CNN the day before the interview was to be broadcast. "It's the biggest roll of the dice of his career. . . . I think it's one of those gutsy moves that you have to make because this story was unraveling on them very fast. He'll either walk out of there as the most viable Democratic candidate or a guy who's not going to be the nominee."

Also on CNN that Saturday, *Newsweek*'s Eleanor Clift said Hillary's performance would be critically important. Calling Hillary her husband's best defender, Clift said, "She does not come across as an aggrieved victim the way some other political wives have. She will make the case that they deserve credit for sticking together, but they will not get into any specifics."

CNN's Gene Randall, however, spoke of anxiety in the campaign. Quite clearly many of the Clinton campaign key strategists believed the whole effort was coming apart, that another front-running Democrat was about to self-destruct.

"There is a recognition that before this campaign can go forward, this issue must be dealt with," Randall said.

Reporters were not allowed to watch the Sunday morning taping of the interview, which lasted almost ninety minutes. Security guards sealed off the entire third floor of the plush Ritz-Carlton Hotel in Boston, where the interview was conducted. Hotel elevators were not allowed to stop on the floor.

In their suite, both Clintons were prepped by campaign aides. Staffers fired potential questions at Hillary, and she gave answers. Normally the strongest member of the entourage, the governor's wife later confessed to friends that she feared she would cry on camera.

Finally, the time arrived for the taping. CBS's Steve Kroft conducted the interview. Some viewed Kroft, less well known than the program's star inquisitor Mike Wallace, Morley Safer or even Ed Bradley, as a softer interviewer, and thought the Clintons should have insisted on facing Wallace with his reputation for toughness or passed on the *60 Minutes* invitation and instead subjected themselves to Koppel's questioning on *Nightline*. Others thought Clinton preferred to face Kroft, that the younger correspondent might be more sympathetic or less combative than the feisty Wallace.

As the Clintons sat next to each other, and Kroft began his interrogation, Hillary and Bill recited lines they had practiced for days—lines about loving each other, lines about commitment, lines about hard times that had been overcome.

In the midst of the taping, a small bank of lights taped to a wall became unstuck, fell and struck Hillary on the shoulder. She was not injured, but everyone in the room—the Clintons and CBS employees alike—clearly were shaken. The tension mounted.

Kroft tried to get the couple to admit to past infidelities. Neither would bite. Twice during the taping, producer Don Hewitt knelt by the governor's chair, trying to get him to bluntly admit adultery.

"I'm not prepared tonight to say that any married couple should ever discuss that with anyone but themselves," Bill said.

"I don't want to be any more specific," Hillary said. "I don't think being any more specific about what happened in the privacy of our life is relevant to anybody besides us."

They described Flowers as an acquaintance whom they had met in the late 1970s when she was a reporter for a Little Rock television station. They said she had called the governor repeatedly through the years as rumors surfaced occasionally that she was involved in an affair with him.

"Bill talked to this woman every time she called, distraught, saying her life was going to be ruined," Hillary said. "He'd get off the phone and tell me she said sort of wacky things, which we thought were attributable to the fact that she was terrified."

Then a sober Bill Clinton took a calculated gamble by seeming to admit to having had extramarital affairs: "I have acknowledged wrongdoing. I have acknowledged causing pain in my marriage. I have said things to you, and to the American people from the beginning, that no American politician ever had. I think most Americans watching this tonight will know what we're saying. They'll get it, and they'll feel that we have been more candid."

Hillary took it from there: "I think it's really dangerous in this country if we don't have some zone of privacy for everybody.... People can ask us a hundred different ways and in a hundred different directions, and we're just going to leave the ultimate decision up to the American people."

When Kroft said the Clintons apparently had reached an "arrangement"—the same assumption many Arkansans had drawn—the governor pounced on him.

"Wait a minute! You're looking at two people who love each other. This is not an arrangement or an understanding. This is a marriage."

Hillary then said something that would dog her for the rest of the campaign. She made the mistake of offending country music fans.

"I'm not sitting here because I'm some little woman standing by my man like Tammy Wynette," she said. "I'm sitting here because I love him and I respect him and I honor what he's been through and what we've been through together, and you know, if that's not enough for the people, then heck, don't vote for him."

The couple said the interview would mark the last time they would talk about the allegations. With the New Hampshire primary still three weeks away, it was time to focus on other issues. But the interview had broken little new ground. Clinton seemed to suggest he had "caused pain" in his marriage through adulterous conduct, but evaded any clear admission. Bill and Hillary said their marriage had not been perfect but was now solid—something both had said in the past. Eventually, they would be forced to talk more about the issue—much more.

"Our message is that we've told you everything we think in good conscience you should know," Bill said afterward. "We did the best we could do. Hillary was magnificent, as she always is. We'll just have to see what happens. This has been a challenge both for the American people and the legitimate press. If you think about it, we are about to lay down a standard here that will take out any candidate in any campaign in the future."

But it wasn't the Clintons's call. The *Star* promised more articles. Officials at the tabloid scheduled a New York news conference the next day at which Flowers would play parts of taped telephone conversations she said she'd held with Bill Clinton.

The rest of that Sunday, dozens of reporters and photographers swarmed around the couple at every stop, shouting questions, demanding answers. Without exception, the questions were personal. If the press held any lingering doubts about the appropriateness of character questions, the Clintons's appearance on *60 Minutes* resolved them. The candidate himself had put the issue into play. The resulting frenzy was so intense, staff members had to physically shove journalists out of the way to allow the Clintons to leave the Ritz-Carlton following the taping.

But the public seemed less interested in the intimate details of the couple's marriage than did the press.

Later that same day at a rally in Portsmouth, New Hampshire, more than three hundred people shouted down an audience member who tried to raise the issue of infidelities. The Clintons flew to Little Rock that evening to watch the program with Chelsea at the Governor's Mansion. When they saw it, they were incensed—especially Hillary—that the segment was shorter than CBS had promised and that what they believed to be the best parts had been cut.

The show was seen by about forty million viewers. The Clinton interview had been the lone topic of the special fifteen-minute telecast, and the initial reviews were not good.

"CBS had a bad night Sunday," political columnist John Robert Starr wrote in the *Arkansas Democrat-Gazette*. "To those of us who keep up, the Bill and Hillary Clinton Show on *60 Minutes* was as big a disappointment as the one-sided Super Bowl. Clinton didn't say anything about allegations of marital infidelity that he has not said before."

Meanwhile, Tammy Wynette—who'd cowritten and sung "Stand By Your Man"—was offended by Hillary's allusion to her.

Ironically, the country singer and the candidate's wife should have been allies. With her frazzled history, Wynette had also been battered by the celebrity-baiting *Star*, but even in her sixties could still muster up some dignity behind a microphone. Wynette was one of those rare singers for whom music is emotional communion; she had always kept faith with the raw, insistent hurt that inhabits a certain breed of fragile-yet-indomitable country woman. Listeners read the progress of her marriage to honky-tonk Picasso George Jones in the frayed timbre of her voice. Though the woman who made "Stand By Your Man" an anthem could never be a feminist heroine, she proved she understood that male insecurity was often the root of misogyny in songs such as the 1967 hit "Your Good Girl's Gonna Go Bad."

The day after the interview was televised, Wynette wrote Hillary about the comment.

"She was totally speechless," Wynette's current husband, George Richey, said of his wife's reaction. "It was totally off base." He added that his wife was "mad as hell, and she probably will be for a time."

Wynette, in her letter to Hillary, demanded an apology on behalf of all the women who are willing to forgive and accept " 'cause after all, he's just a man."

"Mrs. Clinton," the letter read, *"you have offended every woman and man who love that song—several million in number. I believe you have offended every true country music fan and every person who has made it on their own with no one to take them to a White House."*

Hillary, who, following the interview, was in Colorado campaigning for her husband, said she hadn't meant to hurt Tammy Wynette "as a person."

"I happen to be a country music fan," she said. "If she feels like I hurt her feelings, I'm sorry for that."

During that same visit to Colorado, Hillary picked up the pace of the political counteroffensive. She charged in several interviews that the allegations leveled against her husband were part of a Republican smear campaign.

"We now know that when Republicans first offered money to this woman to change her story, she held out, apparently negotiating with the media to change a story she had denied repeatedly," Hillary told the editorial board of *The Daily Sentinel*, a newspaper in Grand Junction, Colorado. "Part of the reason I feel so calm is that Bill and I are stronger today than when we got married. Bill and I will be fine, regardless of what happens. It's not easy running for president. You feel like you're standing in the middle of a firing range, and sometimes they come close to hitting you."

Despite the Wynette flap, Bill's strategists, especially flamboyant Louisiana native James Carville, were pleased with Hillary's performance and urged her to do interviews without Bill. She agreed to tape an interview with the tenacious Sam Donaldson of ABC. Portions of the interview, to be taped in Little Rock at the Governor's Mansion, would be aired on Thursday night's *Prime Time Live*, whose producer, Richard N. Kaplan, had been a friend of the Clintons for more than a decade.

For the second time in five nights, Hillary would be called on to give a crucial performance before an audience of millions of Americans.

In her interview with Donaldson, Hillary fired away at Flowers. "If someone is willing to pay you $130,000 or $170,000 to get your fifteen minutes of fame, and you're some failed cabaret singer who doesn't even have much of a résumé to fall back on ... that's the daughter of Willie Horton as far as I'm concerned," Hillary said. "It's the same kind of attempt to keep the real issues of this country out of the mainstream debate where they need to be."

This was a more forceful—almost bitter—Hillary Rodham Clinton than the one who had appeared on *60 Minutes*. As she had done in Colorado, she laid the entire episode at the feet of Arkansas Republicans. She was quick to point out that she had forgiven her husband long ago.

"If you are married to someone for more than ten minutes, you are going to have to forgive somebody for something," she said.

Donaldson characterized Bill's presidential campaign as a believability contest between Hillary and Gennifer Flowers.

Hillary said she had listened to the taped telephone conversations released earlier in the week during Flowers's New York news conference. But she wouldn't say if the man's voice on those tapes belonged to her husband.

Clinton campaign officials had insisted that the interview cover more than Flowers's allegations. They wanted the segment to be a profile of Hillary, not a single-subject story. So Donaldson allowed Hillary to tell about the first time she met Bill Clinton.

"As I was cutting through the student lounge at Yale Law School, this voice said, 'And not only that, we grow the biggest watermelons in the world.' And I said, 'Who is that?' And my friend said, 'Oh, that's Bill Clinton, that's all he ever talks about. He's from Arkansas.' "

On the air, Donaldson alluded to the "big-city law career" that awaited Hillary following her success at Yale and as a staff lawyer for the House Judiciary Committee's impeachment investigation of Richard Nixon.

"I had to make a hard choice," Hillary told him. "But I also knew that I would be real dishonest to myself if I didn't follow my heart and see where this relationship led, and take that leap of faith."

Realizing that Hillary's support for her husband might be the only thing keeping Clinton's nomination hopes airborne, schedulers worked furiously to line up additional major interviews for her. She even spoke with the upscale New York publication *Women's Wear Daily*, saying that the couple's marital obligations included fidelity but that the details of their relationship were not open to inspection. In an age of electronic voyeurism, Hillary seemed determined to reclaim a measure of privacy, not only for the sake of herself and her husband's career, but for the health of the national conversation.

"We have really collapsed the space in which public people can live, to the detriment of our overall politics," she said.

Asked if one's marriage could be a drag on one's political career, she responded, "It depends on the candidate and the marriage. Any stressful undertaking can either be made better or worse by the relationship between the spouses. But if it's a supportive one, if people believe in each other, if they love each other, if they have a commitment to what each is trying to do, it makes life a lot easier than it is alone.''

How much more of the intense media focus on the couple's personal life could she take?

"My attitude is that if you're doing what you believe in and you think it's important, you have to be ready to defend yourself and you have to be ready to take the offensive when necessary," she said. "We've learned our lesson about how you stand up, answer your critics and then just counterpunch as hard as you can. That's what we'll do in this campaign."

With that, Hillary returned to New Hampshire to counterpunch some more. Tracking polls the Sunday of the *60 Minutes* interview had shown that Bill had dropped twelve percentage points in New Hampshire, into a tie with former Senator Paul Tsongas of neighboring Massachusetts. Before Flowers's allegations were made public, Clinton had been at thirty-nine percent in the state, followed by Senator Bob Kerrey of Nebraska at eighteen percent and Tsongas at fourteen percent.

Flowers's message in her Monday news conference at New York's Waldorf-Astoria Hotel had been simple: Bill Clinton lied. In a ballroom filled with hundreds of reporters and photographers, Flowers said, "The truth is I loved him."

It marked the first time Flowers had appeared publicly to say she'd had an affair with the governor.

"Yes, I was Bill Clinton's lover for twelve years, and for the last two years, I have lied about the relationship," she said. "Now, he tells me to deny it. Well, I'm sick of all the deceit, and I'm sick of all the lies."

Publicly, Hillary directed her anger at Flowers and nameless, faceless "Republican operatives" rather than at her husband. Yet despite Hillary's public support, many political analysts thought Flowers's news conference had doomed the campaign. Many members of the media present believed at least a part of what she had to say.

It seemed only a matter of time before Bill Clinton would follow Gary Hart, sinking indecorously into the muck of history to be remembered only as a vaguely pathetic, mildly risqué joke.

Halfway across the country in Baton Rouge, Louisiana, the man who had trained like an athlete for the presidency since a teenager, was once again reduced to saying obligatory, unconvincing things: "She didn't tell the truth. . . . My wife and I said everything we have to say about this whole subject yesterday. As far as I'm concerned, it's a closed matter."

But as Hillary's willingness to go on *Prime Time Live* with Donaldson three days later would show, it was far from closed. And now there were new fires to put out.

On one of the tapes with Flowers, the voice alleged to be Clinton's had said New York Governor Mario Cuomo "acts like" someone with Mafia connections. He also called the New York governor a "mean son of a bitch."

"This is part of an ugly syndrome that strikes Italian-Americans, Jewish people, blacks, women, all the different ethnic groups," Cuomo said.

And Clinton's attempt at reconciliation was less than satisfying. After seeming to deny that his was the voice captured on tape, he added, "If the remarks on the tape left anyone with the impression that I was disrespectful to either Governor Cuomo or Italian-Americans, then I deeply regret it."

This curious statement served only to heighten Cuomo's anger.

"What do you mean 'if'?" he said. "If you're not capable of understanding what was said, then don't try apologizing."

"This hasn't been a great week for us," Harold Ickes, chairman of Clinton's New York campaign, said in one of the year's most glaring examples of understatement. "Obviously, some people are nervous."

After the *Prime Time Live* interview, Hillary flew back to New Hampshire to help direct the rescue of her husband's campaign. The goal: to get the media focus off the couple's personal lives and back onto the issues.

As part of that effort, hundreds of Arkansans were asked to descend on New Hampshire. Dubbed the Arkansas Travelers, these friends and supporters of the Clintons knocked on doors and told residents about the man and woman they knew, not the man and woman portrayed by the media.

Typical of the Arkansans accompanying Bill and Hillary that final week of January 1992 was David Leopoulos of Little Rock, who had known the governor for more than three decades. Leopoulos said he traveled to New Hampshire at his own expense to "try to talk to people about the human side of Bill Clinton."

Even Senator David Pryor of Arkansas, Clinton's predecessor as governor from 1975 to 1978, headed north from Washington. It was an unorthodox—and some thought desperate—strategy.

With Hillary at his side, Bill addressed a crowd in Portsmouth: "I would say the most gratifying thing has been the number of people who have just come up to both of us and said, 'Hang in there. We appreciate what you are trying to say and we like you. We want to know about what you're going to do about our tomorrows, not your yesterdays.' "

Later, at a Democratic fund-raiser in Washington, Hillary tried to provide a bit of comic relief. The event, a dinner roast of Democratic National Committee Chairman Ron Brown, attracted more than a thousand people. Some of them probably attended just to see how Hillary would respond to jokes about her husband.

STAND BY YOUR MAN . 45

"It's ten o'clock, Hillary; where is Bill Clinton?" asked talk show host Larry King, the emcee, in his opening monologue.

"Bill Clinton is with the other woman in his life, his daughter, Chelsea," Hillary replied.

Clinton had purposely skipped the roast to escort his daughter to a YWCA father-daughter dance in Little Rock. Campaign strategists were thrilled by his decision. For starters, it would look good for the governor to be seen with his daughter. Second, despite the earlier gaffe regarding Tammy Wynette, campaign advisers actually had more confidence in Hillary performing well at the roast than they had in the candidate himself.

After the dance, Bill and Chelsea returned to the Governor's Mansion, where the eleven-year-old taught her father a card game called Spite and Malice—"a game which is quite appropriate for the last few days," Bill said.

Even if some people still had doubts about Bill Clinton's fitness for office, the Flowers episode seemed to increase Hillary's standing with most Americans, many of whom began to wonder if perhaps the wrong Clinton was running for President. In a campaign spot, the candidate himself broached the question, saying "I'm not sure people aren't right when they say she is the one who ought to be running. You know, we like each other. You can watch me watch her speak sometimes, and I've got the Nancy Reagan adoring look. I think she's one good argument for voting for me."

Then, in what *The New York Times* described as a stream-of-consciousness tribute, Clinton said: "If the choice for us is having gotten a divorce a couple of years ago and being single and going up to New Hampshire and winning and being free of this almost unbelievable set of behaviors to which I and my family and our friends have been subjected, but ultimately being nominated and going on to the White House, or just going home to the rest of my life with her and Chelsea, I think now everybody in America ought to be able to see why I would choose to go home.

"I think she has just been extraordinary. One of the reasons that I guess I'm in elected office and she isn't is she always wanted to guard her privacy much more and I've always kind of hated to have to discuss some of the things that we have discussed in the last few weeks. . . . Like every other challenge that I've ever seen her face, she was able to rise to it."

On February 3, Hillary went back to her alma mater, Wellesley College in Massachusetts, and repeatedly fielded the same question: "Why aren't you running for president?"

Hillary assured a packed hall of 1,500 students that she and her husband would work as a team. She scarcely mentioned the Flowers controversy during a thirty-minute speech made without notes. She told the students that the couple remained committed to each other. Mostly, though, she talked about education and child welfare. She credited Wellesley with guiding her away from the conservative politics of her parents, reminding the students that she had come to the school as a "Goldwater Girl."

A former professor, Alan Schechter, introduced her as one of the best students he had ever had. He read from the letter of recommendation he had written, which helped her get into Yale Law School: "Her papers are brilliantly executed, and I have learned from them myself."

During the days preceding the New Hampshire primary, "No Excuses" jeans began running an ad featuring a photo of Bill and Hillary above a caption that read, "To Hillary Clinton—The modern no excuses wife who doesn't care how many ladies there are, as long as she's the FIRST lady."

The Clintons didn't approve. Nevertheless, Hillary

was sent a wardrobe of jeans and sleepwear from New Retail Concepts, which markets No Excuses.

"I think people expected us to use Gennifer Flowers," a New Retail marketing vice president said.

By now the attacks weren't just coming from the right.

Senator Tom Harkin of Iowa, perhaps the most traditionally liberal of the men seeking the Democratic nomination, tried to paint Clinton as weak on abortion rights. Harkin repeatedly attacked Bill's willingness to sign an Arkansas law requiring girls seeking an abortion either to notify a parent or guardian or to receive an exemption from a judge. Harkin supporters distributed leaflets suggesting the Arkansas law was evidence that Bill didn't favor reproductive rights for women.

At a hastily called news conference in Manchester, Hillary defended both the law and her husband, saying he had an unswerving commitment to abortion rights. She was supported by a group of New Hampshire women backing Clinton and also by a letter from the executive director of the Arkansas Coalition for Choice.

"We have our position," Hillary said. "We just want it fully represented. Anyone who cares about choice knows the difference between notice and consent, and that is a significant difference."

Back on the campaign trail, another body blow came February 6 when *The Wall Street Journal* reported that Bill Clinton had deftly avoided an ROTC commitment at the University of Arkansas.

The campaign immediately produced television and radio spots to counter allegations that the governor had avoided the draft. Campaign officials also purchased newspaper ads with the names and telephone numbers of Arkansans who New Hampshire voters could call to ask about Clinton. Another part of the comeback strategy was Clinton's agreement to appear on viewer call-in shows. The final part of the strategy was to have Hillary by the governor's side as much as possible.

Just when it seemed as if things were turning around, another crisis erupted. On Wednesday, February 12, a letter Clinton had written in 1969 was released. In the letter to Colonel Eugene Holmes, former head of the ROTC program at the University of Arkansas, Clinton said he had made himself eligible for the draft because he wanted to maintain his "political viability."

In a Manchester airport hangar, campaign aides made the letter public after learning that ABC News already had obtained a copy of it. ABC had gotten the letter from Clinton Jones, who had been second in command of the ROTC program under Holmes. Jones claimed he had been so deeply offended by Clinton's letter—and had found it so curious—that he had held onto a copy of it for twenty-three years.

Within days of receiving the first copy of Clinton's letter, ABC obtained a second from James Tully, a Republican businessman with ties to Watergate conspirator John Mitchell and Iran-Contra figure Richard Secord. Tully also had close friends in President Bush's administration.

Top Clinton advisers rushed from Little Rock and Washington to Manchester. They convinced the governor to go on ABC's *Nightline* that evening. Suddenly, the *Nightline* appearance was deemed as important as the *60 Minutes* interview had been a few weeks earlier. This time, however, Bill would not have Hillary by his side.

As hundreds of thousands of Americans looked on, Ted Koppel devoted nearly ten minutes of his forty-five-minute program to reading Clinton's astonishing letter in its entirety. At a time when the average television sound bite had shriveled to less than twenty seconds, such an extravagant use of time was both brave and intelligent; it betrayed an uncommon respect for the program's viewers. Koppel obviously thought people could decide for themselves what the letter meant.

It was an extraordinary document. Written December 3, 1969, while Clinton was a Rhodes Scholar at Oxford University in England it described the Vietnam War as a war Clinton "opposed and despised." He thanked Holmes "not just for saving me from the draft, but for being so kind and decent to me last summer, when I was as low as I have ever been."

Although some found the letter touching, the act of a guilt-torn and thoughtful young man, many saw Clinton's concern about his political viability as surpassingly cynical. Others read the worst into Clinton's admission that he "loathed" the military. All in all, it further injured Clinton's bid for the nomination.

Even before the letter's release, surveys indicated Clinton had dropped into second place among New Hampshire voters, losing a third of his support in two weeks. A *Boston Globe* tracking poll showed Clinton support among New Hampshire Democrats had dropped from twenty-eight percent to nineteen percent in five days.

Instead of retreating home following the letter's release, the Clintons and the hundreds of Arkansas Travelers increased their intensity level.

"The people putting this stuff out would have you believe he is a draft-dodging sex pervert," former Arkansas state Representative David Matthews told a crowd at Manchester. "Get real. Don't get sidetracked."

On *Nightline*, Bill said of the previous three weeks, "All I was asked about by the press is a woman I didn't sleep with and a draft I didn't dodge."

Others thought Bill Clinton had lied twice and escaped with his presidential ambitions intact.

Harkin was quick to predict that the draft controversy would doom Clinton's candidacy. Both Hillary and Bill characterized Harkin's comment as an act of desperation. In one television interview, Bill said, "I don't think it has undermined my electability. If you say I'm electable on Tuesday, by definition I'm electable."

Somewhat surprisingly, Paul Tsongas mildly defended Clinton, saying that to dismiss him as inviable would be a "major mistake." The former Massachusetts senator said Clinton's draft status should be "part of the discussion," but that the media frenzy went too far and that "issues got lost in the shuffle."

By Thursday, five days before the crucial primary vote, Hillary and Bill were telling supporters that a good finish—meaning coming in at least second—would revive their campaign. In a strategy advisers likened to a crap shoot, the governor purchased a thirty-minute block on the state's major television station to answer questions from a panel of ten undecided voters. The program, coproduced by native Arkansan and Hollywood television producer Harry Thomason, was televised unrehearsed.

Hillary, a close friend of Harry Thomason and his wife Linda Bloodworth-Thomason, was among those who had suggested the approach.

Remembering past political struggles in Arkansas, Bill said, "I've always been able to come out of it when I stood up to it, fought it and worked it through. And I will with this if there is enough time."

"In New Hampshire, five days is a lifetime," Clinton aide George Stephanopoulos assured Hillary that Thursday.

By Saturday, two tracking polls showed that Bill's slide in New Hampshire had been halted. A revitalized Bill and Hillary Clinton had breakfast at a Manchester restaurant and then helped the Arkansas Travelers canvass a local neighborhood. At each home, they handed out campaign videotapes.

Mary Ellen Glynn, the Clintons's New Hampshire press secretary, called the taped message "very direct.

It speaks to voters without a filter of the news media. It takes Bill Clinton into their homes.''

With charges of womanizing and draft evasion dominating news accounts, the campaign had little choice.

''We always do best when we're talking about the issues,'' said Frank Greer, a campaign media adviser.

Just six weeks earlier, Bill and Hillary had been the darlings of the national media. They were running what political analysts termed a textbook campaign, picking up dozens of endorsements and raising hundreds of thousands of dollars. Bill led his Democratic challengers in the polls. In New Hampshire, he even led President Bush.

But now all of that might be lost. As the final weekend before the primary began, the Clinton campaign continued its aggressive, expensive effort to regain momentum.

''Given the intensity and the volume of coverage, between now and Tuesday is a long, long time,'' strategist James Carville said that weekend. ''There's no shortage of time, events or opportunities for anybody.''

The day before the primary, hundreds of Clinton volunteers, many of them college students, handed out literature, knocked on doors and made phone calls. A *USA Today*-CNN poll showed Tsongas leading Clinton by twenty percentage points. A *Boston Globe* poll, however, had Tsongas's lead at only seven points.

''Someone will turn out to be right,'' a Tsongas pollster said. ''We just don't know who yet.''

Bill and Hillary visited ten southern New Hampshire communities that Monday. At stop after stop, as Hillary looked on smiling, the governor said, ''This is the work of my life, and that is why you should vote for me tomorrow.''

On February 18, 1992, New Hampshire voters saved Bill Clinton's campaign. He finished a strong second, just eight percentage points behind Tsongas, who garnered thirty-three percent of the vote. Clinton immediately dubbed himself the "Comeback Kid."

In prime time, the Clintons walked onto a stage in a Merrimack hotel ballroom and, in essence, claimed victory for finishing second in the nation's first primary. The strategy worked—the media spin in the days that followed was that Bill had confounded the experts simply by surviving.

"He's blown away the polls," Clinton's pollster, Stan Greenberg, said. "There had to be a big, late surge no one detected. He closed very strong."

"This is a guy that was piled on and came back from a free fall," said Washington consultant Jim Duffy. "He can say he took some shots and came back."

In politics, where perception is reality, Bill indeed seemed the winner by having finished a close second. He said he had "proved you don't have to roll up and die if someone says something about you that's untrue."

Bill and Hillary next headed south, where they would rely on strong regional appeal along with organizational and fund-raising advantages. The march to the White House had begun in earnest.

Less than nine months later, Bill would become the first person in thirty-six years to win the presidency without first having won the New Hampshire primary. It was the seventh time a party nominee did not first win the primary, but in each of the previous cases, the nominee did not win in November. Those who had lost the New Hampshire primary, won their party nomination and then lost in the general election were Democrat Adlai Stevenson in 1952 and 1956, Republican Barry Goldwater in 1964, Democrat Hubert Humphrey in 1968, Democrat George McGovern in 1972 and Democrat Walter Mondale in 1984.

In 1972, Senator Edmund Muskie of neighboring

Maine defeated South Dakotan George McGovern, but a smaller margin of victory than expected derailed Muskie. Four years earlier, President Lyndon Johnson narrowly defeated Eugene McCarthy in the New Hampshire primary, and the small margin of victory drove the President out of the race.

In 1992, Clinton finished second and survived against all odds. He survived Gennifer Flowers's highly publicized allegations of a twelve-year affair. He survived the controversy over his Vietnam-era draft status.

Those searching for the turning point in the Clintons's march to the White House might focus on those winter weeks in New Hampshire. During that period, a winning presidential campaign was forged. And Bill Clinton had Hillary Clinton to thank. Had she even once expressed doubt about his honesty and character Bill's bid for the presidency would have gone the way of Gary Hart's campaign after the Donna Rice scandal. No matter how strained things might have been privately, Hillary held firm publicly.

During those long, dark days, she was a rock. In the snows of New England, Hillary stood by her man in a way that should have made Tammy Wynette proud.

CHAPTER TWO
The Good Wife

Bouncing off the second-place finish in New Hampshire and the positive media spin it engendered, the Clinton campaign turned south and west as Hillary faded from the foreground and focused her attention on the drab, often grueling, but always necessary business of raising funds.

In a campaign, convincing the unconvinced is less than half the battle. You must also convince the convinced to open their checkbooks. So, eight days after the rush of the New Hampshire "victory," Hillary attended two Washington fund-raisers—a $250-per-person reception and a $1,000-per-plate private dinner that together provided the campaign a welcome $300,000 infusion.

She flew solo at these events while her husband campaigned in Colorado. The Clinton team had decided that whenever Bill couldn't attend a major event, Hillary was a more than adequate surrogate. At least several reporters thought she was, if not the brighter, at least the more steely half of the team. She also could be counted on to avoid being drawn into what were ultimately tangential issues. Bill Clinton had just survived the worst two months of his political life and emerged intact—and perhaps even stronger after the crises. The lingering, unanswerable questions about the quality of Clinton's character no longer seemed important. At issue was the more pragmatic problem of who among the still-standing Democrats could beat George Bush in November.

"I think the important thing to recognize is that Bill is the only candidate who has done well in every single encounter," Hillary said in Washington. "He's the only candidate who has gotten delegates in every single primary and caucus. When you keep your eye on what is important, which is the delegate count, Bill Clinton is the only candidate who's running a national campaign."

In addition to her fund-raising duties, Hillary remained her husband's closest advisor. When she spoke, campaign strategists knew it was wise to listen, and not simply because they wanted to save her feelings. Nor did she involve herself solely with the campaign's broad themes and general direction. Hillary also had an aptitude for microsurgery.

Little of what is said during a presidential campaign is ever truly spontaneous. As it happened, Hillary was responsible for one of the Arkansas governor's best "ad-libs" during a debate in early March among the Democratic candidates, telecast nationally by ABC.

Just before the debate, as Bill's advisors finished briefing him on some arcane bit of policy, Hillary came over to straighten her husband's lapel.

"Bill, look," she whispered in his ear. "If Jerry Brown goes off on some wild tangent against you, just remind him he's from California and what they say out there is 'chill out.' Just tell him to chill out."

Sure enough, midway through the debate, an overheated Brown attacked Clinton on his civil rights record in Arkansas.

"Bill, you've had eleven years to get through a civil rights act and you're trying to appeal to African-Americans and Hispanics, and I want to see where are your civil rights," Brown said.

Clinton delivered his prepared line perfectly: "Jerry, chill out. You're from California. Chill out. Cool off a little. Nobody has a better civil rights record than I do, and you know it."

Hillary, watching a television monitor in the studio, laughed along with everyone else.

Not everything went so smoothly as the planted riposte. There were, of course, still controversies—some personal, some political. Even Hillary's trademark headbands became a matter for dissection. One journalist said they made her "look like a prim Southern working woman instead of a Wellesley feminist."

A hairdresser noted that "it's lazy, even if it does hide dark roots."

"Hillary Clinton's headbands suggest a woman who opens her own car door," syndicated humorist Erma Bombeck wrote. "She's a woman who would lean across the table in Japan and warn her husband, 'You eat that sushi, Bill, and you're going to make the six o'clock news.' A headband definitely means a strong domestic policy and a withdrawal of more nuclear arms. As the campaign heats up, the thing to watch here is whether Hillary Clinton caves in to public pressure about her headbands. I think she'll 'stand by her bands!' "

Bombeck was wrong. Within months, the headbands were gone, and Hillary's hair reflected a more polished, sophisticated approach to life in the limelight.

The flap over Hillary's headbands must have eventually become a source of great annoyance to a woman who had always—even from her high school days— valued substance over style. While Hillary allowed herself to be groomed for campaign appearances, there is little to indicate she took much of an active interest in the process.

Her style was always professional, but because she lacked the time or the inclination to shop, her clothes were not always carefully thought out. Until the campaign, when she, somewhat reluctantly, submitted to the image maker's advice. As the campaign went on, her hair became blonder, sleeker, more done. But Hillary Clinton had more important things on her mind than hairstyles.

Not so easily banished was the controversy that arose over Hillary and Bill's involvement with an Arkansas business and political figure named James McDougal. In early March, *The New York Times* reported that the Clintons had been business partners with McDougal at the same time his failing savings and loan association was subject to state regulations. In 1978—the year of Clinton's first gubernatorial campaign—McDougal, then a real estate developer, formed a corporation with Bill and Hillary called the Whitewater Development Company, which purchased 230 acres of land situated along the White River in the Ozark Mountains of north Arkansas. Their plan was to subdivide the land and sell the plots as vacation sites.

Whitewater paid $202,000 for the land in August 1978. Most of the Clintons's share of the money came from Hillary's income; as Arkansas attorney general, Bill was making only a fraction of her private-sector earnings.

Like Clinton, McDougal had worked as an aide to Senator J. William Fulbright from Arkansas. McDougal worked on Fulbright's staff from 1967 until Fulbright's defeat in 1974. He then worked in Clinton's first administration (from 1979 to 1980). In 1982, he ran unsuccessfully for Congress in the 3rd District of northwest Arkansas against Republican incumbent John Paul Hammerschmidt—the man who had defeated Clinton in his first try at elected office in 1974. McDougal got only thirty-four percent of the vote.

McDougal later would became an aide to Governor Clinton. In 1982 he bought the controlling interest in Madison Guaranty Savings and Loan Association. Eventually, federal regulators took over Madison Guaranty.

In 1989, a grand jury indicted McDougal on bank fraud charges. Even though the Whitewater venture eventually lost thousands of dollars and McDougal was acquitted on the fraud charges, there was political fallout. The *Times* article suggested that Madison Guaranty should have been closed by the state because of a federal report showing the institution "would result in an insolvent position." But the former state securities commissioner, a Clinton appointee named Beverly Bassett Schaffer, said state officials relied on an independent audit.

"We had in our possession an independent audit with a clear, unqualified opinion showing the institution to be solvent," Schaffer said.

McDougal reportedly had urged Clinton to appoint Schaffer—a member of the law firm representing the S&L—to the securities post. McDougal later played down his involvement, saying he was "among many Clinton supporters who were backing her."

He said Schaffer's appointment "wasn't done on my recommendation, I can tell you that. I don't remember ever calling the governor and putting pressure on him to appoint anybody to anything."

Meanwhile, as a lawyer for Little Rock's Rose Law Firm, Hillary authored two proposals to the state to keep the Madison Guaranty afloat. Both proposals were accepted by the state shortly after Schaffer's appointment.

Madison had hired the Rose firm in 1985 following a federal investigation of the S&L. After publication of *The New York Times* story, Bill Clinton declined to answer questions about the Rose firm's relationship to McDougal, Whitewater Development or Madison Guaranty, instead referring reporters to the Rose firm. Because it was a Sunday, nobody could be reached, and Hillary Clinton was kept out of the public eye by campaign aides.

Hillary and Bill Clinton, the *Times* contended, also improperly deducted at least $5,000 in interest payments in 1984 and 1985 for bank loan payments made by Whitewater.

According to the *Times* article, McDougal said the governor called a mutual acquaintance when he began contemplating a campaign for President and asked whether McDougal held a grudge. Clinton reportedly suggested to his friend that he might find a job for McDougal, who was reduced to living on Social Security disability payments.

The *Times* story was published two days before the crucial Super Tuesday primaries as Clinton campaigned in Texas, a state hit hard by the savings and loan scandal. Once again, the campaign was pitched into crisis mode. At a March 8 airport news conference in Austin, Texas, Clinton aides distributed a packet of materials disputing several points in the article and claiming that at least five statements were clearly inaccurate.

The packet contained a statement from Charles James, Whitewater Development's accountant, stating that the Clintons were liable for loans of more than $200,000 for the Ozarks property. The *Times* article had said the couple largely was protected from financial loss on the investment.

Also included in the packet was a statement from Schaffer saying she did not know McDougal and had not been influenced by the involvement of her law firm with Madison Guaranty.

Bill Clinton told reporters there was ''no impropriety. I was not yet governor, and he (McDougal) did not yet own a financial institution'' at the time their partnership was formed. He further denied any wrongdoing and claimed the investment had been costly to the couple. While such real estate investments had been attractive in the 1970s, Clinton said his and Hillary's involvement came just before "a big collapse in the real estate market."

"I know we lost over $25,000 on this deal and never made a penny on it," he said.

As reporters pressed him, Bill claimed he did not drop out of the venture upon becoming governor in January 1979 because "frankly, at the time, it never entered my mind."

Then things got curiouser.

Susan McDougal, James McDougal's wife, spitefully told reporters that Hillary had personally solicited representation of Madison Guaranty for the Rose firm, contradicting the Clinton campaign's earlier claim that another Rose lawyer handled all issues involving Madison.

And James McDougal's dealings had not been limited to the Clintons. McDougal was a business partner through the years with other prominent Arkansas political figures, including Fulbright, Lieutenant Governor Jim Guy Tucker (who would succeed Bill Clinton as governor in December 1992) and Little Rock attorney Sheffield Nelson (who was Clinton's 1990 Republican opponent). While Arkansas is a small state, where incestuous political and business relationships are inevitable, it soon became apparent McDougal was exceptionally well-connected.

After Clinton lost his 1980 reelection bid to Republican Frank White, McDougal bought controlling interest in a small north Arkansas bank, the Bank of Kingston. Former Clinton aide Steve Smith was also a partner in the bank. Then, in 1982, McDougal bought the controlling interest in Madison Guaranty.

Tucker—the former congressman and future governor—had purchased about thirty-four acres from Madison Guaranty in the Little Rock area in the 1980s. He also had joined McDougal in the purchase of 2,600 acres in northwest Arkansas in the late 1970s. Tucker also briefly owned a small share of McDougal's Bank of Kingston in the early 1980s while Fulbright had bought about four hundred acres near Little Rock from Madison Guaranty and Nelson participated in a McDougal development off the Maine coast—a 3,900-acre development on Campobello Island, President Franklin Roosevelt's summer home.

In an attempt to head off further criticism, the Clinton campaign hired a Denver lawyer, Jim Lyons, to perform a financial review of Bill and Hillary's involvement in the Whitewater partnership. After a few days, the controversy seemed to fizzle, and Clinton was able to pile up big numbers on Super Tuesday.

Next, the couple headed to Illinois, Hillary's home state. Together, they visited Main South High School in Park Ridge, Hillary's alma mater, where the students welcomed her home with a huge banner. Not only was Hillary a native, but Clinton's campaign manager, David Wilhelm, was also playing on his home turf—Clinton was counting on a big victory in the Illinois primary in March.

After having gone underground for several days during the McDougal controversy, Hillary again became highly visible, visiting black churches on Chicago's South Side and marching with her husband in a Saint Patrick's Day parade in an Irish neighborhood.

Clinton's popularity in Chicago's black community was helped by the fact that thousands of Arkansas residents had moved to Chicago in the years following World War II as part of a mass black migration from the Mississippi River Delta to northern industrial cities. Clinton enjoyed enormous support among black Arkansans, invariably drawing ninety percent or more of the black vote in his statewide races.

Hillary spoke at the Saint Paul Church of God in

Christ, telling the congregation, "This is not a campaign about my husband. It is not about me. It is not about any individual. We can no longer ignore what goes on around us. What we have to agree among ourselves is that we have to solve our problems."

Members of the congregation shouted "amen" as Hillary spoke.

That same Sunday, March 15, *The Washington Post* published new allegations concerning Hillary Clinton's dealings on behalf of Madison Guaranty. That prompted Jerry Brown to blast the Clintons during a televised debate that Sunday night, calling the report "a scandal of major proportions."

Brown's attack, in turn, spawned an angry rebuttal from Bill Clinton, who told the former California governor that he should be "ashamed of yourself for jumping on my wife. You're not worthy of being on the same platform with my wife."

Clinton's response humanized him for many people—he appeared to be genuinely angry, a man capable of incautiousness in defending his wife. Unlike Michael Dukakis, who maintained his clinical coolness when CNN's Bernard Shaw asked if he, an opponent of the death penalty, would favor capital punishment for a hypothetical thug who raped his wife, Clinton's defense of his wife seemed impassioned. No matter that it was as calculated as the "chill out" comment, it seemed to work.

Brown may have exercised some political hyperbole that Sunday night, but it had the desired effect on Monday, the day before the primary. Bill and Hillary were reduced once again to defending their business dealings.

"I have done everything I knew how to do to be as careful as possible, including turning my back on funds that were coming into my firm," Hillary said outside a Chicago diner as dozens of reporters crowded around her.

"I think it was really insulting and was unfair that Jerry Brown misrepresented *The Washington Post* article," her husband added. "She is in the oldest law firm west of the Mississippi, and it's just a typical thing men do to professional women. He jumped on her, and I jumped him back, and I still feel good about it this morning. I think most people will identify with that."

Hillary promised to release documents about her work on behalf of Madison Guaranty and other businesses dealing with the state of Arkansas. She said she had performed no state business for a fee as a lawyer and that she had accepted no partnership fees that were tied to state business.

The *Post* article, which received widespread play in other major newspapers, began, "It is an axiom of life in Arkansas that most people who want something out of the state will at some point solicit support from the governor's office, where Bill Clinton runs the show, or from the Rose Law Firm, where Hillary Clinton is a partner. Or quite often both. The power line in Little Rock runs fourteen blocks from the red brick Rose building up to the pillared Arkansas Capitol."

The story went on to contend that rarely in American politics had married partners "played such interconnected public roles, and the convergence of legal and political power in the Clinton family poses several problems for them as they seek to move from a small-town, politically inbred capital to the White House."

Indeed, the Rose Law Firm—which would later supply the Clinton administration with Justice Department appointee Webb Hubbell and the doomed Vince Foster, the White House lawyer who committed suicide in July 1993—was one of the most powerful extra-government agencies in the state, and always had been.

Founded in 1819 at Arkansas Post in southeast Arkansas by Robert Crittenden and Chester Ashley, the Rose firm has been known through the years as Crittenden & Ashley; Ashley & Watkins; Watkins & Rose; U. M. & G. B. Rose; Rose, Hemingway & Rose; and Rose, Hemingway, Cantrell & Loughborough. It made the move west from Arkansas Post to Little Rock along with the Arkansas territorial government in 1821.

Prior to Hillary Clinton, the best-known attorney to come from the firm was Uriah M. Rose. He joined the firm in 1865 and was a well-known jurist, scholar and a recognized authority on international law. In 1917, his statue was added to Statuary Hall at the U.S. Capitol. He was one of only two Arkansans to serve as president of the American Bar Association.

His son, George B. Rose, was considered an authority on art and published several books. George Rose Smith, the last descendant of U. M. Rose to be active in the firm, retired on January 1, 1987, as an associate justice of the Arkansas Supreme Court at age seventy-four. With thirty-eight years of service, he had served longer than any justice in state history.

Its influence in the state is substantial; the firm has supplied six state Supreme Court justices and several members of the Arkansas Legislature. Whenever an Arkansas event draws national attention, chances are someone from the Rose firm is playing a leading role. For instance, Rose lawyer A. F. House was the lead counsel for the Little Rock School Board during the 1957 Little Rock Central High School desegregation case.

Hillary Clinton was one of about fifty-five lawyers at Rose, working in the litigation and labor section, one of four sections at the firm. Most of her work involved copyright infringement cases. She had been included in a list of the one hundred most influential lawyers in America by the *National Law Journal* in 1988 and 1991. Still, *The Washington Post* reported that "although she frequently is referred to in Little Rock and in profiles as a premier litigator, there is little indication that she has appeared frequently in court."

"I didn't think that anyone would presume anything other than that I was trying to do the right thing all the way down the line," Hillary said that Monday morning in Chicago. "Right now, I'm a little confused about what the rules are."

Then, like her husband, she implied that her role with the law firm had become an issue simply because she was a woman. Her choice of words, however, created almost as much of a controversy as had her stand-by-your-man comment in January.

Hillary said, "I've done the best I can to lead my life. I suppose I could have stayed at home and baked cookies and had teas. . . . The work that I've done as a professional, as a public advocate, has been aimed in part at making sure that women can make the choices that they should make. I still think that it is difficult for people to understand right now. This is a generational change."

Boom. The remark about staying home and baking cookies triggered thousands of telephone calls to newspapers and radio call-in shows across the country.

"I can assure her that women who stay at home to raise their children do a lot more than bake cookies and have teas," said one caller to the *Arkansas Democrat-Gazette* the day after Hillary had made the remark.

"I've never had a tea and never expect to have one," said another housewife.

"She has always had an arrogance about women who stay home to take care of their children," said a third. "She has this hostility toward women who do not work. It's fine for her to work, but she offended a lot of women who don't."

Hillary said the remark had been taken out of context and fought back, claiming that when Brown was asked

THE GOOD WIFE . 67

about the money his father, Pat Brown, had made from state business in California through the years, he had replied, "I have no control over my father, but Clinton should have had control over his wife."

Hillary Clinton does not like the idea of anyone controlling her. But she said repeatedly during the remainder of the week that she supported "the woman's right to choose (between a career and staying at home), and I respect all choices. I've always tried to help women who want to stay at home with their children."

On the eve of the Illinois and Michigan primaries, Jerry Brown said Bill Clinton was employing "bush-league politics" by trying to paint his wife as the victim of attacks that actually were aimed at the governor. It was a desperate tactic, and it didn't work.

Clinton carried Illinois easily, and Tsongas suspended his campaign. Although Brown would fight on until July's Democratic National Convention in New York, for all practical purposes the battle for the Democratic nomination was over.

Bill Clinton—and Hillary—had won.

But early victory posed one problem. Because only two Democrats were left—and no one figured Jerry Brown for a miracle—the media would have more time to focus on Clinton's career, his wife's career and their business dealings through the years.

Some doubted they could bear the scrutiny.

Any professional woman married to a well-known political figure must be wary of conflicts.

"If you are going to be a high-powered lawyer, it would be pretty hard to separate yourself from the economic power of the state," Clinton campaign adviser Diane Blair, a political science professor from the University of Arkansas at Fayetteville, told the *Post*.

"Everyone has their own standards and makes judgment calls," Ruth Harkin, an attorney married to Democratic Senator Tom Harkin of Iowa, told *The New York Times*.

"The commonsense approach is the correct one," Harriet Babbitt, the wife of former Arizona Governor Bruce Babbitt and a lawyer in a Phoenix firm, told the newspaper. "You absolutely have to have disclosure. It's a little like financial disclosure. You say to the world that Susie Q. and John Q. Public are man and wife. Then, people can do what they want with the information."

But Sheffield Nelson, by then the Clintons's major in-state nemesis, was telling visiting reporters from across the country that Arkansans who wanted special treatment knew to go to the Rose firm, that it was where the deals were cut.

Sheffield Nelson wasn't supposed to be Bill Clinton's gubernatorial opponent in 1990. Lee Atwater recruited Tommy Robinson, former Pulaski County sheriff turned congressman to run against Bill Clinton. In Washington, Robinson might have looked invincible, a tough-talker who could back it up, a plain-speaking populist with a Buford Pusser streak. Robinson was the anointed one, the guy that George Bush and the national GOP could count on to be as comfortable in the mud as up on the tractor.

Sheffield Nelson, on the other hand, previously headed the Arkla Gas company and was a former Clinton ally, a mild-looking man whose name recognition was, in 1990, generously estimated at fifteen percent.

Born in the microscopic community of Keevil in eastern Arkansas, Nelson became head of his family at sixteen after his father—whom Nelson has described as "alcoholic"—deserted the family. While working to support his mother and three sisters, he attended Brinkley High School, lettering in three sports, graduating with honors and ultimately earning academic and athletic scholarships to the University of Central Arkansas in Conway. While there, Nelson continued to work and send money back to his family. He married his high school sweetheart during his junior year and became president of the student body his senior year.

His undergraduate degree was in mathematics. "I wanted to go to engineering school but I couldn't afford to," he said. "I took all the math classes I could and got minors in English and finance. I found that when I got to law school the math courses had trained my mind to think in a very logical, precise way—I found I was much better prepared than people who had majored in history or political science."

Nelson quickly rose through the ranks at Arkla, resigning from the company's board of directors in 1984 after twelve years of being either president or chairman. Clinton then appointed him to serve on the Arkansas Industrial Development Commission, where he stayed for three years, two of them as chairman, before resigning in December 1988 to travel the state and assess his political future.

Nelson officially joined the Republican Party in August, 1989, *after* he had announced his intention to run for governor. He said that, like most Arkansans, he had been voting Republican for years on a national level. He supported Ronald Reagan during the 1980 election, but insisted his objection to the Democratic Party lay with the national element, not the state guys. His problem was with the liberals—the Teddy Kennedys, the Barney Franks, the, uh, Bill Clintons.

"Clinton's liberalism, his tax-and-spend mentality, is killing us," Nelson said during the 1990 race. "People are beginning to wake up to that."

Hillary joined the Rose firm in 1977 when the couple moved from Fayetteville to Little Rock so Bill could begin his two-year term as Arkansas attorney general. In Fayetteville, both had taught at the University of Arkansas Law School. In 1979, Bill's first year as governor, Hillary became the Rose firm's first female partner.

Despite criticism from Nelson and other Clinton opponents, in recent years the Rose firm has not rated especially high on the list of law firms doing business with the state. From July 1, 1990, until March 1992 when Brown made his charges, the firm ranked twenty-seventh, collecting only $4,226.75 in state fees. Since 1985, the firm had received almost $235,000 from the state, but more than $100,000 of that came from being a bond counsel for the Arkansas Development Finance Authority. Bob Nash, the ADFA director, said four other law firms received more business than the Rose firm. Much of the rest of the $235,000 came from the Arkansas Public Service Commission, which was represented by the Rose firm and several other firms during a dispute over a nuclear power plant in Mississippi.

However, the firm did receive $277,000 in legal fees in 1991 from TCBY ("The Country's Best Yogurt") Enterprises, which listed Hillary on its board of directors. The company, which franchises yogurt stores across the country, had added Hillary to the board in 1989. She also served on the board of Wal-Mart Stores of Bentonville, Arkansas, one of the nation's largest retailers.

Hillary consistently said she did not see a conflict in serving on the boards of two giant Arkansas-based companies because neither company was chartered or directly regulated by the state. The Clintons's financial disclosure forms showed that she made more than $12,500 per year by serving on each of the boards.

As Hillary herself would later acknowledge, her ties with big business have paid off handsomely over the years. Though her critics have snidely alluded to her "Marxist Friends," fellow travelers rarely consort with the likes of Sam Walton.

On March 23, the Clintons released the results of Jim Lyons's investigation into their dealings with

McDougal. In a letter to the couple, Lyons wrote, "The facts confirm that not only was there always the potential that you would lose money, you in fact lost significant sums."

Lyons said the Clintons had lost $59,000 on the land deal and that they had "inadvertently" claimed $5,133 in interest deductions to which the corporation, not its shareholders, were entitled in 1984 and 1985. That resulted in what the review said was a "marginal" tax benefit for the couple. Hillary said she and her husband would pay that tax liability as they had promised.

"Even though you were passive shareholders, you assumed considerable financial responsibility for a corporation whose liabilities exceeded and continue to be greater than its assets," Lyons wrote. Accompanying his letter was a statement of review from a financial consulting firm, Patten McCarthy & Associates of Denver.

Lyons's report, however, did not put an end to stories about possible conflicts of interest involving Hillary. Three days later, *The New York Times* reported that although Bill Clinton had supported an ethics and disclosure law for public officials, he and his advisers altered it so that high-level public officials would be exempt from disclosing potential conflicts of interest. The law, approved by Arkansas voters in 1988, was imposed only on the state's legislators.

According to *The New York Times*, deletion of the provision occurred at a private drafting session in which Webb Hubbell, a senior partner at the Rose firm (and second in command in the Justice Department during the Clinton administration), participated. At the time, an ethics package had been passed by the Arkansas House but was stalled in the state Senate. The package would have required legislators and a broadly defined category of "public servants" to file a report each time they took an action that might affect their family's finances. The revised version of that bill retained the disclosure requirement for legislators but deleted it for the governor, other statewide elected officials and appointed officials on boards and commissions.

"One practical effect was to exempt Clinton from reporting any actions or decisions on his part that affected his wife's clients or the Rose Law Firm," investigative reporter Jeff Gerth wrote in *The New York Times*. "With that language out of the legislation, Clinton also did not have to wrestle with which of his wife's or the firm's activities would require disclosure—a potential quagmire of complex and debatable judgments."

Clinton issued a statement saying the reasons for dropping the provision had "nothing whatsoever to do with possible problems for me, my wife or her law firm, a subject which no participant recalls ever even arising in countless conversations on the ethics bill." Hubbell, meanwhile, acknowledged having participated in writing the law—he was a member of an ethics commission appointed by Clinton—but denied shaping it to shield the Rose firm's work for the state from public scrutiny. A day after the publication of the *Times* article, Hillary received support from an unlikely source—Barbara Bush. The first lady said criticism of Hillary surrounding the Rose firm's business with the state was unfair. Barbara Bush said she believed a first lady should be allowed to have an independent career.

"I think she should be allowed to make a choice," she said.

Meanwhile, more and more Americans were beginning to take notice of Hillary. Writing to *Parade* magazine's popular "Personality Parade" feature, someone asked if Hillary as first lady would turn into "a Nancy Reagan and try to run this country." Walter Scott answered, "The highly intelligent and ambitious Mrs. Clinton could emerge as the most powerful first lady since Eleanor Roosevelt."

Back home in the *Arkansas Democrat-Gazette*, political columnist John Brummett wrote that the discussion centered "on whether Hillary Clinton is a net advantage or a net disadvantage for Clinton's presidential candidacy. The possible disadvantage is that she offends a significant portion of the population—country-western fans, homemakers—whenever she opens her mouth. The advantage is that she is the first candidate's wife to run for co-president, and her intelligence and feminist edge ideally mesh with the current climate. I think she's a net advantage. Country-western fans and homemakers haven't yet emerged as an organized, money-raising political movement."

Bill indicated in late March that his wife would play a major role in his administration should he win in November. At a stop in Milwaukee, the governor said, "We will try to decide what it is she ought to do and then discuss it with ourselves and then tell the American people and give them time to get adjusted to it. It would be unusual. There has never been a. . . ."

He paused without completing the sentence. He then added, "I appreciate your encouragement. I'll sure try to get her in there at some high level. But you've got to get me in first before I can get her in."

The media focus on and public interest in Hillary gave rise to another debate: What should the spouse of a presidential candidate look like, sound like and act like? What role should that spouse play during the campaign? And what should she do if she reached the White House?

Many of the same Wellesley students who cheered Hillary in 1992 had in 1990 protested school officials' decision to award Barbara Bush an honorary degree; students felt a degree wasn't warranted by someone whose only career was as a wife and mother. But thousands of Americans were criticizing Hillary for just the opposite reason—because they felt she hadn't spent enough time being a wife and mother. Similar criticism has been heard almost a decade before in Arkansas when the governor appointed his wife to head a state education commission. By the time she was finished, however, Hillary was receiving rave reviews.

"I think we elected the wrong Clinton," said Lloyd George, a veteran state representative and chicken farmer from a rural county in west Arkansas.

After that success, Bill began telling Arkansas audiences that a vote for him was also a vote for Hillary. He carried that theme into his presidential campaign, telling voters in New Hampshire, "Buy one, get one free."

Part of Hillary's early interest in politics had come from the six months she spent working with the Children's Defense Fund after law school. In 1986, she was named chairman of the CDF board, one of seventeen civic and corporate boards on which she was serving by the time her husband announced his presidential candidacy.

Ironically, the amount of time that candidacy was taking forced Hillary to ask for a leave of absence in February 1992 from her job as chairman of the CDF board. She also had decided that her role in the campaign would compromise her position with the advocacy group. The CDF's stated policy was to put children before politics. Other board members worried that Hillary's visibility would cause the group to be aligned with one political party.

"I think Hillary is very sensitive about the perception issue," said Donna Shalala, the board's vice president and Clinton's future secretary of Health and Human Services. (Many contended—probably correctly—that Hillary made the call on that and several other Cabinet appointments.)

Shalala emphasized that leaving the CDF board was entirely Hillary's decision. "She has been a wonderful chair," said Shalala, who was chancellor of the University of Wisconsin at Madison. "She brings a combination of high intelligence and pragmatism, and she has carefully thought through how to deliver services and the role of government. Hillary is passionate about issues involving poor children."

As a non-profit charity, the CDF by law cannot endorse candidates or engage in partisan politics. But under the leadership of Marian Wright Edelman, the organization's president and founder, the CDF built a reputation as a powerful and effective lobby. Edelman and Hillary had become close friends and political allies through the years. With Hillary as chairman, the CDF was able to place children's issues high on the government's priority list.

Hillary's involvement brought her several awkward moments such as in 1989 when the CDF attacked Clinton and other governors for supporting a two-year freeze on the enactment of additional Medicaid mandates. Early in the presidential campaign, Tom Harkin cited CDF studies to support a conclusion that "the nation is doing poorly by its children, particularly in states like Arkansas."

Such criticism became part of life for Hillary. She learned to temper her responses. By late spring, she was somewhat less outspoken than she had been during the *60 Minutes* interview in January. Asked at a fundraising reception in Little Rock why she put up with life in a fishbowl, Hillary answered, "The first time I was asked that question, it just sort of struck me. And I just looked at the man who asked me and I said, 'You know, this may sound real corny to you, but I really love this country. And I believe that we can do better than we're doing.' "

During March and April 1992, an old controversy would resurface and some new ones would arise. The old controversy concerned Hillary's involvement with Jim McDougal's Madison Guaranty Savings and Loan.

The conservative *Washington Times*, quoting unidentified sources, reported in late March that Hillary received $2,000 per month in legal fees from Madison during a fifteen-month period beginning in the summer of 1984. According to the newspaper, McDougal deposited the $2,000 each month into a bank account for legal fees. The Rose firm then billed the account for the legal work, the sources were quoted as saying.

Hillary and Webb Hubbell disputed the assertion that the governor's wife had received $30,000 from the troubled S&L. Both maintained that Hillary had only a peripheral role in legal matters involving Madison. Hillary confirmed the firm was paid monthly by McDougal but said the $2,000 figure was too high. She and Hubbell also said the money paid to the firm went directly to Rose and was not funneled through a bank account. Hillary said she received no payment for legal services directly from Madison, but she declined to say how much the firm was paid, citing the attorney-client privilege.

Compounding the resurfacing McDougal problem were comments Hillary made in the May issue of *Vanity Fair* magazine concerning a rumor that President Bush had had an extramarital affair. In an interview with Gail Sheehy, Hillary suggested that reporters should look into the long-rumored but never substantiated reports about a Bush affair. The distracting controversy came just before the New York primary.

In the interview, Hillary named the woman rumored to have had the affair with Bush. The magazine only printed the woman's first name, Jennifer. The rumors long had floated around Washington, but during Bush's 1988 presidential campaign, his oldest son, George W. Bush, had said his father never committed adultery. When Hillary's *Vanity Fair* interview was released Bush's campaign press secretary, Torie Clarke, responded by saying Hillary's allegations were "absurd, irresponsible and wholly out of line." The interview led to a new series of lurid headlines in New York's tabloid newspapers.

Campaigning in Albany, Hillary told reporters the comments had been "a mistake. People were asking questions at the time, and I responded. Nobody knows better than I the pain that can be caused by even discussing rumors in private conversations, and I did not mean to be hurtful to anyone."

While Hillary was backing away from the comments, Bill was saying nothing. He said all questions should be addressed to his wife. "I will stick by what she says," the governor stated.

Clearly, though, Clinton was angry that the release of the interview had taken the media's focus off a meeting with Mario Cuomo at Albany. At that meeting, the Arkansas governor played down the earlier disagreements between the two. Meanwhile, Cuomo, often mentioned as a potential Democratic nominee should there be a brokered convention, said that was "not going to happen. It is not the way to produce the strongest Democratic candidate."

Clinton complimented Cuomo at length, calling him "one of the most brilliant and insightful political leaders this country has produced in my lifetime." He said that if Cuomo had decided to run for the presidency, the New York governor would have been the favorite.

Clinton also played down his comments on the Flowers tape in which he had called Cuomo a "mean son of a bitch."

"I don't want to reopen old wounds, but I'll tell you, after what I've seen the last two weeks, every now and then, the governor of New York ought to have to be a little mean to survive in this atmosphere," he said.

Yet all reporters seemed to care about on those "mean" streets of New York were Hillary's comments to *Vanity Fair*. The interview with Sheehy actually had

taken place in late January. At that time, Hillary was
upset because the allegations about her husband's sex
life seemed as though they might end his campaign.

Hillary said she had received her information from
Anne Cox Chambers of the Cox communications em-
pire of Atlanta. She promised to write Barbara Bush a
letter apologizing for the comment. The letter would
add emphasis to the public apology she had issued at
Albany. Meanwhile, Clinton aides said Hillary had
thought the part of the interview in which the controversial statement was made to Sheehy was an off-the-
record conversation.

The *Vanity Fair* article, spread over fourteen pages,
painted Hillary as an ambitious, almost unfeeling person. Ironically, two days after the excerpts were released, Barbara Bush was in Little Rock for a fund-
raising event. She brushed aside Hillary's comments
with a single word: "Baloney." When reporters per-
sisted in their efforts to get the first lady to talk about
Hillary, she said, "I'd rather talk about George Bush."

"You're starting rumors," she said to one reporter who
kept asking questions. "You are, too," she said to another.

One of the first people to come to Hillary's defense
was close friend and Hollywood producer Linda
Bloodworth-Thomason, who charged that *Vanity Fair*
had rejected a more positive profile in favor of the one
printed in the May issue. She said she had seen the
first draft of Sheehy's article.

"This is a different picture of Hillary than what it
originally portrayed," Bloodworth-Thomason said.
"The editors felt it was too positive. They didn't believe they had that good a marriage. Tina Brown (*Vanity Fair*'s editor at the time) instructed her (Sheehy) to
go back out and get some dirt."

A *Vanity Fair* spokesperson responded that Sheehy
wanted to continue reporting the story right up until
the time of publication on April 1. The spokesperson
said that if Bloodworth-Thomason saw a draft, it was

"obviously a work in progress" and "was by no means a final draft. . . . I have no idea what Linda Bloodworth-Thomason saw or when she saw it."

Within a week, there would be another minor controversy involving Hillary. When Wellesley chose her as its commencement speaker some students spoke out against Hillary, contending that she was not among those nominated by graduating seniors and that her selection was a "breach of democratic process."

"I think a lot of people are unhappy she is speaking," said Sara Gross, a Wellesley student. "We're concerned the media will see this as more of a political issue than just a commencement speech and will interrupt our commencement." Gross also said she did not want the country to get the impression that Wellesley was endorsing Bill Clinton's candidacy.

Hillary apparently had been chosen at the last moment after a nominating committee had difficulty scheduling any of the twenty speakers on its list. Students had complained two years before that the ceremony had become a "media circus" when Barbara Bush spoke.

"Some students may be unhappy with the process by which she was selected, but that's to be expected at Wellesley," said Laurel Stavis, a spokesperson for the school. "We have a tradition of choosing prominent, sometimes controversial speakers."

"I'm sure Hillary Clinton will be a fabulous speaker," Gross said of the 1969 alumnus. "But she has already spoken here once this semester, and her husband is in the middle of a presidential campaign. It's not that we don't like her. It's the fact that we weren't consulted."

Still, Hillary gave the commencement address as planned on May 29. She called on the 534 graduates to help improve the lives of children, saying to laughter and applause that they could accomplish the task by "making policy or making cookies." She then attacked

the Bush administration for not responding to women
and their concerns.

"Women who pack lunch for their kids, or take the
early bus to work, or stay out late at the PTA or spend
every spare minute tending to aging parents don't need
lectures from Washington about values," she said.
"They, and we, need understanding and a helping hand
to solve our own problems."

Barbara Bush's address two years earlier had centered
on the central role of the family in a meaningful life. But
Hillary said it was a "false choice" to feel forced to
choose between a family and work. Hillary, the first former student ever allowed to address the school's commencement   ceremonies,   also   faulted   the   Bush
administration for not meeting the needs of the nation's
children.

"The shrinking of their futures diminishes us all,"
she said. "Whether you end up having children of your
own or not, I hope each of you will recognize the need
for a sensible national family policy that reverses the
absolutely unforgivable neglect of our children."

As summer and the general election campaign approached, Hillary began to hit her political stride. But she
dismissed reports that she might run for office herself
someday. The *Vanity Fair* story suggested that Hillary
had wanted to run for governor in 1990 if her husband
had not run. Sheehy described a phone call from Hillary
to a friend, Dorothy Stuck, in which Hillary asked what
would happen if she chose to run. Stuck reportedly told
Hillary she should wait several years so she would not
be saddled with her husband's baggage.

"She's talked to me about running for governor or
hoping I'd run for something as long as I've known
her," Hillary said of Stuck. "That was one of the millions of conversations she has had with me, but it
wasn't anything serious."

Hillary's focus clearly was on getting her husband
to the White House and, in the process, becoming the
most powerful woman in the world.

CHAPTER THREE
The Emerging Co-President

Any doubt that Hillary Clinton was, at least in fiscal terms, the dominant partner in her marriage was erased in April 1992 when the Clintons released their tax records. Her private-sector earnings dwarfed her husband's income and raised some questions about the appropriate role of a public servants's spouse.

The Clinton's 1990 federal return reported a gross income of $268,646, up from $197,651 the previous year. As governor of Arkansas, Bill made only $35,000. In 1991, the Clintons made $235,401 with Bill earning just $46,854. Together they declared $13,466 in interest income as well as $11,000 in honoraria for speeches. Hillary also earned $64,700 in fees for serving on corporate boards.

A week after the release of the returns, Clinton opponents and the press began to focus on Hillary's service on these boards. Hillary had joined the TCBY board in 1989 and the Wal-Mart board in 1986 and had been a fairly high-profile representative of both companies, frequently appearing at store openings and other corporate ceremonies.

Her affiliation with another corporation, however, was not so well known. In fact, given her liberal credentials, some supporters were quite surprised to learn

Hillary was earning $31,000 per year for serving on the board of Lafarge Corporation.

Headquartered in Reston, Virginia, Lafarge is a Fortune 500 company with a subsidiary engaged in the controversial practice of burning hazardous wastes to fuel cement plants. Hazardous wastes burned in cement kilns include everything from carcinogenic solvents such as acetone and benzene to paint, ink and waste oils. Lafarge was operating sixteen full-production cement plants, four cement grinding plants and more than one hundred distribution facilities throughout the United States and Canada.

The subsidiary, Systech Environmental Corporation of Xenia, Ohio, had been targeted by environmentalists and community activists in Texas, Indiana, Alabama, California, Michigan, Ohio and Kansas.

In 1991, the citizens of New Braunfels, Texas, a small town about midway between Austin and San Antonio, voted by a wide margin to oppose a Systech plan to burn hazardous wastes at a cement plant there. In March 1992, in Alpena, Michigan, a township board of supervisors voted to oppose plans to increase burning at the Portland Cement plant on the shores of Lake Huron.

Lafarge communications director, Katrina Farrell, said she assumed Hillary knew of the company's involvement in hazardous waste burning when she joined the board in 1990. But she couldn't say at the time whether Hillary had made any board decisions affecting Systech.

"What we're basically doing is recycling, which is what society wants us to do," Farrell said. "We don't have problems at the federal level. It's at the local level. I think it's a question of communications."

Asked about her association with Lafarge, Hillary said she believed the company had taken steps to ensure that hazardous wastes were disposed of safely. She noted that in 1991, Lafarge had destroyed seventy-seven million gallons of hazardous wastes that otherwise could have been deposited in landfills.

Her explanation did not satisfy everyone.

"How can you be concerned with the environment and sit on the board of a French-owned company that has only one thing in mind—to make money?," asked David Wallace, the founder of a grass-roots organization in Texas that was fighting the Systech burning plan. "I think it's atrocious. Mr. Clinton and Mrs. Clinton have both come out as environmentalists. Lafarge is not a company that promotes the environment. If Mrs. Clinton really was an environmentalist, she would resign tonight."

"If she's sitting on the board, she obviously has a vested interest in what they're doing," said John Pruden of the Huron Environmental Activist League. "And what they're doing is polluting."

On May 4, Hillary abruptly left the boards of Lafarge, Wal-Mart Stores and TCBY Enterprises. Her stated reasons for resigning, however, ignored the questions incurred by the financial disclosures.

"I have concluded that my full-time participation in my husband's presidential campaign prevents me from fulfilling my responsibilities as a director in the public companies," she said in a statement released by the campaign. "I have appreciated my association with these companies, each a leader in its respective industry."

To spare her husband further political embarrassment, Hillary was apparently willing to give up quite a chunk of the family's income. In addition to the $31,000 from Lafarge, Wal-Mart was paying her $18,000 per year in quarterly increments, as well as $1,500 for every meeting attended. TCBY paid her $5,000 per year and $1,000 for each meeting attended.

"Hillary's contribution in improving hiring and promotion practices for women and minorities was instrumental in advancing Wal-Mart as an industry leader," said that company's chairman, Rob Walton, son of the late Sam Walton. "Her proactive stance on environmental issues prompted Wal-Mart's deep, long-term commitment to preserve and protect our land, air and water."

In light of her concurrent service on Lafarge's board, some scoffed at Walton's comment.

"Hillary Clinton did the right thing for the wrong reason," *Arkansas Democrat* managing editor John Robert Starr wrote. "She said her husband's presidential campaign was keeping her so busy she couldn't do justice to the jobs. That convenient excuse masks the real reason for the resignations, which is that Hillary's connections with these big businesses had become an embarrassment for the campaign because of the inherent conflict of interest."

After her resignations, Hillary's aide Kim Hopper advanced the disingenuous spin that "no specter of conflict of interest had influenced Hillary's decision."

"If Hillary and campaign officials do not see that conflict, it is because they will not see," Starr responded in print. "She should never have accepted these appointments. I've always thought that Hillary's corporate connections represented a conflict of interest, even for a governor's wife, but I didn't fuss about it too much because she is, after all, the principal breadwinner for the family. Certainly it would not do for the first lady of the nation to be sitting on corporate boards."

In April, the Clintons took a day off from the campaign to fly to tiny Bentonville, Arkansas, to attend the private memorial service for Sam Walton, the famed Wal-Mart founder. Reputedly the nation's richest man, Walton had died at age 74 following a long fight with bone cancer.

"I wouldn't have been anywhere else today," Hillary said in Bentonville.

*   *   *

The image of Hillary as a cold and calculating elitist began to fix in the public imagination. People from across the country were still sending cookies to the Governor's Mansion in Little Rock in response to her careless "baking cookies" remark. Given the vituperation some aimed at her, it was probably wise that most of the cookies were thrown out. But dozens of chocolate chip cookies provided a temptation some couldn't resist.

"I had one, against some better advice," Clinton aide Trey Schroeder acknowledged.

Repairing the damage caused by the cookie gaffe led the normally no-nonsense first lady of Arkansas into some rather trivial pursuits as she and the campaign staff sought to soften her dragon lady image. In the days leading up to the Democratic National Convention, she dressed in pastels and talked about child-rearing and the Fourth of July.

Family Circle magazine requested chocolate chip cookie recipes from both Hillary and Barbara Bush for a national reader's choice bake-off. Hillary's recipe called for "more democratic" vegetable shortening instead of butter, and added rolled oats to stretch the dough and serve more people. Old-fashioned Barbara Bush used old-fashioned butter in her version.

"Obviously we were responding to some extent to the great furor over whether Hillary Clinton bakes cookies at all and whatever that is supposed to represent," Jaqueline Leo, *Family Circle* editor-in-chief said. In Little Rock, a local taste test—the brainchild of a radio personality—found that 60 percent of grocery shoppers preferred Barbara's butter-laden cookies to Hillary's more politically correct version.

In an editorial, *The New York Times* pleaded for the Democrats to "Let Hillary be Hillary." And the Pulitzer-Prize-winning voice of Pine Bluff, Arkansas, Paul Greenberg, told an interviewer from *W*:

"The first time I met Hillary Rodham, she was angry about injustice and not fearful or calculating about saying so. She was more ideologically committed, less fashionably attractive. Now she's tough, controlled, cosmetologized, intense, with something contradictory under the surface. You have the idea she's holding back."

In yet another distraction, Hillary was asked if she had ever smoked marijuana. The question came following her husband's clumsy admission that he had once smoked marijuana but "didn't inhale." Hillary answered the question by saying, "No, I don't like smoke, cigarettes or anything," a response that anticipated one of her first actions as first lady—declaring the White House a "No Smoking" zone.

Asked if she thought it was fair to raise the question of whether she had smoked marijuana, Hillary said, "It's tough to judge fairness.... It is not really on target with what is going on and what the future of this country is dependent on."

No, but inquiring minds wanted to know.

Meanwhile, Joan Quigley, the astrologer and advisor to Nancy Reagan who had helped set dates for Ronald Reagan's treaty signings, news conferences and travel, predicted in Washington that Bill and Hillary might separate if he did not win the presidency. She also predicted that another scandal involving the Arkansas governor would be revealed toward the end of the campaign.

The way things were going that seemed like a safe bet.

The cover of an April 27 issue of *U.S. News & World Report* asked the question: "Does Hillary Clinton help or hurt husband Bill in his quest for the presidency?"

The poll inside showed these responses:

•Thirty-eight percent of respondents thought Hillary helped her husband's campaign and thirty percent thought she hurt it.

•Seventy-nine percent of respondents thought Barbara Bush helped her husband's campaign and only four percent thought she hurt it.

•Asked what kind of job they thought Hillary would do as first lady, ten percent of respondents said excellent, thirty-six percent said good, twenty-four percent said fair and nine percent said poor.

•Twenty-five percent of respondents said they would like to see Hillary in the Cabinet if her husband were elected President, sixty-six percent said they would like her to be able to continue practicing law and fifty-eight percent said they preferred a traditional first lady.

Meredith Oakley of the *Arkansas Democrat-Gazette*, who had covered Hillary since she burst onto the state political scene in the 1970s and who had often antagonized the governor, answered the question thusly:

"She wants the presidency for her husband as much as he does, and being more level-headed, she has taken fewer detours and suffered fewer distractions. As best I can tell, Hillary's negative rating is highest among classes of people who rarely vote and, when they do, rarely vote Democrat.

"There isn't much she wouldn't do to live in the White House, but there are immovables in her makeup. She can change her name, she can change her hairdo, she can change her mind. She can even make a concerted effort to temper her brusqueness. She cannot change who and what she is. That is a brilliant, determined, focused, quick-witted but sometimes impetuous person who doesn't buy into the notion—shared by too many people, male and female alike—that this is and ought to remain a man's world. The American public doesn't quite know how to take her. Many Arkansans

don't, either. Perhaps it is that they are more familiar, hence more comfortable, with her ambivalent husband.

"I don't think our first lady has an indecisive bone in her body. Maybe at one time, as a young, well-educated, single woman with seemingly limitless options spread before her, she paused, or stumbled or stalled. But once Bill Clinton began to figure in those options, I don't think she ever really looked sideways. Theirs is not merely a marriage, it is a partnership, and she's a full partner in the dream. The questions about Hillary's effect on the campaign are inspired largely by her attitude and the public perception of and reaction to it, not by any of her political or professional deeds.

"Nothing aggravates a weak ego or low self-esteem quicker than a self-confident, assertive female. If she is misunderstood, oftentimes it is because her detractors refuse to hear what she is really saying. If Hillary made a mistake with her tea-and-cookies remark, it was in failing to remember that not everyone knows how many women assist a husband's political career by orchestrating and presiding over social and fund-raising events. To the uninformed and the already antagonistic, it was just another haughty retort from an uppity woman who thinks she's better than women for whom homemaking and child-rearing are full-time occupations."

Despite unlikely defenders such as Oakley, Hillary was forced to explain herself constantly. Modern political campaigns seem to lurch from controversy to crisis, and new crises seemed to erupt constantly for the Clintons.

During the spring, Hillary had to defend a November 1973 academic dissertation she had written at age 26 for the *Harvard Educational Review*. In the lengthy, dry dissertation on the rights of children, Hillary advocated additional legal rights for young Americans. That was interpreted by some as giving children the right to sue their parents.

In 1979, an obscure monograph she wrote called "Children's Rights: A Legal Perspective" was published in a collection of writing on children's rights. In that monograph, Hillary wrote that parents should not unilaterally have the authority to make decisions "about motherhood and abortion, schooling, cosmetic surgery, treatment of venereal disease or employment."

In March, historian and social critic Gary Wills had published a largely sympathetic overview of Hillary's writings in the area of children's rights in *The New York Review of Books*. Wills wrote:

> *"Millions of Americans were first exposed to Hillary Rodham Clinton as she sat loyally by her husband. . . . (She) denied that she was like Tammy Wynette standing lachrymosely by her man; yet that is exactly what she seemed at that humiliating moment. It would be a shame for people to continue thinking of her only in that role, since she is one of the more important scholar-activists of the past two decades."*

Wills contended Hillary's "attempt to undergrid practical activity with legal theory" set her apart from other successful, pragmatic litigators. Yet her legal theorizing gave her husband's political enemies plenty of fodder. Her work with the Children's Defense Fund and extensive writings challenging the hegemony of the father, under which wives and children were basically treated as chattel, were subject to interpretation and distortion by those who sought advantage by raising the colors of "family values."

While the conservative *American Spectator* and radio talk-shows hosts decried Hillary's "antifamily positions," *U.S. News & World Report* sensed in Hillary Clinton a kind of "national Rorschach test on which Americans can project their views of gender and equality.''

While some first ladies have been controversial in office—Eleanor Roosevelt, Betty Ford, Rosalynn Carter—none has engendered such spirited public debate ahead of time. For some, she's an inspiring mother-attorney. Others see in her the overbearing yuppie wife from hell—a sentiment that led GOP media guru Roger Ailes to say that Hillary Clinton in an apron is like Michael Dukakis in a tank.

Despite all the distractions, and the perception that the campaign had muzzled her, Hillary kept up a busy late-spring schedule of campaign appearances nationwide and traditional first lady of Arkansas appearances inside the state.

In Arkansas, she joined the other members of the 1983 Education Standards Committee, which she had chaired, in appearing before the state Board of Education. She urged the board to solicit ideas from academic and education-related organizations, from schools and from parent-teacher associations in its attempt to better implement the state standards for school accreditation. Her 1983 committee, after holding public hearings in all seventy-five Arkansas counties, had developed standards that mandated minimum course offerings, set graduation requirements, required competency tests, set limits on class sizes and required elementary schools to hire counselors.

''We went to all the curriculum groups and asked for recommendations,'' Hillary told the board. ''I hope you will ask the same groups to reconvene and to assess what was done and what is needed to improve.'' She said every provision of the state standards had come from ideas suggested by the public.

Out on the campaign trail, Hillary said she would like to use the job of first lady to be a voice for children in education and other areas. She said she had no inter-

THE EMERGING CO-PRESIDENT . 91

est in serving in her husband's Cabinet and would not accept a paying post in a Clinton administration.

"What I did in Arkansas was to be a volunteer, basically," she said during a visit to the Missouri Democratic Party convention. (Her job as chairperson of the Education Standards Committee nine years earlier had paid nothing.) "That's what I'd like to be in a Clinton administration. I'd like to be a voice for children."

In addition to improving public education Hillary promised she would work to improve child and prenatal health and expand the Head Start program. In a speech to the Missouri delegates, Hillary said Bush had contributed to "a spiritual crisis" in the country through his lack of vision. "It is very difficult to lead a great country without a vision of what that country should be," she said, warning that the U.S. faced losing an entire generation to "alienation, violence and despair."

With her husband virtually assured of the Democratic nomination, Hillary's attacks on Republicans became more aggressive. She said they were attacking her personally in an effort to distract the public "from the real issues facing the country. They can't fight on the issues. If they fight on the issues, Bill Clinton wins. The Republicans know that."

Hillary said the GOP's efforts to discredit her as an antifamily harridan were part of a "Big Lie technique" and that she was counting on most people having better sense "than to buy into that again."

She called for Americans to first "get mad," and then "get even" with the GOP for what twelve years of Reagan-Bush trickle-down policies had wrought. She spoke of the millions of people hurt by the slumped economy.

"Vote against the policies that have neglected this country and destroyed its future for millions and millions of Americans," she said in Jackson, Mississippi.

Hillary also blamed the Republicans for the constant controversies that had dogged her husband's campaign.

"It's true that this campaign has been unlike anything we've ever seen in presidential politics," she said. "I have never seen anything like it, and I don't think anybody who's a follower of presidential politics has. . . . Our message is a progressive message. I think once we're able to focus on that message, it is going to be clear that is what will win in November."

Hillary even entered the fray when Vice-President Dan Quayle attacked fictional TV character Murphy Brown. During a May speech in San Francisco, Quayle criticized the character, an unmarried television anchor in her forties, for choosing to have a baby even though she was not married. Quayle cited the TV show as an example of moral decay.

"He's trying to blame the Los Angeles riots and the social problems in this country on a TV sitcom," Hillary told the *San Francisco Examiner* during a visit to California several days after Quayle's remarks. "I think that's kind of sad because we have serious issues that need to be addressed." If Bush and Quayle really cared about family values, she said, the administration would not have vetoed the family leave and child-care bills. Quayle simple wanted to "point fingers and allocate blame."

"I wonder if he lives in the same America we live in, if he sees the same things we see," Hillary said. "Part of what it means to believe in family values is to value every family. I wish people in high office understood the real problems people in this country face."

Hillary mentioned that her husband's father had been killed in an automobile accident two months before Bill was born and that Bill's mother left him with his grandparents for several years while she attended nursing school.

Increasingly it became a battle fought in pop culture venues. In early June, Hillary joined her husband on the syndicated *Arsenio Hall Show*. It was during this program that Bill, wearing Ray-Bans and a garish tie, opened the show on saxophone, playing "Heartbreak Hotel" with Arsenio's band. When the talk show host asked Hillary why people should vote for her husband, she answered, "He's got the right combination of a good heart and a good mind. That's what the country needs right now."

During a visit to Little Rock the week of the Arsenio appearance, former First Lady Rosalynn Carter offered Hillary some advice about the campaign: "Enjoy it if she can—it's a once-in-a-lifetime adventure." She said she had been given the same advice from another former first lady, Lady Bird Johnson, during Jimmy Carter's 1976 presidential campaign.

"Campaigning is hard work, but there's a momentum that goes along with it that makes you not want to stop," Rosalynn said. "It's a tough but really wonderful experience where you get to meet people across the country. When I first started campaigning, I would be very nervous about going out of Georgia. What I found was that people are concerned about the same things across the country. They want a better life for their children than they had for themselves, they want a good community to raise their children in and they want to make ends meet. Every time I saw Lady Bird, she said, 'enjoy, enjoy.' It's such a fleeting time in your life. One thing that is important is to know what is true. You have so much that is said about you that is not true, and if you know what is true and you're comfortable with yourself and you know what you've done is good and right, then don't worry about it."

Whether Hillary actually enjoyed herself on the campaign trail is subject to debate. But no one had ever accused her of being "nervous" about leaving Arkansas. The closer the Democratic National Convention got, the more evident it became that a Bill Clinton presidency could indeed turn out to be a co-presidency with Hillary. She was no shy Rosalynn Carter.

In many ways, she was more harsh in her criticism of Republicans than her husband, and often more quotable. As Democrats began to patch up their differences and set their sights on the general election campaign, the fascination with Hillary increased. The country had never seen such attention focused on the wife of a major party nominee.

Hillary began July by telling *Working Mother* magazine that if her husband were elected president, it would be "hard, if not impossible, for me to continue to practice law. There are legitimate questions of conflict of interest."

In a small state such as Arkansas, business and politics are so intertwined that what might seem like conflicts to outsiders are considered normal by those who live there. When everybody knows what everybody else is doing, some allowances can be made.

In national politics though, Hillary discovered she had to be more careful about potential conflicts. She found that even her most offhand remarks would be taken seriously, dissected by the media and often blown out of proportion. But she also discovered that the intense scrutiny was well worth the potential reward of becoming first lady and redefining that role.

In speeches leading up to the Democratic National Convention in New York, Hillary continued to talk about being an advocate for children. As the convention drew closer Hillary began toning down her remarks in other, more controversial areas.

During a July 8 appearance at the Arkansas Governor School, a summer program for the state's most gifted high school students, Hillary was asked if she had been told by campaign advisers to stay quiet.

"Nobody ever said that to me," she replied. Whether it was her idea or James Carville's, she was choosing her words much more carefully than several weeks before.

Hillary gained a new campaign partner on July 9 when Clinton announced that his running mate would be Senator Al Gore, Jr., of Tennessee. Gore's wife, Tipper, had been outspoken during his 1988 presidential campaign but on far different issues than those that interested Hillary. Immediately, the media began comparing the two women, their wardrobes, their hairstyles and their political beliefs.

The *Arkansas Democrat-Gazette*'s Meredith Oakley wrote:

"There will be snide remarks about balancing the ticket between the wife who doesn't bake cookies and hold teas and the one who does." "The ensuing media blitz will have a decidedly sexist tone that ought not obscure the fact that the astute presidential contender gives the spouses of potential running mates as much scrutiny as he gives the ones who would be Vice-President. Don't kid yourself that the women beside the men cannot play a significant role in advancing both the candidacies of their husbands and their political agendas.

"There are, to be sure, significant differences between Hillary Clinton and Tipper Gore in both substance and style. Hillary is the tough careerist, Tipper the fluffy traditionalist. Yet both are highly ambitious political women, quite at home in the public eye. Both have been activists, launching personal crusades embracing issues of public concern. That they approach related issues in dramatically different ways will garner a great deal more ink."

Hillary's crusades had been children rights and education reform. Tipper, meanwhile, had written the book *Raising PG Kids in an X-Rated Society* and led a questionable drive to make record companies place warning labels on albums containing explicit lyrics. Many rock 'n' roll fans considered her an enemy of free expression.

Hillary wasted no time, though, in attempting to convey the impression that she would get along with Tipper. On the afternoon the announcement was made in Little Rock that Al Gore would be Bill Clinton's running mate, Hillary brought Tipper to a ceremony honoring the medical director of Arkansas Children's Hospital (for which Hillary was a board member). Hillary spoke on children issues while being photographed with Tipper and the children being treated at the hospital.

The national media was out in force for the photo opportunity. Hillary called Tipper "someone who shares with so many of us a commitment to the children of America." Tipper did not speak, choosing only to smile for a score of photographers.

During the week of the Democratic National Convention, Hillary kept a busy, high-profile schedule and avoided addressing controversial subjects. Although her husband was kept under wraps early in the week, Hillary attended five events that Sunday. She began the day at an afternoon event sponsored by the Children's Defense Fund and then gave brief remarks at an American-Israel Public Affairs Committee reception. From there, Hillary went to the Arkansas delegation party, a reception for Texas Governor Ann Richards and a reception for the party Hispanic caucus in Congress.

All of Sunday's public events went well. The next day, however, supporters of Jerry Brown interrupted Hillary with chants of "Let Jerry speak" as she appealed for party unity in a speech to the 406-member California delegation. Brown had 153 delegates from the state, and many of them joined in the chants even as the chairperson of Brown's delegation (San Francisco

County Supervisor Angela Alioto) and Brown's sister (Kathleen Brown, the state treasurer) urged the Californians to unite behind Clinton.

The former governor of California was tying his endorsement of Bill Clinton to securing promises such as Democratic Party support for raising the minimum wage and lowering the amount of money that could be donated to political campaigns. But Clinton campaign officials said they would not schedule a convention speaking time for Brown until he endorsed the party nominee.

Hillary's speech was conciliatory in nature as she began her twenty-minute visit with the delegation. She referred to Brown as an "old friend" that she had known since his days as governor of California. She promised that the party stood for campaign finance reform and said Brown would have to continue to "stress the need to reform the political process if America is to reform itself. Both my husband and Al Gore are committed to see those changes through."

About ten minutes into the speech, though, Hillary became more aggressive in response to the constant chants. Clearly aggravated, she said, "I've never known Jerry not to speak when he wanted to speak. He's always speaking as far as I can tell."

Despite the anger Hillary displayed at the California caucus, the media profiled her as the kinder, gentler Hillary during convention week. *Family Circle* magazine brought thousands of cookies to town to publicize its bake-off between Hillary's cookie recipe and Barbara Bush's recipe.

A smiling Hillary told reporters she found the controversies that had trailed her since the first of the year "surprising" and "bewildering."

"I thought women were beginning to develop a framework for the kind of life we could lead—still married, still committed to the family, still engaged in the outside world," she told columnist Ellen Goodman of *The Boston Globe*. "And I've just been surprised, I guess, by the assumptions that bear little resemblance to how all of us—not just me—make our way through this uncharted terrain. . . . We're all trying to work this out. We're all trying to find our way, and we don't have a common language."

Later that day, Bill would agree that "building up women does not diminish men."

Although Bill Clinton had become one of the most recognizable faces in America over the past few months, Hillary did not make her solo magazine cover debut until the August issue of *Working Woman*. In a four-page article, she reiterated her promise not to hold a Cabinet post in her husband's administration but to "engage in public service." Almost six months before her husband would appoint her head of a commission to redesign the country's health care system, Hillary said she might be interested in heading a special commission similar to the 1983 committee on education standards in Arkansas.

The *Working Woman* story was written by Patricia O'Brien, author of the novel *The Candidate's Wife*. The novel explored the role of candidates' wives and the public expectations of them. O'Brien noted in her profile of Hillary that in this so-called Year of the Woman in American politics, it actually was easier for a strong, independent woman to be a candidate than to be a candidate's wife.

"Hillary Clinton has been criticized and sniped at, some say, even though she is precisely the kind of competent, outspoken, caring human being that voters appear to want," O'Brien wrote.

After the convention, Hillary accompanied Bill, Al Gore and Tipper Gore on the first of what would become a series of well-publicized bus tours. The initial six-day tour took the four all the way from New York to St. Louis. They made more than twenty stops for rallies.

After the first bus tour, Hillary headed off on her own to address the two thousand delegates to the National Federation of Business and Professional Women Club's annual convention in Minneapolis. She told the delegates that she would not be pigeonholed as a mother, wife, community volunteer or lawyer.

"I am all of those things, and I am more than the sum of the parts," she said. "I am me. I've refused as best as I can and will continue to refuse the kind of stereotyping that tries to strip from me or tries to strip from any of you your individual dignity and your identity. . . . What I want is a community where we celebrate one another and where we recognize the complexity of who we are."

The federation president, Pat Taylor of St. Louis, introduced Hillary as "the prototype woman of the nineties." Hillary's thirty-minute speech was interrupted frequently by applause, and the federation's political action committee unanimously endorsed the Clinton-Gore ticket.

"If the Republican Party does not change its platform on the choice issue and all the other women's issues—family value issues that have been ignored the past twelve years—they are going to lose women's votes," Taylor said. "The gender gap is real, and it will be a career-affecting decision for the President."

Hillary garnered the loudest applause that day when she said, "It is absolutely possible, and I would argue imperative, to be pro-family and pro-choice." She also said it was possible to be both pro-business and pro-labor and both pro-economic growth and pro-environmental protection.

From there, it was off to join Bill, Al and Tipper on the second bus tour of the year, this one taking the four through the American heartland of Missouri, Iowa and Minnesota. With each public appearance, Hillary received more and more of the audience's attention. On the second bus tour, she found her appeal wasn't limited to politics. At a stop in Burlington, Iowa, a teenage boy carried a sign declaring, "Hillary is a babe." A drawing of a heart punctuated the message. Hillary eventually made her way to the sign and several excited young male admirers. She autographed the sign "for the boys."

After the second bus tour, Hillary flew west to San Francisco to attend the annual convention of the American Bar Association. While there, Professor Anita Hill, Supreme Court Justice Clarence Thomas's accuser, urged her and other female lawyers to speak out against sexual harassment.

"We must, even at some individual risk, participate in the education of our colleagues," Hill said. "Whether we move forward to change or revert back to the status quo is most assuredly up to us as a profession."

The University of Oklahoma law professor was honored by the ABA's Commission on Women in the Profession for testifying against Thomas during his 1991 Supreme Court confirmation hearings. Hillary said Hill's testimony had "transformed consciousness and changed history. All women who care about equality of opportunity, about integrity and morality in the workplace are in Professor Anita Hill's debt."

Hillary was the keynote speaker at the commission luncheon, attended by an overflow crowd of 1,200 people, where she presented awards to Hill and five other women.

While in San Francisco, Hillary was immortalized in song by a songwriter known only as Latch. He sang:

"From the great state of Arkansas
She looks like she just got off the set of L.A. Law
And that's cool by me
Vote for Hillary!

She got the guts to stand by her man
If she can't do it, nobody can.
She's blonde and a lawyer, too
Think of all the laws she'll push through.
Her mate is adulterous that true
But he ain't done nothing that Bush hasn't tried
    on you.
Think of the great political wives of history
Who outshine their husbands just like Hillary
Imelda, Cleopatra and Eva Peŕon
But next to Hillary, they're all outshone.''

Utterly forgettable, the song failed to dent the charts. But it was another manifestation of Hillary-mania—businesswomen were cheering her in Minneapolis, female attorneys were cheering her in San Francisco, and teenage boys were declaring her a babe in Iowa, so why not a song?

While Hillary-mania grew during the late summer of 1992, the Republicans were planning a well-orchestrated, unprecedented attack on the wife of the Democratic nominee. Never before had a major party gone after an opposing candidate's wife in such a manner. But never had a major party nominee had such a high-profile spouse.

During the week prior to the Republican National Convention in Houston, GOP Chairperson Rich Bond began the attack on Hillary, twisting her legal writing to suggest she had "likened marriage and the family to slavery." Bill Clinton labeled Bond's remark "pitiful" and said it proved the Republicans had no ideas of their own to talk about.

Bond was attempting to rally party leaders, who clearly were worried about Bush's chances for reelection. He said the gloves were going to be off during the convention. Bond even referred to Hillary as "that champion of the family" in a mocking tone.

"She has referred to the family as a dependency

relationship that deprives people of their rights,'' Bond said.

Bond's source was the essay on children's rights in which a much younger Hillary had written this sentence: ''Along with the family, past and present examples (of when an individual's rights are superseded) include marriage, slavery and the Indian reservation system.''

Bond quipped that the nation's toughest job belonged to ''the person in the Clinton campaign who is charged with keeping Hillary Clinton under wraps.''

Fred Meyer, the Texas Republican chairperson, said Bond's attack was not out of line as ''an introduction to the Republican National Committee to get their juices flowing.'' George Bush himself wandered into the fray, saying Hillary would ''encourage kids to hire lawyers and drag their parents into court.''

Hillary responded to the attacks, calling the President's suggestion ''preposterous.''

''Any fair reading of the work that I've done just doesn't support that,'' she said.

In an interview with *The Washington Post*, she charged that the Republican strategy was ''to say that the work I've done for more than twenty years on children's issues is somehow out of the mainstream or (is) undermining family values. And I think that is regrettable. . . . One of the things I've learned in the last seven or eight months is that meaning is imputed into things I say and do that's beyond me.''

As she had done earlier in the campaign, however, Barbara Bush came to Hillary's defense. When asked about a newspaper report that Bush's campaign associates were urging reporters to look into Hillary's life, the first lady said, ''I think that is outrageous. I hope that is not a true story. I think that's disgusting.''

She also said she did not agree with Bond's attacks. Asked if she would convey her feelings to the Republican National Committee chairman, Barbara Bush said,

"If I see him and he asks me. If I don't, I won't. Maybe you will. I love Rich Bond, but I read the headlines. I think that's not my kind of campaign. He got the world's best candidate, why not talk about it."

While Bond's remarks stirred up the controversy, a conservative publication, the *American Spectator*, printed a lengthy article by Daniel Wattenberg alleging that Hillary was associate editor of a special 1970 edition of the *Yale Review of Law and Social Action* that contained drawings depicting policemen as pigs.

"In one, rifle-toting, hairy-snouted pigs with nasal drip march in formation emitting 'oinks' and thinking to themselves 'niggers, niggers, niggers, niggers,'" Wattenberg wrote. "Another shows a decapitated and dismembered pig squealing in agony. It is captioned 'Seize the time.'"

Wattenberg also delved into Hillary's legal writings, noting that in one article she proposed reversing the legal presumption of incompetence of minors, extending to children all procedural rights granted to adults and permission for competent children to assert interests independent of their parents' in court.

Hillary had written that she preferred intervention by a court "into an ongoing family be limited to decisions that could have long-term and possible irreparable effects if they were not resolved. Decisions about motherhood and abortion, schooling, cosmetic surgery, treatment of venereal disease, or employment, and others where the decision or lack of one will significantly affect the child's future should not be made unilaterally by parents. Children should have a right to be permitted to decide their own future if they are competent."

On the third night of the convention in Houston, the Republicans decided to showcase what many considered their best asset—grandmotherly Barbara Bush. They wanted to portray the conservative, matronly first lady as everything Hillary was not. They also wanted to show that in this highly publicized political Year of

the Woman, their nominee's wife would be allowed
to address the convention, which didn't happen at the
Democratic National Convention the previous month in
New York.

"In one glorious evening, hardly anybody but fe-
males got to speak," John Robert Starr wrote of the
Democratic National Convention in the *Arkansas
Democrat-Gazette*. "They even invited some Republican woman to heap verbal abuse on Bush's stand on
abortion. At one time or another, or so it seemed, every
woman even vaguely connected with the Democratic
Party got a chance to be heard. Everybody, that is, but
Hillary Clinton.

"In the Democrats' 'Year of the Woman,' the wife
of the Democratic presidential nominee stands one step
behind her man, smiling and applauding almost every
word he says. That's the position good little Republican
wives have always occupied. Good little Democrat
wives, too, for the most part. But in the Year of the
Woman?"

Hillary denied that she had been asked by convention
planners to take a backseat to her husband. Starr speculated that "the male chauvinist pigs who run the Democratic Party pander to women, but they were not about
to abide a liberated woman upstaging the candidate."

In Houston at the Republican National Convention,
however, Hillary took center stage. She wasn't there,
of course, but her name was mentioned at almost every
event. From a fiery—some said mean-spirited—Pat Buchanan's speech on a Monday night to a family values
theme on Wednesday, the GOP tried to portray Hillary
as a radical feminist.

"What does Hillary believe?" Buchanan asked as
millions of Americans watched on television. "Well,
Hillary believes that twelve-year-olds should have a
right to sue their parents, and she has compared marriage as an institution to slavery and life on an Indian reservation."

On the same night Barbara Bush addressed the Republican National Convention, Marilyn Quayle, the wife of Vice-President Dan Quayle, also spoke. Almost seventy Bush relatives were in attendance. They assumed a high profile to help hammer home the message of family values.

Bill said later in the week that he was "beginning to think that George Bush was running for first lady." While the quip drew laughter, there was real anger in the Arkansas governor's voice.

He again accused Republicans of being unable to run on their record and said the Bush administration was "the worst in fifty years economically."

"They just intend to run me down and even run against my wife," he said. "It's sad. All this business about co-president, accusing Hillary of running for co-president, that's pathetic. Neither she or I ever said that. It's an outrageous distortion of her work, her writing. These are people who've made life much worse for most children and families in this country. Because of the policies of this administration, the average American people are much worse off. The working poor are worse off. There are a lot more poor kids in America."

Hillary, Bill and Chelsea flew to Atlanta later that week to help former President Jimmy Carter build a Habitat for Humanity house. One of Carter's pet post-presidential good works, Habitat for Humanity is a non-profit group that works to reduce poverty by building housing throughout the world. Volunteers build houses for families living in substandard housing. The families then buy the homes at cost and donate five hundred hours of labor to the organization. The Clintons thought helping Carter build one of those homes would provide a nice photo opportunity to offset the family values message coming out of Houston.

"They haven't done anything to promote values," Bill Clinton said of the Republicans. "My wife has spent twenty years trying to build up families and kids in this country, working hard and being recognized by all kinds of people. Now when they're in real deep trouble, they think they can twist around and willfully distort things that she's written in the last twenty years and try to turn her into an issue in this campaign. It's just another Willie Horton deal. It shows the panic and the lack of vision and commitment and real character in the whole Republican campaign.''

Although Hillary wasn't responding publicly to the GOP attacks, the Clinton campaign quickly developed a convention-week strategy. That strategy was to paint the Republican Party as a party that had been taken over by hard right personalities such as Buchanan, Pat Robertson, Jerry Falwell and House Minority Whip Newt Gingrich of Georgia, who on the second night of the convention had called Democrats supporters of ''multicultural nihilistic hedonism.''

Clinton communications director, George Stephanopoulos, pointed out that Barbara Bush had said'''attacks on the family, attacks on Hillary specifically were out of bounds.''

Still, a lot of commentators thought Hillary's ideas were fair game. As John Brummett wrote in the *Arkansas Democrat-Gazette*:

"You get a first lady with almost every president, true, but Clinton seemed to be offering Hillary, a lawyer with a public policy record, as part of a trailblazing co-presidency. The record in Arkansas suggests as much. To any who doubt that Hillary would function as an occasional co-president, consider the centerpiece of Clinton's claim to fame in Arkansas: the new education standards. Hillary wrote those, and she did so masterfully. She had every right to apply her skills to public policy on behalf of her husband.

"But she can't have it both ways—policy leader for her husband yet immune to Republican criticism. To

*say she is immune is to be sexist. It is to suggest
that politics is only a men's scrimmage in which the
women wear yellow vests to signify that they can't
be touched. . . . Clinton's campaign staff was shaken
up a bit in June and July, largely on the recommendations, if not orders, of Hillary. So don't try to tell me
she's not relevant.''*

Hillary was, in fact, the most relevant spouse of any
man who had ever run for President. And the strategists
were learning that she couldn't be held down for long.
They were going to have to let Hillary be Hillary,
whether or not it seemed politically wise.

CHAPTER FOUR
Hillary Triumphant

In American politics, political wives long enjoyed immunity from direct attack. But, as the Republican National Convention illustrated, in 1992 the GOP decided Hillary Clinton was a campaign issue. Some people thought that because Clinton had shoved his wife into the arena with his early suggestions of a two-for-one deal, Hillary was fair game. However not everyone thought the assault on Hillary appropriate. Many of the statements made by the Republicans seemed ugly and misogynistic, the kind of comments often made by insecure men ambivalent about, and sometimes hostile to, power in the hands of women.

Pat Robertson claimed she was a "radical feminist," and defined "the feminist agenda" as a "socialist, anti-family political movement that encourages women to leave their husbands, kill their children, practice witchcraft, destroy capitalism and become lesbians."

In fact, the conflagration of two paticularly vicious themes of the GOP convention—the danger of an encroaching "homosexual lifestyle" and the demonization of Hillary Clinton—was at least partially responsible for a rash of unsubstantiated nasty rumors about Hillary's sexuality. Hillary portrayed as lesbian, picking others of her kind such as Attorney General

Janet Reno, Department of Health and Human Services head Donna Shalala and assistant Housing and Urban Development secretary Roberta Achtenberg—the only confirmed homosexual in the crowd—for her ineffectual husband's administration was a favorite image of the more dunderheaded elements of the right wing.

But while the lesbian rumors were a whispered campaign, never acknowledged by the Bush forces, Hillary's paper trail was deemed suitable for comment. Bush's labor secretary, Lynn Martin, said on CNN's *Larry King Live* that she didn't think spouses should be an issue unless—like Hillary—they asserted their opinions on campaign issues. She said there were "certain things I don't like at all. . . . I used to think Nancy Reagan took such punishment from Democrats."

Referring to recent Republican jabs at Hillary, however, Martin said, "You know, if you talk on the issues, you have a right to be criticized. The Democrats, I think, have to be careful. They can't keep saying that any criticism is negative campaigning."

Martin's comments quickly were challenged by the junior senator from Arkansas, Democrat David Pryor, who was also a guest on the show. Pryor called the Republican attacks a "very, very familiar pattern, that you allow people to get up there and make these statements and then you say, 'Well, we don't have anything to do with it. We disassociate ourselves.' What is being said from the convention floor, from the podium, is absolutely, in my opinion, preposterous. It brings down all of us in politics."

"I think there's another set of values that we've got to talk about," Pyor continued, "and that is the value of telling the truth, and what is being said about Mrs. Clinton is simply not the truth."

In an appearance on ABC's *Prime Time Live* the week following the GOP convention, Vice-President Dan Quayle said some of the Republican attacks against Hillary might have been unfair but that she was still a legitimate target.

"She's going through a fairly difficult time," the much-maligned Vice-President said. "I've got a lot of empathy for her." Still, both Quayle and his wife, Marilyn, said Hillary's views would remain an issue in the presidential race. In fact, they said Hillary should be flattered that her views were being taken seriously enough to come under fire.

"We, as women, have wanted to be taken seriously for what we say and what we write as professionals," Marilyn said, adding that she thought the fact that people were talking about Hillary's background and legal writings was "wonderful."

"That's a new threshold. It shows that she's equal with all the other advisers. It might not be pleasant. She might not enjoy the digs that are coming in, but they're not personal," she said.

Quayle added, "This is to her credit and to the credit of women of her generation that have a profession, have a so-called paper trail."

Other Republicans, however, admitted that the attacks on Hillary and the polarizing convention rhetoric about abortion and sexuality had not given the Bush campaign momentum. Charles Black, the President's senior campaign adviser, said the Bush campaign would no longer attack Hillary. Polls showed that a majority of working women were offended by the GOP attacks and that women were turning in greater numbers than men away from Bush. Despite the widespread attention given to the Republican National Convention by the media, Clinton's lead over the incumbent remained in double figures as August came to a close.

"There's nothing that has approached the attack on Hillary Clinton," James Reichley, a political historian and senior fellow at Washington's Georgetown University, told *The Dallas Morning News*. He noted that many of the delegates had worn buttons critical of her and that a new book called *Hillarious* was widely distributed at the convention. One Republican group planned to have an elephant crush a doll representing "the antifamily values of Hillary Clinton."

Lewis Gould, a University of Texas history professor who teaches a course on first ladies, told the Dallas newspaper, "as you start to get wives who have their own careers and are more out front, they become fodder for attack. You also have for the first time a potential first lady who has a paper trail."

In the week following the GOP convention, the wraps came off Hillary again, as the Democrats attempted to put their own spin on "family values." Three days after the GOP convention, Hillary said, "The undeniable fact is that our children's future is shaped both by the values of their parents and the policies of our nation. And it is time we recognize that fundamental truth that, yes, every family and every parent has to assume the responsibility for the most sacred trust they are given—the nurturing and care of the next generation."

In an appearance two days later in Little Rock to kick off a statewide prenatal care program, Hillary made a substantive statement, discussing whether families could and should be required to obtain basic preventive health care before receiving government benefits.

"One of the real problems that we have in this country is the failure during the past twelve years of people to recognize the importance of primary and preventive health care and the lack of understanding at the national level that a dollar invested in prenatal care, a dollar invested in immunizations, will help us control health care costs at the other end," she said. "We've been talking about doing everything we can to make sure that health care is delivered to children. And it may be

necessary to make those kinds of linkages. But those
are kind of last resort steps.''

During the final week of August, the Clinton campaign chose Texas for its fourth bus tour. Hillary received much better reviews than she had received in
Houston the week before. Bill Clinton did not have to
defend his wife, and she did not have to defend herself,
as the buses made their way from San Antonio to the
east Texas city of Tyler.

At a rally in Austin, which was attended by almost
fifteen thousand people, she was greeted with chants of
''Hillary, Hillary, Hillary.''

The Arkansas governor added a new twist to the line
he had been using about President Bush running for
first lady. ''As a person with nearly two decades of
experience in that contest, I can tell you he would not
have a chance,'' Bill said. ''He'd better stay in there
and run against me.''

No longer was Hillary relegated to standing alongside her husband, smiling and waving benignly. At each
Texas stop, she spoke. Judging from the signs and comments along the way, the GOP assault had generated
sympathy for her.

Among the hand-lettered signs were those saying:

"Hillary For First Lady."
"Hillary, Mrs. President."
"We love You Hillary."
"Elect Hillary."

''We're not die-hard feminists,'' said twenty-two-
year-old Merri Heigher, of San Marcos. ''But we want
to be treated fairly.''

Kelly Krause, age twenty-one, of Georgetown, said
the GOP attacks were ''totally uncalled for.'' Her
thirty-two-year-old sister, Kim Krause, said of Hillary,
''I think they're real intimidated by her. She represents

a lot of us. We can relate to her. She is very aggressive and very tough, and I love it. And her husband doesn't seem to mind.''

All along the campaign trail, women, especially young women, expressed similar feelings. Peter Hart, a Democratic pollster who helped conduct the NBC-*Wall Street Journal* poll, said attacks on a working woman were risky since forty-six percent of women who work said they do so because they have to.

Democratic strategists believed the GOP convention had given the President only a temporary lift while giving the Democrats long-term opportunities. In addition to saying that Bush was really running for first lady, the Arkansas governor even began mocking his opponent's speech patterns.

Reporters started noticing the new Democratic attack strategy, including Hillary's higher profile. Adam Pertman wrote this in late August for *The Boston Globe:*

"The Clinton campaign has apparently decided to showcase his wife, who gets loud applause from her audiences, after months in which she had taken a decidedly subordinate role on the stump. A week ago, for example, she gave an unusually long speech for a spouse, fifteen minutes, on the subject of family values. Meanwhile, the governor and his aides have taken to repeatedly describing the Republican Party as having sold out to its most intolerant and conservative elements while honing in on the suburban voters who the Democrats believe will be essential to victory in November. . . . Senior advisers to Clinton said they believe the Republican Party's catering to its right wing and scathing attacks on Clinton's wife will backfire. Both tactics, they asserted, will eventually alienate progressives, moderates and even some conservatives."

A *New York Times* poll showed Bush trailing Clinton by only seven percentage points among men but by twelve points among women. In the same survey, seventy-six percent of respondents said the Republicans had gone too far in chastising Hillary. Only seventeen percent thought the GOP attacks were fair.

In an early September appearance in Boston, Hillary said Republicans had inadvertently expanded the audience for her concerns by targeting her during their convention.

"It may be one of the good effects to come out of the Republican Convention," she said at a news conference. "It is nice to see the issues we have been concerned about getting additional attention. It is hard for children's voices to be heard."

Hillary's visit to Boston provided evidence that the GOP attacks on her personal views and legal writings had heightened her visibility and prompted a backlash among women. She attracted a large press corps. There were eight television crews, including one from German television, covering Hillary's tour of the Boston Children's Museum. After the tour, almost 1,300 supporters heard her speak at a $250-per-person fundraising luncheon. Planners said they originally had expected to draw only about 400 people.

"After the Republican Convention, people wanted to be there for Hillary," Steven Grossman, chairperson of the Massachusetts Democratic Party, said.

Elaine Guiney, state director of the Clinton-Gore campaign, said the Boston headquarters had received almost three hundred telephone calls per day during the convention from area residents, most of them women, wanting to support the Democratic ticket. She said the female callers were as upset as they had been during the Senate Judiciary Committee's cross-examination of Anita Hill. Guiney said, "their feeling is if they can do that to her, what can they do to me."

Hillary also began responding publicly to the attacks, saying they were totally dishonest and bore no relation to her actual beliefs and opinions. In an interview with

NBC's Jane Pauley on the program *Dateline*, she said, "They were not saying anything truthful about me. They were doing it for political purposes. I knew that some of the people knew better."

Pauley said, "They are using your words, your own words against you in a rather shrewd way."

Hillary responded, "In a rather dishonest way. I mean totally dishonest. . . . They knew the kinds of things that I cared about and that I stood for and worked for."

She said her comparison of marriage to slavery referred to a time when women and children literally were the property of men. Hillary explained that her writings on children's legal rights applied to severe situations such as instances in which children were chained to radiators. She also mentioned in the interview that she had once received a note from Bush, a prolific note writer, thanking her for bringing the problem of infant mortality to his attention.

Hillary said she had become a lightning rod in the presidential campaign because women do have opinions. When Pauley asked her if a first lady could be both popular and opinionated, Hillary answered, "Given the challenges we face, maybe we need to do with a little less popularity and a little more courage."

Hillary's views on children's rights received even wider attention in September when a twelve-year-old Florida boy went to court to "divorce" his parents. Gregory Kingsley, who had been in and out of foster care three times, had asked to be adopted by his most recent foster family despite the desire of his biological mother to have him back. The child charged that the biological mother had abused him and argued that she should be stripped of her rights. But the mother said she was thwarted by social workers in her attempt to stay in touch with her son. Following a two-day hearing, a Florida circuit judge came down on the child's side, saying he could stay with the foster family that had raised him for almost a year.

Such legal cases usually are brought by government agencies, but in this case the child had retained his own lawyer, who accepted the case on a *pro bono* basis. The events in Florida reflected Hillary's legal reasoning that children have rights and might require independent counsel when their interests differ from those of the parents.

"Gregory's case points out exactly what Hillary Clinton was writing about," said Howard Davidson, director of the American Bar Association Center on Children and the Law.

In late September, Hillary was questioned at length about her views on children rights during an hour-long appearance on the ABC daytime talk show *Home*. A woman called to say she was concerned that Hillary's legal views could mean that people would have to "give up their authority to be parents," echoing the pre-convention rhetoric of Rich Bond.

"People who said I advocated that were not being truthful," Hillary responded. "They took what I said out of context." She went on to say she believed in strong families that take care of their children's problems, but added that in some cases this was impossible.

"We're not doing a good job in those extreme cases when families break down with difficult cases of abuse or when a child's medical needs are pressing but—for whatever reason—the family won't tend to them," she said.

In the September issue of *McCall's*, Washington-based political reporter Joan Mower questioned whether Hillary was too controversial to be an effective first lady. She noted that Richard Nixon once told *The New York Times*, "If the wife comes through as being too strong and too intelligent, it makes the husband look like a wimp."

"While Bush and Clinton may come from different ends of the political spectrum, it is not their political views per se that have set them apart," Mower wrote. "The divide is not one between liberal and conservative. It is between a woman who seeks a powerful, activist role for herself and one who envisions herself primarily as her husband's supportive helpmate. First ladies with wildly divergent views on issues have found themselves in hot water for having too much power and influence."

She recalled that Abigail Adams mockingly was referred to as "Mrs. President" because of her putative influence and that Edith Wilson shielded her husband, Woodrow, from the public after his stroke, leading a senator to say the country had "a petticoat government." A member of FDR's cabinet had urged Eleanor to "stick to her knitting." Rosalynn Carter was dubbed the "Steel Magnolia" after her habit of sitting in on Cabinet meetings became public knowledge. And, of course, Nancy Reagan was subject to her share of criticism—*The New York Time*'s William Safire once accused her of "extraordinary vindictiveness" as she meddled in affairs of state.

Mower quoted third-party candidate Ross Perot, who "found it fascinating that grown men (were) hiding behind their women" in the ongoing campaign. She also interviewed GOP consultant Roger Stone who admitted that Hillary appealed to a "definite socioeconomic group."

"To some younger, professional and working women, she is a heroine," Stone said.

Newspapers and women's magazines weren't the only ones dissecting Hillary. The United Methodist News Service explored her religious life, with veteran reporter Jean Caffey Lyles interviewing Hillary and ministers who knew her well. Hillary told Lyles that her family's devotion to Methodism went back to the days of the "camp meetings and the Wesleys."

Even though she had married a Baptist, Hillary said she remained a Methodist because of Methodism's tradition of meshing evangelism, social action and intellectual inquiry. Lyles reported Hillary regularly read the Bible and devotional books such as those by Episcopalian Madeleine L'Engle. "What surprised me was how specifically she knew the words of the founder of Methodism," Lyles said of Hillary's familiarity with John Wesley's writings.

The Reverend Don Jones, a Methodist minister who is a professor of social ethics at Drew University in Madison, New Jersey, told *The Chicago Tribune* he first met Hillary when she joined his youth group while she was a teenager growing up in Park Ridge, Illinois.

"My impression was of a strong spiritual and intellectual quest," he said, adding that he had maintained ties with Hillary to this day. "There's absolutely nothing phony about her spiritual commitment. It's interwoven in the fabric of her private and public (life)." Jones remembered that Hillary had, several years before, sent him a book about the renewal of the Methodist Church.

"It was underlined and annotated thoroughly," Jones said. "And I thought how unusual it was" for a woman of Hillary's prominence to take time to study such a work.

Nancy Wood, the director of the Arkansas Education Association, who is a member of the same Little Rock Methodist church as Hillary, said she heard Hillary always travels with her underlined, marked-up Bible. In Little Rock, Hillary also taught an adult Sunday School class.

"She's great, she never uses a note," Wood said. "It just pours out. She would set up a position, then draw reactions from the class. It was a big discussion class. She also handled people who disagreed with her well. She never made them feel stupid or unimportant."

During September, Hillary returned to a heavy schedule of solo appearances. In Window Rock, Arizona, she told American Indians that her husband would uphold their sovereignty and attempt to improve educational and health care opportunities for them. Hillary had been invited to the forty-sixth annual Indian fair by Navajo President Peterson Zah.

Zah urged Hillary not to be discouraged by Republican attacks, and compared her to Annie Wauneka, who was awarded the Presidential Medal of Freedom for her work eradicating tuberculosis on Indian reservations in the 1950s.

"It seems to me if she were Navajo, she would be the Annie Wauneka of our time," Zah said of Hillary. "She's a breadwinner in the family. We want her to know here on the Navajo reservation, we have some very, very strong Navajo women."

Riding alongside Zah in a parade, Hillary wore a headband under a red cowboy hat. She also wore a red Navajo-style skirt and black cowboy boots. She waved to almost one hundred thousand American Indians on that day. Many of them sat in the back of pickup trucks, wrapped in blankets. The five-day fair annually attracts about two hundred thousand people.

In other speeches she gave during the next two weeks, Hillary chose to focus on welfare reform. "In the last few years, it has turned into a huge bureaucracy with its own rules," she said in Cincinnati. "It doesn't seem to be geared to helping people get off welfare anymore. . . . People need to feel good about themselves. It's hard to feel good about the future if you don't have hope."

On October 3, Hillary marked the one-year anniversary of her husband's presidential campaign by flying to Knoxville, Tennessee, to address 1,200 delegates to the national meeting of the predominantly black Christian Methodist Episcopal Church. She spoke of her husband's "consistent campaign for change" while denying that her appearance at the meeting was simply an attempt to bolster her husband's position among minorities.

"The kind of record my husband has on behalf of all Americans, but particularly with respect to African-Americans, is one that has not only garnered him support in Arkansas but throughout the primaries and will again on election day," Hillary said. "My husband's campaign, which has been consistent since he announced one year ago today, has stayed on the issues that are important, and he has set forth a plan that will really help America recover. . . . Most people are anxious to vote for somebody who not only stands for change but can make it happen. There is a great deal at stake in our country."

A week later, Hillary chastised hecklers as she campaigned in Ohio. She was greeted at a University of Akron rally by about two thousand people, including a small group of Bush supporters. At one point, she stopped to say she hoped her husband's supporters were more courteous at Bush's appearances.

As election day neared, Hillary began to liken the Bush-Quayle ticket to an incessant bore. "We've all had the experience, you know, when you're trapped in a corner by somebody who just keeps talking and you want to get away," she said during a speech made in Kansas City on October 14. "The American people are just kind of caught in this corner by the Bush-Quayle campaign, that somehow thinks that we can ignore the last twelve years. And they just keep talking at us." She predicted that on election day, the Democrats would "send them away."

By late October, it was evident that, barring a catastrophe, Bill Clinton would realize the ambition he had trained for since his teens. Clinton was winning. Ron Fournier, an Associated Press reporter based in Little

Rock, told of an incident late in the campaign. Hillary was chatting with aides as their small private plane flew from Arkansas to Tennessee.

"How are you doing?" she asked an aide.

"We're winning," the aide replied.

"I know," Hillary said. "I keep thinking we'll wake up from a dream in a week and say, 'What happened?' "

It wasn't a dream. Everything was going Bill and Hillary's way in those final days of the campaign. They were going so well, in fact, that Hillary even won the *Family Circle* baking contest against Barbara Bush. In the chocolate chip cookie contest, Hillary's vegetable shortening-based recipe got 55.2 percent of the votes, compared with 44.8 percent for the First Lady's butter-based recipe. Barbara complained that the recipe printed by *Family Circle* wasn't really hers but one released earlier by the White House chef. The first lady wanted another bake-off, using her personal recipe. But the magazine said it was too late for that.

It was too late. In those final days, Hillary became giddy at the prospect of her husband's victory. Fournier said Hillary was known by her friends as "the funniest of the bunch, a woman with an all-too-average singing voice who loves to croon, especially when she gets punchy after a long day."

"I don't care about the critics," Hillary said. "I'm not going to stop singing."

Hillary accompanied her husband on a triumphant, final campaign swing that began the day before the election. The trip lasted twenty-nine hours and covered eight states, nine cities and 4,106 miles. There were stops in Philadelphia; Cleveland; Detroit; St. Louis; Paducah, Kentucky; McAllen, Texas; Fort Worth; Albuquerque and Denver.

The couple arrived home in Little Rock at mid-morning Tuesday, November 3, and headed to vote. It was over quickly, though the networks had agreed not to call the race until voters on the West Coast had had their chance to cast their ballots. Finally, a few minutes before 10 P.M. central standard time, they made their call. In a hotel room in Houston, George Bush turned to Barbara and whispered, "It's over."

He then placed a phone call to Little Rock to wish Bill Clinton the best of luck.

At downtown Little Rock's antebellum Old State House, which was bathed in brilliant white light, Hillary's husband declared victory. The two were obviously emotional when they took the stage at the Old State House. As millions of people watched worldwide, the Arkansas governor thrust his fist into the air at 11:22 P.M. central standard time. Hillary, standing beside him in a brilliant blue dress, smiled broadly. The roar from the crowd was deafening. Both Bill and Hillary waved and pointed at friends.

"My fellow Americans, on this day, with high hopes and brave hearts, in massive numbers, the American people have voted to make a new beginning," Bill Clinton told the thousands of people who had gathered on the cool night to hear his speech. He talked about the same things he had spoken of thousands of times during the previous thirteen months—improving the economy, requiring more personal responsibility and rebuilding the nation's infrastructure.

Then, he looked at his wife and said she would "be one of the greatest first ladies in the history of the republic." The crowd responded with chants of "Hillary, Hillary, Hillary."

Bill Clinton would have given the speech somewhat earlier if not for his reliance on his wife. Before leaving the Governor's Mansion for the Old State House, he had given his copy of the speech to his wife for safekeeping. And Hillary Clinton had left the most important speech of her husband's career in the backseat of a limousine.

*   *   *

Bush, who promised to "get very active in the grand-child business" knew early what kind of night it would be. States that Bush needed were awarded to Clinton before the polls had closed in western states—Pennsylvania with twenty-three electoral votes, New Jersey with fifteen electoral votes, Michigan with eighteen electoral votes and Missouri with eleven electoral votes. Weeks before, Republicans had written off three of the largest states—California, New York and Illinois—a total of 109 electoral votes.

Clinton, in fact, became the first Democratic presidential nominee since 1964 to win California, the nation's largest electoral prize. For the first time in years, the Democratic nominee also carried states such as Kentucky and Vermont.

It was, of course, a campaign that at the start most experts had felt Bush wouldn't and couldn't lose. The Republican President had soared to record approval ratings in early 1991 following American victory in the Persian Gulf War. Some polls showed the president with approval ratings as high as ninety percent.

One after another, the men considered the top Democratic contenders said they would not enter the race. Senator Lloyd Bentsen of Texas, Michael Dukakis's running mate in the disastrous 1988 Democratic campaign, bowed out. So did Representative Richard Gephardt of Missouri, one of seven Democratic candidates in 1988. Even the Reverend Jesse Jackson refused to make his quadrennial run. For a time, it appeared as if former Massachusetts Senator Paul Tsongas would be the lone Democratic candidate. Tsongas entered the race in April 1991 with an economic platform that sounded more like that of a pro-business Republican than of a Democrat.

As the recession took hold, however, the Democratic field grew to six. Tsongas was joined by Senator Tom Harkin of Iowa, Senator Bob Kerrey of Nebraska, Governor Douglas Wilder of Virginia, former Governor

Jerry Brown of California and finally Clinton. Wilder was the first to drop out of the race; Brown the last.

With Hillary by him every step of the way, the Arkansas governor eventually survived allegations of infidelity, draft dodging and financial improprieties. Yet despite Hillary's support, polls showed that voters didn't trust Bill Clinton from the time he entered the race in October 1991 until the July 1992 Democratic National Convention in New York. Going into the convention, in fact, he was viewed as the least popular Democratic nominee in four decades. But Bill and Hillary Clinton worked relentlessly, wearing out aides and the media alike with a succession of eighteen-hour campaign days.

In an effort to keep their names before the public, Bill and Hillary had depended on such nontraditional, pop culture outlets as MTV and the syndicated *Arsenio Hall Show*. They also had made an effort to distance themselves from traditional Democratic interest groups such as Jackson's Rainbow Coalition. Bill Clinton went as far as to criticize rap singer Sister Souljah while speaking to a meeting of the Rainbow Coalition.

Bush had been a war hero, a diplomat and, for eight years, Vice-President in the popular Reagan administration. Yet as the economy soured, so did voters' opinions of the Republican President. Increasingly, Americans viewed Bush as a blue blood who was unaware of the depth of the nation's economic problems.

"It was a combination of a no-feel-good economic recovery and a basically inept party leader who could not articulate his policies," said Terry Eastland, a former Reagan administration official. "He had no capacity to advance or defend his political philosophy."

Bill and Hillary, meanwhile, advanced their philosophy at every stop. Critics argued that they also altered their philosophy to match the changing winds of public opinion.

"Never let it be said that we did not turn over every

possible stone,'' Bill Clinton had said as his chartered jet flew back into Little Rock on election day. Now, it was time for the Clintons to decide what they would and wouldn't do in the White House.

Hillary had not been a mannequin as a political wife. She had provided much more than window dressing for her husband's campaign and would do the same as first lady. Never before had an incoming first lady been a working mother who earned more than her husband. Barbara Bush had filled the traditional image of the first lady as a hostess. Hillary would be a political activist.

''There hasn't been the kind of opportunity until now for someone of Bill's age and generation to be contending for the White House with the kind of changes it represents, including a lot of the issues and questions about the responsibilities of women,'' she said.

Hillary said she had been surprised by some of the issues that had arisen during the campaign. She said that in Arkansas, she had ''just gotten used to people knowing who I was. . . . If someone opposes you at home, it is for substantive reasons. They don't go into all this other stuff. For nine or ten years, the kinds of questions I was asked were, 'how is education reform going?' They were very substantive. They weren't about me personally so much as they were about what we were trying to do. I realized, after thinking about it, that our whole political process at home for the last decade had been substance driven, and I miss that.''

But Marilyn Quayle, the wife of Vice-President Dan Quayle, said, ''In her situation, the scrutiny came because her husband made her an issue. The governor said, 'You buy one, get one free. Vote for me, you get Hillary.' ''

Looking back on the campaign, Democratic strategist James Carville said Republican attacks had backfired: ''It was one of the most foolish acts of the campaign. Why on God's green earth would they attack the candidate's wife?'' He said voters' reaction to criticism from the likes of Pat Buchanan and Pat Robertson was, "If these goofballs think she's bad, she must be great."

Harriett Woods, a former Democratic Senate candidate from Missouri and president of the National Women's Political Caucus, said, "The more she was flogged by the Republicans as a symbol of the career woman, the more value she had. . . . Initially, she stumbled a bit trying to balance her role as a member of the support team and her own skills as a professional. I think she went from (being) a potential liability to a tremendous asset."

Betsey Wright, Bill Clinton's longtime gubernatorial chief of staff and the deputy campaign chairman, said Hillary had embodied "the concept of grace under fire. She is without precedent or without role models. She is blazing pathways for a lot of women to come."

Columnist Ellen Goodman wrote in *The Boston Globe:*

"The backlash backfired. The shopworn attempts to divide women along the great home front battleline mommies at work from mommies at home failed. The attempt to demonize feminism flopped. The Republican convention—that weeklong barrage aimed at women whose lives have changed—misfired. The attacks on Murphy Brown didn't work. Hillary-bashing didn't work.

"But it must be said that the Year of the Woman was not the Year of the Wife. It was easier for a strong woman to run for office than to be a running mate. We saw many portraits of this lawyer, wife and mother: Hillary the feminist harridan, Hillary the headband, Hillary the family-buster and the cookie-maker. Now we have a partnership marriage of two professionals heading for the White House. She may not be the President. But she ain't no Barbie doll, either."

*   *   *

Hillary, however, was reluctant to describe herself as a trailblazer.

"I'm more focused on what I can get done and what kind of changes I'd like to see," she said. "What we ought to be doing is trying to figure out how to support women who want to be full-time homemakers, women who want to have full-time careers and particularly the majority of women who balance work and family obligations."

The country had not come so far, however, as to be able to disregard Hillary's looks.

"Whether she buys from an unsung sportswear house or from a high-profile designer, she will be watched, imitated, criticized and held to a much higher standard than a woman who has to worry only that her shoes and stockings match," Cathy Horyn wrote in *The Washington Post*. "Ultimately, Clinton will be regarded as an unofficial ambassador of American style, a mantle not always worn well or with much distinction by her predecessors. It is perhaps a pity that so much attention is focused on what a first lady wears. And yet appearance counts for a lot in Washington, from the senatorial red ties that brighten sound bites to the alleged indifference to fashion expressed by women, including first ladies, who quietly spend a fortune on their clothes.

"On the evidence of what has been written about Clinton, she cares about her appearance to the extent that she has consulted a fashion stylist, modified her hairstyle and makeup, and accepted advice from her closest friends. And while the idea of being courted, if not co-opted, by the fashion industry might seem a bit bothersome to a new first lady, Hillary Clinton may just find that fashion moves in ways more mysterious than she had imagined."

In January 1987, Hillary had told an *Arkansas Democrat* reporter she didn't think much about clothes until her husband was elected Governor.

"It changed," she said at the time. "I think being the spouse of a governor, I have to look good." She began to place more emphasis on her clothes, her hair and her overall appearance. That emphasis intensified during the campaign.

"Judging from pictures of her over the years, she has tried a variety of looks since her husband was first elected governor," *People* reported. "The style she has arrived at is studiedly informal: combed but not manicured, attended to but not fussed over. If Jackie Kennedy was jet set, Hillary Clinton is frequent flyer—someone who can live out of one bag if necessary and still look on arrival as if she hadn't made the trip in cargo."

When Hillary arrived in Arkansas in the early 1970s, she had frizzy brown hair and wore horn-rimmed glasses. When she stood by her husband on the night of November 3, 1992, she was slimmer and wearing a designer suit. Her hair was blond and the glasses had been replaced with soft contact lenses—she looked more like her high school photo than any picture taken of her during the 1970s or 1980s.

There was a worldwide focus on the blonder, slimmer first-lady-to-be. The Germans especially were fascinated by Hillary. A left-wing German newspaper, the *Tageszeitung* of Berlin, carried a large, front-page headline that read, "Hillary's Husband Elected." Another Berlin daily, *BZ*, ran a front-page story on the first lady, proclaiming her "the most powerful woman in the world."

Back in the states, a New Hampshire desktop publisher announced plans to compile opinion and satire on the incoming first lady in a new publication to be called *The Hillary Clinton Quarterly*.

"It's not *Time* magazine," publisher Frank Marafiote of Concord, said. "It's not even the *Concord Daily*

Monitor.'' He said the newsletter-sized publication would be similar in scope to *The Quayle Quarterly*, which was started by a Connecticut couple in January 1990. Unlike the Quayle publication, which consisted mostly of hostile jokes, *The Hillary Clinton Quarterly* was balanced, or even pro-Rodham. Marafiote said readers could expect an eclectic mix of stories, ''sort of a cross between *The New Republic* and the *National Enquirer.* . . . Whatever dirt or petty details we can find about Mrs. Clinton, we'll publish that, too. Even though she's an attorney, we have no intention of boring our readers. My sense, though, is that she has a pretty good sense of humor. She might even be willing to help judge our annual Hillary Clinton Bake-off.''

Immediately after the election, Hillary began wrapping up her obligations at the Rose Law Firm. Her association with the firm had lasted almost sixteen years. She also began a long goodbye to friends in Arkansas. Most of her time, though, was spent helping her husband put together his administration. From start to finish, Hillary played a key role in the transition process.

Her first public appearance during the transition period didn't come until a week after election day when she picked up the Woman of the Year award from a Little Rock YWCA. The event turned into a mix of awards luncheon, fashion show and national media happening.

''I think we have a lot of challenges ahead of us, all of which we can meet if we recognize how important it is for our various institutions to work well together to support individuals and families,'' she said after accepting her award.

But she left quickly after the luncheon, taking no questions from the reporters who had turned out in force. Press secretary Lisa Caputo explained that Hillary needed time to ponder her role as first lady before answering questions.

"She's taking her time and thinking everything through," Caputo said of Hillary, who had just been named one of several Women of the Year by *Glamour* magazine for "bringing our country's First Relationship into the '90s."

Despite her history as a close adviser to the governor of Arkansas, some were surprised when Hillary took an active role in the transition. They shouldn't have been.

"We just sort of sit out here around a table every day and talk," the President-elect said. "She's part of it. There isn't any real structured decision-making process. Other people come in and out depending on what we are talking about. It is pretty much the way I've always done things."

During a mid-November dinner meeting with Democratic congressional leaders, Hillary spoke up on a number of topics. Asked about her role the next day, Bill said, "She knew more than we did about some things."

During the couple's first post-election visit to Washington, though, she played a much more traditional role. It was Bill Clinton and Bill Clinton only who met for ninety minutes with George Bush in the Oval Office. Hillary, meanwhile, toured the White House with Barbara, who had just returned to Washington from a house-hunting trip in Houston.

Barbara gave Hillary a big hug and cautioned her about reporters. Pointing to reporters and photographers on the South Lawn of the White House, the outgoing first lady said, "Avoid this crowd like the plague. If they quote you, make damn sure they heard you."

"That's right," Hillary replied. "I know that feeling already."

Photographers shot frame after frame of film as the two women held hands and, at one point, even put their arms around each other. Inside, though, there were no aides or reporters. It was just Barbara and Hillary for an hour, visiting each room.

An aide was later quoted as saying that Hillary showed no interest in redecorating the rooms, but was instead preoccupied with how to accommodate her huge library. Perhaps she shouldn't have worried. In Little Rock, the private quarters of the Governor's Mansion had eighteen hundred square feet of living space—two bedrooms, four bathrooms, a den and a sitting room. In Washington, the private quarters at the White House had fourteen thousand square feet, plenty of room for Hillary's copies of Tony Hillerman and Olive Ann Burns novels, and her collection of Dorothy Sayers and Perri Klass.

Hillary Clinton was on the threshold of a limitless and pitiless place, fraught with possibility and peril.

CHAPTER FIVE
The Unofficial Chief of Staff

Had any Democrat other than Bill Clinton been elected President in November 1992, Hillary Clinton probably would have been considered for a Cabinet post, possibly even for the position of attorney general or for the Supreme Court. Like her husband, since childhood she had seemed destined for great things. Betsey Wright, who served as Bill's chief of staff while he was governor of Arkansas and later helped keep tabs on the media during the presidential campaign, said she had opposed Hillary's marriage to Bill on the grounds that it could stunt the political career of a bright and talented woman.

When she became first lady, Hillary became one of—if not the—most powerful women in the world. Not only is she the wife of the President of the United States, she is almost certainly his closest adviser. And unlike other first ladies, she seemed quite comfortable asserting herself on matters of public policy—attending White House meetings, talking to strategists and interviewing candidates for top administration posts.

More than a month before inauguration day, the conventional wisdom had determined Hillary would be what Bobby Kennedy had been to John Kennedy and what Jim Baker had been to George Bush. In a sense, she would be the co-president. And she would be the first woman to play that role.

"The expectation among friends and aides is that she will act as an unofficial chief of staff," Eleanor Clift and Mark Miller wrote in *Newsweek* soon after the election. "She will find a way to oversee everything. And having an old family friend like Mack McLarty as chief of staff makes it an easy fit. Hillary Clinton is Bill's Daytimer, the gentle lash who keeps him focused, who doesn't mind making decisions and refereeing disputes when Clinton would rather stall."

Featured in the same issue of the magazine were several of Hillary's friends and advisers—including Tipper Gore, the Children's Defense Fund's Marian Wright Edelman, Democratic fund-raiser Pamela Harriman and media consultant Mandy Grunwald. *Newsweek* predicted all these women would play important roles in shaping the direction of the new administration. An accompanying poll of 750 women showed forty-nine percent of them had a favorable opinion of Hillary with seventeen percent unfavorable. A surprising thirty-four percent claimed to have no opinion of the woman who would soon be the new first lady.

"At a White House Christmas party last week, the guests joked that President Clinton would appoint Hillary to the Cabinet and give Barbara Bush a four-year contract to be first lady," Clift and Miller wrote.

In an interview with *Newsweek* conducted by Clift, Hillary commented on the changing expectations of and for American women: "I think the '90s is a time when we're trying to reconcile a lot of the changes that we've lived through in the past twenty or thirty years, where we acknowledge that we have a right to have control over our own destinies and to define ourselves as individuals."

In an accompanying article, Washington author Sally Quinn, the wife of former *Washington Post* Executive Editor Ben Bradlee, wrote that Hillary had become "topic A among Washington's professional female community of her generation. Women lawyers, lobbyists, reporters, producers, economists, environmentalists and health-care experts are watching with a mixture of pride and apprehension to see how she is going to handle the position. These are women who have worked their way up in Washington, which has always been and still is to a certain extent a man's town."

Quinn, who made her name producing scathing profiles of Washington's power elite for the *Post,* advised Hillary to know her constituency, and to realize she was not elected President. Quinn counseled her to find her own job, not attend her husband's meetings, not allow herself to become a scapegoat, not make her husband look like a wimp and not betray the electorate by actually establishing a co-presidency.

And Sally Quinn was something of an ally. *Human Events* magazine described Hillary as "the Evita Perón of American politics." *American Spectator* dubbed her "the Lady MacBeth of Little Rock."

"I'm a little indignant that they ran around the country claiming she wasn't a doctrinaire leftist," the *American Spectator*'s R. Emmett Tyrrell, Jr., told Howard Kurtz, the *Post*'s media writer. "Hillary Clinton actually is making moves toward having a role in the formulation of policy. We should be able to criticize her without being called antifeminist."

But would a hard-core feminist have sublimated her own public policy career in order to support her husband's ambitions? In an interview with *Good Housekeeping* magazine, Hillary defined a feminist as someone who supports "equal political, social and economic rights for women" and not the "rejection of maternal values, nurturing children, caring about the men in your life."

She told writer Carl Sferrazza Anthony, the author of the book *First Ladies,* that she would like to be able to point to "real progress" once her husband left the White House. The goal was to see "fewer children in poverty, fewer children going without health care and missing immunizations."

In his highly favorable piece, Anthony wrote that Hillary's "dignity under fire during the campaign, when her husband's opponents were showering her with abuse, led many voters to take a second, more favorable look at Bill Clinton."

Anthony quoted the President-elect: "Hillary has helped a generation of children and inspired a generation of women. It's really amazing how much she has accomplished."

Magazines weren't the only media outlets paying attention to Hillary during the transition period. Major newspapers featured her on their front pages, while ABC's *Nightline* devoted an entire program to speculating on Hillary's role in the new administration.

"In short, millions of trees have been felled and hundreds of talk shows devoted to what cover stories in both *Time* and *U.S. News & World Report* have dubbed 'The Hillary Factor,' " Howard Kurtz wrote in late November. "And this orgy of coverage may reveal more about the media than about the first lady to be. The press loves to personalize complex issues, and first family members fit the bill nicely—Billy Carter as the wayward sibling in a Hee Haw White House; Nancy Reagan as the designer-crazed symbol of the greed decade; Neil Bush as the poster boy of the savings and loan scandal.

"In a larger sense, Hillary Clinton has become a blank canvas upon which ideologically inclined authors paint their brightest hopes and darkest fears. Some conservative writers have portrayed her as a feminist shrew."

Kurtz and other media critics explained the Hillary-mania of November and December as a symptom of a news vacuum. With the campaign complete and the new administration not yet in place, there was little to write about. In the weeks immediately following the election, Hillary received hundreds of interview requests and several book proposals.

She turned down almost all requests for interviews, with her protective press staff even turning down requests for interviews with her mother—who wouldn't speak without White House approval—and cutting short photo opportunities with shouts of "No questions!"

Interview requests were generally rejected with the explanation that Hillary was too busy, although press staffers were always careful to let reporters know Hillary herself made the decision. But while the first lady's appointment book was probably full, there was also a sense among Washington reporters that Hillary felt she no longer needed them to get out her message.

Most of the interviews she gave were to women's magazines or other "soft" publications. A *New York Times* interview was strictly limited to her household plans, including what kind of food she planned to serve. Through her press staff, she flatly refused to discuss such things as health-care reform or her goals for the next four years.

Even so, there were still plenty of news stories covering every aspect of Hillary's activities, her writings and beliefs. The CBS affiliate in Washington reported that she preferred to be known as "presidential partner" rather than first lady. Hillary's aides quickly denied the report.

The Boston Globe even did a story about what it meant that Hillary's zodiac sign was Scorpio. It called Scorpio "the most feared and misunderstood sign of the zodiac" and Hillary had "a typically intense Scorpio way of making her point—with a sting—and this can be used against her. Even her writings are not safe. Look what the Republicans did with her scholarly tract defending children's rights. In their hands, it wound up being a call to arms for every kid in the country to sue his parents. . . . But it is possible for a Scorpio to win over the public. Katharine Hepburn has pulled it off, although it did take roughly fifty years. Unfortunately, Hillary has only four—maybe eight—to turn it around.''

While negative stories appeared in conservative journals such as the *American Spectator* and *Human Events,* much of the coverage was as favorable as the *Good Housekeeping* story. In fact, some of the coverage late in the campaign had been fawning as reporters scrambled to get on Hillary's good side.

At the end of 1992, the conservative Media Research Center of Alexandria, Virginia, gave ''The I Am Woman Award For Hillary Rodham Hero Worshipping'' to NBC's Jane Pauley for a question she asked on the program *Dateline.* Pauley had asked, ''When you hear yourself held up, as you were at the Republican convention, some people have used the word 'demonized,' does it make you hurt or make you mad? What was the worst thing you've heard said about you? . . . What was the grossest distortion of your record?''

One runner-up for the award was a *Time* cover story by Margaret Carlson that began, ''You might think Hillary Clinton was running for President. Granted, she is a remarkable woman. The first student commencement speaker at Wellesley, part of the first large wave of women to go to law school, a prominent partner in a major law firm, rated one of the top one hundred lawyers in the country—there is no doubt that she is her husband's professional and intellectual equal. But is this reason to turn her into Willary Horton for the '92 campaign, making her an emblem of all that is wrong with family values, working mothers and modern women in general?''

Another runner-up for the award was a question

Katie Couric of NBC's *Today* show asked Hillary: "Do you think the American people are not ready for someone who is as accomplished and career-oriented as Hillary Clinton?"

In a mid-December profile, *The New York Times* reported that although Hillary "is not yet first lady, her influence is already evident as her husband assembles his administration. She has a place at the table when the President-elect and his three other closest advisers decide whom to cross off or add to the Cabinet list. And she is increasingly seen, by both admirers and critics within the transition operation, as an important force behind the choices of people like Donna Shalala (who had just been named secretary of Health and Human Services)."

"Some people in Arkansas trust Hillary's judgments more than her husband's," the magazine reported.

The next month, during a joint interview with her husband, Hillary told *People* that as first lady she would "try to do the very best that I can do. It is something that I've thought a lot about. But Bill and I haven't had a real chance to talk very much about it because he's been so busy. I love my husband, and I love my country, and I can't imagine a better place to be than where I will be after January 20. I want to make a difference."

The celebrity magazine even profiled Hillary's two younger brothers, Hughie and Tony Rodham of Coral Gables, Florida. Hughie has been a public defender in Coral Gables since 1980. Tony was a process server and private detective until selling his business, Rodham Investigating Services, to work in the Clinton campaign. The brothers lived together for three years until 1986, when Hugh married Maria Arias. Tony is a bachelor who lives just a few blocks from Hugh and his wife. The magazine reported that Hillary's brothers "still watch football games together, play golf and hang out at Duffy's, a scruffy Miami bar."

Even *Advertising Age* weighed in during the transition with a story headlined "What's Hiding in Hillary's Closet?" "Jackie Kennedy gave America pillbox hats," the story said. "Nancy Reagan gave a boost to the color red, and Barbara Bush made faux pearls chic. Now everyone is wondering what Hillary Clinton's fashion legacy will be."

In the midst of all the national media attention, there was a short-lived tempest in Little Rock during the transition period when it was revealed that the Little Rock Airport Commission was considering renaming Little Rock Airport in honor of Hillary. She had represented the commission for several years in her role as a private attorney.

"I don't have anything against Hillary, but she hasn't done anything out there she hasn't been paid for," said Seth Ward, a commission member. "I have always liked Hillary. I was instrumental in hiring her as our attorney. But I don't see that she has done anything outstanding to warrant renaming the airport after her."

Four of the five commissioners had ties to the Clintons. Donna McLarty is the wife of Arkla Chairman Thomas F. "Mack" McLarty, who would be named Clinton's chief of staff; John Flake managed the downtown Little Rock building in which the transition team was housed; Les Hollingsworth served for a time on the state Supreme Court after being appointed by Clinton; and Ward's son-in-law, Webb Hubbell, was a colleague of Hillary's at the Rose Law Firm.

"She has done tremendous things for the people of Arkansas and she has been a consistent adviser and supporter of the airport, working well beyond what one might expect," Hollingsworth said. "I think Hillary has performed extraordinary service. I can't speak for the other commissioners, and I don't know where the commission intends to go from here. But I'm in favor of it. I think it's a very appropriate honor.''

The Rose Law Firm was paid about $360,000 for Hillary's professional services to the commission during two stings totaling more than twelve years. Those stints began in the late 1970s and ended when she became too busy with her husband's campaign to practice law. In Little Rock, there was a public outcry against naming the airport for someone who was still alive and was not a native Arkansan.

"We haven't kept count," the airport manager, James Rodgers, said of the calls that poured in once the possible name change was revealed. "But it's safe to say we have had more calls con than pro here."

The complaints killed the idea. Ward said on November 19, "I know the airport manager's office got at least 150 calls asking them not to change the airport's name. I've since heard, through a fellow commissioner, that Mrs. Clinton is not interested in having the airport bear her name. At home, I've received a whole lot of calls asking us not to change the name. Without the newspaper bringing this to light, I think the name change already would have gone through. . . . Now, it's all history. I think we should just let it quietly lie.''

While that minor controversy swirled in Little Rock, Barbara Bush had kind words in Washington for the next first lady. Her comments came during the annual ceremony held to mark the arrival of the White House Christmas tree.

"I wanted to talk to you about that," she said, sounding like a stern grandmother when reporters asked about Hillary. "She was wonderful, really nice, and I hope you all treat her like you treated me. Wait until she makes her mistakes. You waited until I made mine. I mean, give her a break.''

As a horse-drawn cart delivered an eighteen-foot Oregon fir to the Blue Room of the White House, Barbara Bush said she disagreed with those who said the news media had been fair to Hillary. "I don't think you have yet. The cartoons are ugly and I think she does not deserve it—let her make her own mistakes. She's great. She was just the warmest, nicest, friendliest person."

Yet as the inauguration neared, speculation—and in some quarters anxiety—increased as to the exact role Hillary would play in the administration. Would she focus on education? Would she devote her time to children and families?

Since 1967, there has been a federal law prohibiting government officials from putting relatives on the federal payroll. Whatever Hillary was about to do for the administration, she would not be paid for it. Some, including Martha Burk of the Center for Advancement of Public Policy in Washington, said the law should be repealed. Burk said it was a "bad law, passed in a fit of presidential pique" because Lyndon Johnson did not like John Kennedy's appointment of his brother, Bobby, as attorney general.

Burk argued that Hillary should be attorney general. "To prevent a talented individual from serving the American people because she is married to the President is not fair to her or the nation," she said.

Columnist John Robert Starr answered her in the *Arkansas Democrat-Gazette* by writing, "Unfortunately, we cannot make an exception for Hillary without allowing future Presidents—and current congressmen—to put onto the government payroll wives, relatives and in-laws who may not be as talented as Hillary. She can, and will, serve her country without portfolio, just as she served Arkansas without an official title for so many years. Bill Clinton needs her at his side, not off somewhere wrestling with the day-to-day problems of running an agency. She apparently will remain Bill's Number One and most trusted adviser, a

role she played so well during the campaign and
throughout his tenure as governor of Arkansas."

The first of several emotional farewells came December 12 when Bill Clinton formally resigned as governor
and turned over the office to his lieutenant governor,
Jim Guy Tucker. Hillary accompanied her husband to
the state Capitol, where they spent several hours shaking hands with the bureaucrats and legislators with
whom they had worked for years. The Clintons's last
break before the inaugural onslaught came when they
flew to Hilton Head, South Carolina, the week after
Christmas for an event known as the Renaissance
Weekend. There, they would be just Bill and Hillary.

"We made it clear to the guests that (the Clintons)
are on vacation," said Jackie Kiss, an organizer of
the annual retreat. Started in 1981 by Phil Lader, a
businessman and unsuccessful gubernatorial candidate
in South Carolina, Renaissance Weekend combines recreation with seminars on subjects ranging from public
policy to personal finance. Journalists who are invited
must agree not to write about what takes place.

Hillary and Bill were old Renaissance hands, having
attended the event for the past eight years with the
likes of former Kennedy administration adviser Ted
Sorensen and humorist Art Buchwald, and they had
formed several lasting friendships with people they had
met there. Lader told *The Island Packet,* a Hilton Head
newspaper, "It has become a support group for Bill."

Until the 1992 retreat, though, Bill had been one of
the more anonymous participants. It was Hillary who
rated a mention in the local newspaper five years earlier
when she was chairperson of the Children's Defense
Fund. The story noted that she had happened to be the
"wife of Governor William Clinton of Arkansas."

Inaugural preparations continued, and Hillary received her share of the attention. In Park Ridge, Illinois, the Main South High School band decided it would not play standard marching band fare at the inaugural parade. Instead, the band from Hillary's alma mater would play a new composition called the "First Lady March."

"She's a very, very lovely lady," said composer Erbin Litkei, who had written every official Presidential march dating back to Franklin D. Roosevelt.

While Litkei was composing his march, the national discussion over the best place for Hillary to utilize her talents continued. Americans wondered how she would balance her independence and outspokenness with the job's traditional obligations.

"They say she must not fail because, as symbol of societal evolution, she carries the hopes and aspirations of modern womanhood on her shoulders," columnist John Brummett wrote in the *Arkansas Democrat-Gazette*. "It's funny that in Arkansas we didn't think much about her as a pioneer. She was a smart career woman who supported her husband, period. She was widely accepted when appointed by her husband to lead the way for education reform. But the presidency is something else entirely because it symbolizes and defines an era, a generation, even a culture."

Like the seventy-two percent of mothers with school-age children, Hillary knew what it was like to juggle a job with family obligations. For many of those women, who were unable to identify with Barbara Bush, Hillary was a symbol.

Working mothers were a reality of the baby-boom generation, who had grown into a world where two incomes were a requisite for raising a family. For a generation that harbored illusions of having it all, Hillary Rodham Clinton was the epitome of yuppie achievement as well as a mother with whom other working mothers could identify.

As Igna Saffron wrote in *The Philadelphia Enquirer:*

"American working women are rooting as never before for Clinton to transcend the traditional restrictions of her job and, in the process, demonstrate how they too can balance the conflicting obligations of modern life. . . . It won't be easy, and not just because Clinton will be under a national microscope. One of her first public acts after the election was to resign from her partnership at a Little Rock law firm, where, like twenty percent of American working women, she earned more than her husband. She had little choice in the decision, given the unlimited possibilities for conflict of interest engendered by being married to the world's most prominent public servant. Federal Law also prohibits her and any other relative from being appointed to the President's Cabinet.

". . . Whatever contributions Hillary Clinton makes on the pressing issues of our day, this accomplished twentieth-century woman is still expected to perform all the usual nineteenth-century hostessing tasks associated with the role of first lady, from managing the White House cooks and butlers to organizing the annual Easter egg hunt. All gratis, of course.

"Bill Clinton will go straight to his office and roll up his sleeves after inauguration day. Not his wife. The details of the family's relocation will certainly fall to Hillary Clinton. . . . When Bill is engaging Congress in the debate over his economic recovery package, Hillary will be tangling with the movers over missing boxes. In doing all this—quitting her job, detouring her career, assuming more of the traditional household responsibilities—Hillary Clinton will face many more of the ordinary concerns than her fancy new address would suggest."

Asked whether Hillary would ever sit in on Cabinet meetings, her husband said, "I hope so. She knows more about a lot of this stuff than most of us do."

When pressed to expound on that comment, Clinton's communications director George Stephanopoulos said Hillary would be "free to attend whenever she think she can make a contribution."

On January 5, 1993, Hillary visited Rockefeller Elementary School in Little Rock to pick up a collage of photographs from the presidential campaign. The collage had been assembled by pupils and teachers at the school.

"She is a hard worker, and she is our hero," Faye Reynolds, an auxiliary teacher at the school, said that morning, "We cry when we look at some of the pictures."

Teachers had collected the newspapers from which the photographs were taken and had pupils cut the photos out. Every student at the school had signed the back of the collage.

Ann Pollard, whose fifth-graders did much of the work, told visiting reporters that shaking hands with someone as important as Hillary meant a great deal to students from low- and middle-income families.

"A lot of these kids don't ever have any connection with events like this," she said. "Being part of something like this, especially in this neighborhood, makes them feel like they are part of the United States."

Hillary's visit to the school was ironic in that it came only hours before the Clintons released a statement saying they had decided to send twelve-year-old Chelsea to a private school in Washington. Thus the television cameras that had followed Hillary to Rockefeller Elementary School were recording her concern for public education after she had, in fact, decided against public education for her own daughter.

Chelsea would attend an exclusive private school in the nation's capital, The Sidwell Friends School. The Clinton's daughter had attended public schools while growing up in Little Rock. At the time of the family's move, she was in the eighth grade at the Mann Arts/

Math-Science Magnet Junior High. Neither Bill nor Hillary would comment publicly on their decision the day it was announced, but a spokesperson said the couple was more concerned about what was best for their daughter than they were about possible criticism.

The Clintons's choice set off a firestorm of debate nationwide. Radio talk shows were flooded with calls, and editorial writers weighed in. Many pointed to the fact that the Clintons had made improving the nation's public education system a key plank in their campaign.

"After many family discussions and careful consideration, we have decided that our daughter Chelsea will attend The Sidwell Friends School," the Clintons's to-the-point statement said. "As parents, we believe this decision is best for our daughter at this time in her life based on our changing circumstances."

Sidwell Friends officials pointed out that their school stressed the Quaker traditions of peace and justice. Situated on a fifteen-acre campus in northwest Washington, the school has about 750 students in grades five through twelve. Many are the children of members of Congress, diplomats and other prominent Washington residents.

That afternoon, Stephanopoulos was grilled by the press at Little Rock. He said the school was chosen because of its "academically challenging environment" and "service component" such as the annual "soup days" at which the poor are fed. Asked if the decision meant the Clintons were rejecting the public schools, Stephanopoulos replied, "Of course not. They didn't reject public schools. What they did as a family was choose Sidwell Friends. It's a good choice."

A Washington-based reporter pointed out to Stephanopoulos that Sidwell Friends is "one of the most exclusive private schools in the country." Another reporter from Washington noted that many in the nation's capital blame the deteriorating condition of the public

schools there on the decision of high-income parents
to send their children to private schools.

"The important point was to make the right choice
for Chelsea," Stephanopoulos said. "You can't put
politics in a personal, family situation."

And Washington's public schools had lobbied for
Chelsea. Amy Carter, nine years old when her father
became President, had attended Stevens School, a public elementary school with a predominantly black student body located on a downtown street eight blocks
from the White House. She spent 1977 and part of
1978 at Stevens, dancing in a chorus line at one assembly, before transferring to Hardy Middle School in one
of the city's better neighborhoods. When her father left
office in 1981, she enrolled at Woodward Academy, a
private school in suburban Atlanta.

If 1600 Pennsylvania Ave. were a normal address,
an eighth grader living there would attend Francis Junior High School, which is in a commercial neighborhood about fourteen blocks from the White House.

"I'd love it," the school's principal, Gary Geiger,
had said. "It would be exciting to have her. We have
students from forty countries. About 350 are black students, 150 Hispanics, fifty Asians and fifty whites. We
have five computer laboratories. Our test scores probably rank fifth or sixth among the thirty-odd junior highs
in the city."

There also was a chance that Chelsea might have
attended Jefferson Junior High School, a public school
in southwest Washington. Attendance there would have
given Chelsea an edge in her area of special interest,
astronautical engineering, since the school has ties to
COMSAT, a satellite communications company. Bill
Clinton once had visited Jefferson and shown an interest in its programs.

Al and Tipper Gore, meanwhile, already were sending their three photogenic children to the prestigious

St. Albans School for boys and the National Cathedral School for girls in northwest Washington. Annual tuition at St. Albans was $11,050. Annual tuition at National Cathedral was $11,340.

R. David Hall, president of the District of Columbia Board of Education, said he would respect the Clinton's decision. Keith Geiger, president of the National Education Association, a powerful lobbying force for public education, also refused to criticize what Hillary and Bill had done. He said the NEA "does not have a problem with private and parochial schools. We believe there's a place for them. What we oppose is public tax dollars going to them."

Geiger surmised that concerns about security and "fitting in," had influenced the Clintons's decision. He estimated that "probably half the kids (at Sidwell Friends) are from the rich and famous already. She won't get gawked at by so many kids. I happen to know they asked her where she wanted to go, and she said that's where she wants to go."

Sid Johnson, president of the Arkansas Education Association, said the Clintons had talked to him and others about their daughter's schooling. He said the couple "personally hoped that something could be worked out where she could attend public school. The child did attend public school in Little Rock. But she was only the governor's child. There are certain things that, once you become the relative of a President, are difficult to do."

Stephanopoulos said the public "knows about Clinton's commitment to public education" and would not change its opinion of Bill and Hillary. He said Chelsea was "deeply involved" in the decision.

While a student in Little Rock, Chelsea had been one of two sixth-graders to take an advanced mathematics program run by the University of Arkansas at Little Rock. Chelsea Clinton had always been more interested in math and science than in politics.

Betsy Ebeling of Arlington Heights, Illinois, who had known Hillary since they were in the sixth grade together in Park Ridge, told *The Chicago Tribune* that "to meet Chelsea is to understand Bill and Hillary. She's very unspoiled; she truly is. They've done a wonderful job."

Growing up the child of a governor and a public policy attorney may have exposed Chelsea to more adult conversations and situations, Ebeling said, but Bill and Hillary had worked to ensure she "could go to school, make lifetime friends. She's not a media child."

Both Bill and Hillary had been regular attendants at Chelsea's softball games, ballet recitals and school performances. Nancy Wood, chairperson of the Arkansas State Board of Education, said she remembered Hillary arranging to meet her at Little Rock Park Plaza Mall because Chelsea's school group was going to be singing there.

One Christmas, Chelsea played Joseph in their church pageant, because she was the tallest kid in the class. "That fits in exactly with what Bill and Hillary raised her to be—an individual," Wood said. "What Hillary said was she wanted Chelsea to be normal but also to be the best she can be with no limits."

Of course, inauguration week could not begin without another controversy. *The Wall Street Journal* reported that a representative of Hillary's brothers had been calling executives at some of the nation's top corporations and soliciting donations to cover the cost of inaugural week parties. Spokespeople for several major corporations said they were approached by Thomas Mellon, a Pennsylvania lawyer working on behalf of Hillary's two brothers. Among those solicited were executives from the Mobil Corporation, Ford Motor Company and the Chevron Corporation. All three companies declined to participate.

Hugh Rodham, Hillary's oldest brother, told the newspaper he saw nothing wrong with the fund-raising activities. "We obviously need to pay for it somehow. . . . We're just small fries. That's all we are," he said.

Luddy Hayden, Chevron's federal relations representative in Washington, said Mellon indicated he was calling "on behalf of the family" and asking "the top ten corporations in America to contribute to the tune of ten thousand dollars each to sponsor a set of events, including a dinner dance, a dinner, a brunch and a breakfast."

Hayden was told sponsors would receive a luxury box overlooking the dinner dance and tickets to the three other events. Already that week, Ron Brown, Clinton's choice for commerce secretary, had canceled a lavish party and two other dinners planned in his honor by some of the largest American and Japanese corporations. After *The Wall Street Journal* story ran, the Rodham brothers backed away from their fundraising effort.

Another controversy having been extinguished, Hillary headed for Washington with her husband, their daughter and thousands of Arkansas friends. On the Monday evening before Wednesday's inauguration, she stopped by a reception in the grand ballroom of Washington's elegant Mayflower Hotel to bid a nostalgic farewell to her former associates from the Rose Law Firm. As almost 700 guests—including actors Ed Begley, Jr., and Richard Dysart—looked on, Hillary was introduced by the firm's Bill Kennedy.

Hillary accompanied her husband to many of the week's events and went to some activities on her own. The biggest stir of the week came on inauguration day when the new first lady, who rarely wears a hat, emerged that Wednesday morning from the Blair House in a huge blue velour hat. Ever since Jackie Kennedy made the pillbox hat famous in January 1961, hat designers had vied for the honor of coming up with something for the first lady to wear on inauguration day.

Hillary's hat was designed by Darcy Creech of Southport, Connecticut. New York hat designer Elaine Armstrong, a friend of Creech's, said the cadet was intended to frame Hillary's face and had a "very flattering, off the face, simple style."

Lou Boulmetis, the owner of a men's hat shop in Baltimore known as Hippodrome Hatters, described Creech's creation as a feminized version of two men's styles, the gambler and the derby. The wide brim was turned up in front and down in the back. The matching wide blue band surrounding the crown was fastened in the back with a large hatpin.

Tipper Gore wore a classic, deep purple hat to match her coat that day. Neither Barbara Bush nor Marilyn Quayle wore hats.

Unkind reviews followed. Milliner Leo Marshall of New York said, "It was a terrible-looking hat. No style, no pizzazz, no nothing. It didn't become her. She picked the wrong hat."

Designer Cherie Jefferson-Lawrence said, "She blew it big time." Even less kind was the *New York Daily News,* which described the hat as "a cross between Paddington Bear's preferred headgear and 'Bowery Boy' Leo Gorcey's mashed-brim fedora."

"I thought it looked appropriate," said Mary Lou Luther, a fashion columnist for The *Los Angeles Times.* "But my husband, he talked about that hat as if it was a mortal sin. My husband said even Barbara Bush had the sense not to wear a hat."

Soon there was more to worry about than the relative silliness of the hat. On the first full day of the Clinton administration, it was announced that Hillary would break with tradition and work out of the West Wing, along with the President's senior staff members rather than in the East Wing. She stood beside her husband that Thursday as they greeted the public during an open house at the White House and was right behind the President when he made his first appearance in the Oval Office.

In an interview that day on NBC, White House Chief of Staff Mack McLarty said Hillary had "been a strong advocate over the years as first lady of Arkansas on a number of domestic issues. She'll be involved in a very constructive way, and I look forward to working with her."

Janet Cawley, in *The Chicago Tribune,* repeated this version of the quintessential—and apocryphal—Hillary Clinton joke:

Chelsea needed to take some medication at school, a situation that required phoning a parent for permission. "Don't call my mom," Chelsea reportedly said. "She's too busy. Call my dad."

In an effort to show voters that the new occupants of the White House were of the people, the Clintons invited average citizens from across the country to an open house. More than two thousand people passed through the White House that Thursday to shake hands with the first couple. Old friends, campaign aides and other acquaintances traded greetings with the Clintons. Hillary received some unwanted publicity when a microphone captured her telling her husband that hundreds of additional people had been admitted through the White House gates on a cold, rainy day and would have to be let inside. "We can't screw all these people," she lectured the president.

On a more substantive level, it was evident that Hillary was having her say on who received key administration positions. Webb Hubbell, one of her former partners at the Rose Law Firm, landed at the Department of Justice. When attorney general-designate Zoe

Baird ran into problems for having hired illegal immigrants, Hubbell took over the Justice Department for all practical purposes. He continued running the department until March, when Janet Reno finally was confirmed as attorney general. Another former Rose partner, the ill-fated Vince Foster, was deputy White House counsel.

Bill Kennedy of the Rose Law Firm admitted that the firm could profit with Hillary in the White House. "We're always looking for new business," he told *Arkansas Business*. "We're always looking to try to get ahead in the world. One would have to assume that if one's partner becomes first lady, the focus on the law firm should increase."

In a later interview with the Scripps Howard News Service, Kennedy was careful to point out that Hubbell and Foster were under strict government ethics regulations. "They are not in a position to confer any direct benefits to us, and that's how it should be."

Still, no one doubted that Hillary was helping to fill administration jobs. She soon received her own job, which was to head a new health-care task force. The President was disturbed that his advisers had not found an affordable way to expand adequate medical care to all Americans and thus turned to his most trusted adviser—Hillary.

The first lady's new role was disclosed to the transition's health-care policy team two days before the inauguration. The disclosure came during a three-hour meeting with Ira Magaziner, a longtime friend and adviser to the Clintons.

A week before, during a January 11 meeting in Little Rock, Clinton had decided to use his wife's talents in the area of health care. At that meeting, he learned that his advisers were planning to use a concept known as "manager competition," in which the government utilizes incentives to encourage competition among health-care providers.

The President-elect preferred combining managed competition with a system of strict price controls. Sources told *The Los Angeles Times* that Bill, known for his volatile temper, became angry when one of the advisers said it was impossible to combine the approaches since one approach depends on a free-market environment and the other is based on a government-imposed budget.

Since the start of his campaign, Bill had been saying controlling health-care costs would be a central part of his deficit-reduction agenda; when told his idea was impossible, he decided that he could no longer trust these advisers.

"This isn't what I want," he reportedly told them. "You don't get it! I'm looking for something different."

Hillary and her staff would immediately have far more influence on administration policy than any previous first lady. From the outset, her staff included five commissioned officers appointed by the president, compared with just one for Barbara Bush.

"Inside the White House culture, that carries a lot of weight," Anna Perez, Barbara Bush's spokesperson, said when asked about the size of Hillary's staff and the fact that the new first lady would be working in the West Wing.

Americans had mixed feelings about Hillary's influence. A *U.S. News & World Report* survey found that forty-seven percent of respondents thought a major advisory role for Hillary would help her husband's presidency while forty percent thought it would hurt. Meanwhile, seventy percent said they would favor her being a traditional first lady. Just thirty-four percent thought she should be "a major adviser on appointments and policy."

"They feel she should have a voice, but there's a line there they don't want her to cross," Republican pollster Ed Goeas said. With the campaign over, how-

ever, it was full speed ahead for Hillary. In those heady
first days of the administration, public opinion surveys
didn't seem to matter.

The President officially announced five days after the
inauguration that his wife would be the nation's health-
care czar. He said she was "a first lady of many talents" with a gift for cutting through complex issues
and then forging consensus. It was the first time a U.S.
president had ever allowed his wife to formulate domestic policy, but the new chief executive said he was
grateful Hillary would "be sharing the heat I expect
to generate."

"I want it done—now," the President said following
a one-hour meeting with Hillary, several Cabinet secretaries, the director of the Office of Management and
Budget, senior White House aides and other members
of the President's Task Force on National Health-Care
Reform. He noted Hillary's education efforts in Arkansas as an example of what she could accomplish, and
White House aides handed out press clips on her work
in the state.

"We're going to work day and night until we have
a health-care plan ready to submit to the Congress that
we believe we can pass," the President said. "We've
talked about it long enough. The time has come to act."

What he described as a "war room" would be set
up in the Old Executive Office Building adjacent to the
White House. From there, advisers would attempt to
come up with proposals by the end of May and then
sell those proposals to members of Congress and the
American public.

Reaction was favorable on Capitol Hill. Representative Henry Waxman of California, chair of the House
Energy and Commerce subcommittee on health, said,
"This move shows that health care is going to be a
very serious priority for the Clinton administration."

Senate Majority Leader George Mitchell of Maine
said, "I think it's a very positive development and

brings greater attention and her great ability to the issue.''

Arkansas residents long ago had become accustomed to Hillary helping shape policy. But in the early days, as evidenced by the *U.S. News & World Report* poll, it took some getting used to for other Americans.

''I think she is an object of enormous curiosity and interest,'' said Diane Blair, a political science professor at the University of Arkansas at Fayetteville and a close friend of Hillary's.

Hillary's appointment to head the health-care task force earned front-page coverage in *The Washington Post* and *The New York Times*. Both newspapers also supported the decision editorially. The editorials pointed out that Hillary's position would make her publicly accountable for a policy role she likely would have played regardless of whether she had been given a title.

The Times said the public reaction to the job done by Hillary would test how much times had changed for American women. ''This is a test of the national psyche,'' the newspaper said of what it called ''this latest and most riveting experiment in the Age of the Clintons.''

The Post, noting that Hillary would assume the traditional duties of the first lady along with a policy job, editorialized, ''She should be judged by how well she does each, not by whether she should be performing either set of duties or what is fitting for her to do.''

Callers to radio talk shows were more skeptical. They wondered whether other task force members would feel comfortable criticizing the President's wife and if doing so might endanger their careers.

Stories ran daily about things ranging from Hillary's office in the West Wing to her decision to include her maiden name ''Rodham'' between ''Hillary'' and ''Clinton'' when signing her name.

''If she can help address this pressing problem of

health care, I don't care if she sits on top of the Washington Monument,'' Blair said.

Among those criticizing Hillary's appointment as health-care czar was Sheila Tate, a Washington public relations executive who had been Nancy Reagan's press secretary. Tate said, ''She is not just another staffer. She has a relationship with the President that makes everything different.''

A day after being selected to head the health-care task force, the first lady flew to New York, leaving Washington for the first time since the inauguration. The sales job had begun for Hillary Rodham Clinton, a first lady unlike any Americans had ever seen.

II

Chapter Six

From Methodism to Mayhem

Scranton is a smoke-choked coal and steel town located 134 miles west of New York City, in a valley bounded by the ridges of the Allegheny Mountains. Named for the Scranton family, which founded an ironworks there in 1840, it is still the largest city in Pennsylvania's anthracite coal region. During the late 1800s and early 1900s, thousands of immigrants landed in New York and then came to Lackawanna County to work the mines.

Hugh Rodham's father had come to the United States from England at age four, and ended up working at the Scranton Lace Company. Hugh, one of three boys, went to work for the lace company after finishing school at Pennsylvania State University, which he had attended on a football scholarship. Hugh majored in physical education and played football for the Nittany Lions.

At the height of the Great Depression, Hugh was convinced he could earn more than the low wages he was paid in Scranton. He left Pennsylvania for New York in search of a better job. From New York, he moved to Chicago, where he went to work as a curtain salesman for the Columbia Lace Company.

Dorothy Howell, the daughter of a Welsh father and a mother with Scottish, French and Indian blood, had been raised near Pasadena, California, in the town of Alhambra. One day in 1937, she came into the Columbia Lace offices to apply for a job. She met Hugh. Apparently, they hit it off immediately, and wrote each other long letters while Hugh was away in the Navy. When he returned in 1942, they were married.

Hillary Rodham was born October 26, 1947, at the Edgewater Hospital on the north side of Chicago. She weighed more than eight pounds at birth and, from all descriptions, was an exceedingly bright, good-natured child. When Hillary was three, the family's second child, Hugh Rodham, Jr., was born. To relatives, he was known as Hughie. With two children, the Rodhams needed more room, so they left their one-bedroom apartment in Chicago.

"I was born in Chicago and my parents moved to a suburb of Chicago called Park Ridge when I was very young," mostly because they wanted to be in a good school district, Hillary told her husband's biographer, Charles Allen, in early 1991. "I mean that's what the motivation was for the ex-G.I.'s after World War II—to try to find a good place to raise your kids and send them to school."

In the early 1950s, Park Ridge was the sort of tree-thick, sidewalked suburb that attracted a more prosperous sort of returning G.I. and their families. Built on land formerly given over to apple orchards, blessed with wide sidewalks and street signs carved from stone, it resembled nothing more than the idyllic, lily-white neighborhoods of the family sitcoms of that period— Park Ridge was a place in which Jim and Margaret Anderson, or Ozzie and Harriet Nelson, would have been proud to raise their above-average kids.

Most of the families were young. Most of the fathers were Republican and commuted into the city every day to work. Most mothers stayed home, took care of the kids and voted the way their husbands suggested.

"I've often kidded my father, who has never been a fan of taxes or government about moving to a place that had such high property taxes to pay for school," Hillary said. "But even though it was a very conservative Republican community, there was just no griping during the '50s and '60s about paying for a good education."

It was a relatively new suburb, annexed into the city only years before, largely because "Hizzoner"— Chicago Mayor Richard J. Daley—decided in the early 1950s that the city needed a new airport. Park Ridge was one of the bedroom communities that grew up around the airport. Hillary Rodham grew up in the flight path of O'Hare International Airport.

Park Ridge in the '50s was pleasantly suburban. People sat on front porches on spring and summer evenings. They grilled steaks and hamburgers in their back yards on Friday and Saturday nights. They went to church on Sunday mornings. There were kids, lots of kids. For entertainment, there was the Pickwick Theater. For soft drinks and milkshakes, there was Ted & Pearl's Happy House.

"There must have been forty or fifty children within a four-block radius of our house and within four years of Hillary's age," Dorothy Rodham told *The Washington Post.* "They were all together, all the time, a big extended family. There were more boys than girls, lots of playing and competition."

Four years after Hughie's birth, a third child arrived. It was another boy, Tony. Meanwhile, Hugh was working day and night to establish his own drapery-making business and save enough money to pay off the mortgage on the family's Georgian-style home on the corner of Wisner and Elm streets. The house in which Hillary was raised had a front porch on which family members often spent their evenings. Hillary's bedroom, painted yellow, sported wooden floors and a sun deck.

Hugh and Dorothy Rodham would live in the same house for nearly thirty-eight years. In 1987, Hillary finally persuaded them to move to Little Rock where they would be near their only grandchild, Chelsea.

While Hugh was proud of his three children, expectations were high. When Hillary brought home straight A's from Eugene Field Elementary School, Emerson Junior High School, Maine East High School and Maine South High School, Hugh would look at those report cards and teasingly say, "You must go to a pretty easy school."

"I was always interested in school," Hillary said. "And always believed, from my parents impressing it upon me, that education was absolutely the key to personal growth, development and success. My mother didn't go to college so she was particularly anxious that her children would go to college. My father went to college on a football scholarship and was sure if it hadn't been for that . . . he might not have been able to go to college, so he was very intent on providing that opportunity for us."

Hugh's company never had many employees. He chose to do almost everything himself. He would buy fabric, print the designs on it, sew it and then hang it in homes, hotels and offices. Hugh expected his children to work just as hard as he did.

"Our parents didn't just pay attention to our grades," Tony Rodham told *The Washington Post*. "They cared about everything we did."

Both sons played junior high and high school football. Hughie was a quarterback. One night he completed ten of eleven pass attempts only to have his father's joke, "I got nothing to say to you except you should have completed the other one."

"My parents really set high expectations for me and were rarely satisfied," Hillary said. "I always felt challenged. I always felt there was something else out there I could reach for. They expected us to do well and work as well as we knew how. And I felt very fortunate because as a girl growing up I never felt anything but support from my family. Whatever I thought I could do or be they supported. There was no distinctions between me and my brothers or any barriers thrown up to me that I couldn't think about something just because I was a girl. It was just 'if you work hard enough and you really apply yourself then you should be able to do whatever you choose to do.' "

Hugh always drove a Cadillac and always voted Republican. He fit in well with the other young, grayflannel types pulling themselves up through the ranks in their various organizations. In the 1950s, Park Ridge rejected egg-headed Adlai Stevenson and embraced the anticommunism of Joe McCarthy. During her final year of high school, Hillary worked as a volunteer in the unsuccessful 1964 presidential campaign of Republican Barry Goldwater.

Although Hillary's political beliefs would eventually move far to the left of her father's beliefs, political differences never affected their relationship. "He was so fond of his daughter, anything she did was OK with him," said Manny Gelb, a childhood friend of Hugh's from Scranton.

When Bill Clinton ran for Congress in 1974, Hillary's parents and two brothers all came to Arkansas to help out. "Dad answered the phones," Tony told *People* magazine. "Hughie and I were the official sign putter-uppers. We'd go out and nail 'em on anything that didn't move and some things that did."

Hughie stayed in Fayetteville. He obtained an advanced degree in education from the University of Arkansas and then got his law degree at the school. It was Hillary who talked Hughie into continuing his education and becoming a lawyer. Tony was less settled, bouncing from job to job through the years despite his sister's steady insistence that he settle down.

Robert Compton, Jr., a neighbor of the Rodhams after they moved to Little Rock, remembers Hugh Rodham—who died in April 1993 at the age of eighty-two—as a master of the lost art of just visiting. Compton remembers Rodham as a man who loved to sit in a rocking chair in his carport and talk with passersby. Just as he had in his younger years, Hugh had strong feelings about everything.

"He would hold forth," Compton said. "I always enjoyed stopping by to visit him, particularly in the heat of a political controversy. We would watch Bill and Hillary on the national news, then go visit Hugh and talk about it."

Few people ever knew Hillary's father well. Even close associates of the President and his wife had little contact through the years with Hillary's parents. When rare interviews were granted, it was Dorothy Rodham who did the talking. The couple rarely made public appearances, although Hugh made a cameo appearance in 1992 on the television program *Hearts Afire,* which was produced by the Clinton's friends Harry Thomason and Linda Bloodworth-Thomason.

While Hillary was growing up, Hugh spent long hours in the city. Dorothy stayed in the suburbs and spent her days with the children.

"I spent all my time in the car then," Dorothy told *Paris Match* magazine. "I had three children, and each one had his or her little activity. I always encouraged them to do what they wanted to do. So I spent my time driving back and forth across town."

Hugh relished the summer weeks spent with his family at a cabin on a lake near Scranton. "He loved that more than anything," Manny Gelb said.

Even after the kids had grown, the Rodhams remained a tightknit family. Beginning in 1980, Hughie and Tony lived together for nearly three years in south Florida, where Hughie had a job as a public defender. In 1986, Hughie married Maria Arias and moved out of the apartment he shared with Tony but not before both tried to convince her to move in with them.

"I never told Maria this, but I waited until the day before our wedding to find another apartment for us," Hughie told *People*. "I was hoping that maybe I could change her mind."

Tony was a process server and private detective until 1992, when he devoted himself full time to the Clinton campaign. In early 1993, he moved to Washington.

The Rodhams regularly attended the First United Methodist Church of Park Ridge. Hillary said the religious foundation laid in Park Ridge helped prepare her for the controversies, personal attacks and stress of the presidential campaign.

"The combination of my upbringing and my work for more than twenty years on behalf of causes I believe it has made me aware that change is a difficult process," Hillary told Diane Huie Balay of the *Reporter,* a Methodist publication. "One has to be grounded in faith and understanding of your place in the world to get up every day and keep going. That has been a very big comfort and support to me in the last year."

She talked of feeling "lonely" when advocating changes "that for you are rooted in scripture and religious experience and for others are viewed as coming out of some other motivation. . . . Just to know that there are many people who see the world in the same way and are committed to creating better opportunities here as part of their expression of faith is very comforting and supportive to me."

As a teenager, Hillary's view of the world was shaped in part by the Reverend Donald Jones—now on the faculty of Drew University in Madison, New Jersey. Jones, who has remained close to Hillary through the years, was the youth minister at Hillary's church. It was Jones's first job after receiving his master of divinity degree, and he had taken it in large part to be near the southern Wisconsin school his girlfriend was attending.

In 1961, as the Eisenhower '50s gave way to the tumultuous '60s, Jones seemed the embodiment of the fighting young minister who could speak to the young. It was Jones who, slowly and carefully, introduced Hillary to the work of theologians such as Paul Tillich—under whom Jones had studied—as well as secular writers such as J. D. Salinger and Stephen Crane. He led his youth group into the worst neighborhoods of Chicago, meeting with black gang leaders and Hispanic delinquents. He introduced his kids to the new culture of protest and social activism, studying the lyrics of Bob Dylan and Beat poetry. He screened Truffaut's *The 400 Blows* and had his group discuss Picasso's *Guernica.*

"The fact that we were exposed to different points of view and different people's experiences at a relatively early age was really important to me," Hillary said. "For many of the people who we came into contact with during those years—like migrant farm workers or inner-city young people—faith was something they really had to hang onto. . . . That made a big impression on me."

Prior to meeting Jones, Hillary had been a typical suburban girl. She had studied piano and ballet. She had earned money as a baby sitter. Now she was organizing "baby-sitting brigades" to care for the children of migrant farm workers while their parents worked the fields.

"He was relentless in telling us that to be a Christian did not just mean you were concerned about your own personal salvation," Hillary told *Newsweek.*

In such a conservative community, it was perhaps inevitable that Jones would create a stir.

"He didn't get along with the powers that be at the church," said Leon Osgood, a member of the Park Ridge church. "He was probably too social-minded. He did have a lot of influence on the young people at that time."

In 1962, Jones took a group that included Hillary into downtown Chicago one Sunday evening to hear the Reverend Martin Luther King, Jr., speak. Afterward, Jones took the well-to-do white boys and girls from Park Ridge backstage to shake King's hand.

Jones left Park Ridge in 1963. Hillary began writing him and they corresponded until she entered law school at Yale. She contacted Jones again years later after reading a New Jersey newspaper that reported on a trial at which Jones was testifying. Jones, who teaches religion and ethics, was an expert witness at the trial of a woman who had sued the state of New Jersey to have Medicaid pay for her abortion.

Jones received a message in his office one day in 1979 that said, "Please call Hillary Rodham." The number had an unfamiliar area code. Jones dialed the number, and a deep voice answered, "Governor's Mansion."

It was a state trooper speaking. Jones thought he had dialed the wrong number. No, the trooper said, the number was correct. Hillary Rodham was the lady of the house, married to Arkansas Governor Bill Clinton.

"That was all a big revelation to me," Jones said. "When you think of Hillary's career, much of it was in voluntary work. She was meeting Martin Luther King at the same time that Bill met John F. Kennedy. Bill took the political route, and Hillary took the volunteer route."

Jones remembers her as someone who was not as interested in boys as other girls her age and didn't mind debating the boys at church. "What I recall is that when we got into heavy discussions on retreats, Hillary was right in the midst of everything,'' he said. ''Hillary was fifteen and sixteen years old, even younger than the juniors and seniors. She held her own in discussions.''

After getting to know Bill, Jones visited Arkansas on several occasions after that 1979 phone call and campaigned for Bill in early 1992 in New Hampshire. Jones said he wasn't surprised Hillary married Clinton.

''I think she has always been intrigued and attracted to his intelligence, his moral commitments, his love of life and his political life,'' Jones said. ''I think she shares all of those things. Love of life may be the least because I think he is more fun-loving than Hillary. She has less time for frivolous things.''

''Historically, my father's family was always Methodist and took it very seriously,'' Hillary told the *Reporter*. ''Mine is a family who traces our roots back to Bristol, England, to the coal mines and the Wesleys. So as a young child, I would hear stories that my grandfather had heard from his parents, who heard them from their parents who were all involved in the great evangelical movement that swept England.

''When my personal experience in church as a child was so positive—not only the youth ministry work that I was part of but a really active, vital, outreaching Sunday school experience, lots of activities for children—there was a sense in which the church was our second home. We would walk up to the church, not only to go to church but to play volleyball, to go to potluck dinners, to be in plays. . . . It was just a very big part of my life. And that kind of fellowship was real important to me.

''As I grew older and had an opportunity to learn more about other theological approaches, I became more and more comfortable with the Methodist approach, the marrying of faith and works and the role of grace. You know, people made fun of the Wesleys

(English evangelist John Wesley founded Methodism in the 1700s along with his brother Charles) because of their method, but for me it's helpful. It's not for everybody, obviously, that's not what appeals to them. But for me, thinking about scripture and tradition and reason and experience really helps me order a lot of thoughts about faith and religion.

"I also like the social mission of the church. I like the way the church has grappled with hard issues over the years. I believe that for a period of time in the late '60s, '70s and '80s there really was too much of an emphasis on social mission to the exclusion of personal faith and growth. But I think the balance is being struck again. I still love the fact that we grapple with the issues that other people don't want to talk about, that they wish would go away, because I think that is being a part of the world. But I also am comforted to know that there is a greater awareness of how the church has to feed the individual soul as well."

Asked by the reporter what she would tell a group of children who had just been confirmed in the Methodist church, Hillary said, "I would say I hoped their decision to be confirmed for church membership carried with it a commitment to grow as a Christian, that they would confront many challenges to their fundamental beliefs and attitudes as they moved through life. And that I hoped they would find comfort and strength from both the scriptures and from their own upbringing in the church. But no matter what happens in their lives, the decision they had made is one that will always be there for them even if they stray from it. . . . That is something that I think, particularly for young people, needs to be stressed because so many of them fall away from the church and suffer doubts about faith."

Hillary said she had gone through periods of intense spiritual examination and growth followed by quieter times.

"About ten years ago, I began to speak at a number

of churches around our state ... about why I was a Methodist,'' she said. ''And then I did a series of Sunday school classes in my church (the First United Methodist Church of Little Rock) over a couple of years about Methodism and about issues of faith that were not necessarily denominational but were more universal. When Chelsea was just a little baby, the minister who married Bill and me, Vic Nixon, came over and we had a picnic in the back yard. Vic and I loved to get together and talk about theology. He gave me a copy of the new *Book of Discipline,* and we had a great conversation. I was really ready to focus on spiritual matters again.''

Vic Nixon met Hillary for the first time in 1974 in the town square at Berryville, the small north Arkansas town where he was the Methodist minister. Hillary had come to Arkansas that fall to be with Bill, who was running for Congress. They would not marry until a year later.

''It was a campaign event, one of those county things where all the Democratic candidates get together, stand out there in front of the courthouse and give their speeches to the crowd,'' Nixon said.

Hillary Rodham stood in the back of the crowd that day.

''She was not calling attention to herself,'' Nixon sad. ''She was rather inconspicuous. I didn't even know she was teaching at the law school.''

Upon learning that Nixon was a Methodist minister, though, Hillary told him that she also was a Methodist. It was the beginning of an important friendship. Not only did Nixon marry the Clintons, he conducted the Little Rock memorial service that followed the death of Hugh Rodham in 1993.

Nixon also gave the invocation at the Democratic National Convention in New York City's Madison Square Garden on the night Bill accepted his party nomination, July 16, 1992. And he gave the invocation at the special prayer meeting at Washington's First Baptist Church the day before Bill's inauguration as President in January 1993.

Methodist ministers such as Don Jones and Vic Nixon always have been important to Hillary, and so have those with whom she has attended church through the years.

In November 1992, during the final days of the campaign, members of Hillary's Sunday school class in Little Rock mailed letters to newspapers complaining that the Republicans were portraying her unfairly. She was not some militant feminist lacking in family values, said John Gill, a prominent Little Rock attorney and a member of the class.

"She has been a good mother because she is intelligent and caring enough to follow, as she taught us, the wonderful line from a book by Rabbi Kushner that says, 'no one on their deathbed ever regretted not spending more time at the office,' " Gill's letter read.

Members of the class took turns teaching. Hillary would teach four to six times a year. The letter said Hillary also regularly attended church functions with Chelsea, resulting in a "fine, wholesome girl despite the abnormal stress of constant exposure to public life." It also noted that Hillary carried scriptures in her address book.

It was a complicated young woman who headed to Boston and Wellesley College in the fall of 1964. She combined the conservative political roots of her father, the religious roots of Methodism and the social conscience given her by Don Jones.

Hillary had considered attending college at three exclusive schools in Massachusetts: Wellesley, Smith and Radcliffe. "I don't really know why I chose that, other than my senior year I had two teachers," Hillary told Charles Allen. "One had graduated from Wellesley, the other graduated from Smith . . . and they were both so bright and smart and terrific teachers and they lobbied me hard to apply to these schools that I had never heard of before. Then, when I was accepted, they lobbied me hard to go and be able to work out all the financial and other issues associated with it. So I went to Wellesley and it was another educational experience for me.''

Hugh drove her there in his Cadillac.

"Aside from a few trips away with girlfriends, Hillary hadn't really been away from home," Dorothy Rodham told *The Washington Post*. "I loved having kids around, and when she went to Wellesley, well, it was really, really hard to leave her. After we dropped her off, I just crawled in the back seat and cried for eight hundred miles.''

As was his custom, Hugh said little on the long ride back to Park Ridge.

Wellesley changed Hillary. She had left Park Ridge behind. Soon, she would leave behind her father's beliefs on Vietnam, civil rights and other issues. She would go home to Illinois each summer, and with each passing year, it became more evident to her friends that the Goldwater Girl had changed.

"I was exposed to a really broad education," she said in an 1990 interview. "It was very difficult for me to understand when I first started working (on educational standards in Arkansas) that the vast majority of the students here would never be exposed to what I was exposed to.''

Alan Schechter, Hillary's political science and law professor at Wellesley, remembers the bright young lady from Illinois. But most of the young ladies at Wellesley were bright. And like Hillary, many of them came from comfortable backgrounds in the suburbs.

"It's wrong to paint Wellesley as some far-left bastion," Schechter said. "It was then, and is now, pretty much mainstream. Most of the students here are liberal to moderate in their political beliefs. But all in all, it is a pretty dull place. There are no real radicals here.''

Of the 2,200 students at Wellesley, there were few blacks and a lot of upper- to middle-class whites. Still, it was not like the world in which Hillary had grown up. There were Jews. There were liberals. There were Southerners. And there were ''real radicals'' in nearby Boston.

''Young and old people alike were challenging authority and saying they didn't agree with the way things had always been done,'' Schechter said. ''You have to recall what it was like in the fall of 1965 when she came here. We were less than two years removed from President Kennedy's assassination. We were in the middle of President Johnson's War on Poverty. There was the Civil Rights Act of 1964 and the Voting Rights Act of 1965. And that was the year that saw the escalation of American involvement n Vietnam.''

Schechter himself had come to Wellesley in 1962 at age 26, living in a college apartment with his wife—''a women's college was not about to hire a single man.'' For Hillary, he would become what Don Jones had been back in Park Ridge—a mentor of sorts, a shaper of her thoughts.

''Looking out the window of my office, this is almost as idyllic a setting as one could imagine,'' Schechter said in the spring of 1993. ''We have all of these outstanding young women from across the country who are gathered in one place. Hillary was not unique. That's not to say she wasn't exceptional, but she wasn't unique. The value system you see in Hillary is characteristic of the value systems you see in hundreds of Wellesley graduates. She has lived out that value system through the years with her involvement in the Children's Defense Fund and other organizations. Her philosophy and her world view have been very consistent since she left here in 1969. I don't think they have changed that much at all.''

Patsy Sampson, the president of Stephens College in Missouri, was Hillary's child psychology professor at Wellesley. She remembers Hillary as someone who, unlike a lot of other freshmen, knew where she was going. Although Hillary dated, she was never serious about any of the Harvard or MIT students she went out with.

''She was very much her own person, very independent,'' Sampson said. She was never one to follow the crowd. ''Whereas others would do things as a group, Hillary was not afraid to go out on her own and do her own thing. She had a strong intellect and a strong social conscience.''

Like many women's schools at the time, Wellesley had curfews. There was a ban on having men in the dormitories. Certain required classes were unpopular with students. Hillary—the little Methodist from the Midwest—led the fight against the rules.

''The changes were not as great as what was going on at Cambridge, but it was still a period of social awakening at Wellesley,'' Sampson said. ''For example, the school for the first time made an active attempt to recruit minority students. Hillary was supportive of that effort.''

As a member of the admissions committee, Schechter spearheaded the attempt to recruit minority students for Wellesley. Sampson, meanwhile, set up a program in which students would work at a Head Start center in the Roxbury area of Boston. Hillary Rodham was part of that program.

''Students were learning what it meant to be active,'' Sampson said.

Hillary decided early to major in political science and go on to law school. But unlike her classmates who planned to attend law school, her goal was not to

Arkansas Democrat-Gazette

April 1979: Hillary Rodham, hard-charging corporate attorney and wife of the Governor of Arkansas, watches first-grader Amanda Gross paint a dolphin. Amanda soon moved on to her hand.

Once and future first ladies: Rosalyn Carter with Hillary Rodham during a visit to Little Rock in 1979.

Arkansas Democrat-Gazette

Hillary Rodham greets Clinton supporters at the Camelot Inn, scene of the 1980 Victory Party that never came off.

January 1981: Bill Clinton, soon to become the youngest ex-governor in U.S. history, hugs his wife after bidding the state's General Assembly farewell.

Hillary with two-year-old Chelsea in 1983.

Arkansas Democrat-Gazette

January 1983: Clinton returns to the Governor's office with a reconstructed Hillary in his wake.

Arkansas Democrat-Gazette

March 1990: To the surprise of almost everyone, including perhaps Hillary, Bill Clinton announces he will run for a fourth term as Governor of Arkansas.

Hillary Clinton addresses hundreds of "at-risk" college students on the grounds of the Arkansas Governor's Mansion in July 1990.

Arkansas Democrat-Gazette

Arkansas Democrat-Gazette

Vermont fans respond to a Hillary appearance during the 1992 presidential campaign.

Bill, Chelsea and Hillary together on the campaign trail. (Note Chelsea's Endangered Species T-shirt.)

Arkansas Democrat-Gazette

Arkansas Democrat-Gazette

Hillary and Tipper Gore at the 1992 Democratic Conven-

Hillary and her husband at the 1992 Democratic Convention.

make big money as a corporate attorney—she wanted to change American society.

When Martin Luther King, Jr., was assassinated in April 1968, Hillary wore a black armband and walked in a memorial march in Boston. She spent part of 1968 campaigning for antiwar Democrat Eugene McCarthy. Just four years after having campaigned for Barry Goldwater, she had left the Republican beliefs of her father behind.

That summer, back home in the oasis from unrest that was Park Ridge, Hillary read of the upheaval across the country. There was the assassination of Bobby Kennedy in Los Angeles, the civil rights battles, the antiwar protests and the riots in the cities. One night, while the Democratic National Convention was taking place in Chicago, Hillary and a friend decided to take a train into the city to see what all the commotion was about.

We saw kids our age getting their heads beaten in,'' that friend, Betsy Johnson Ebeling, would later tell *The Washington Post*. "And the police were doing the beating. Hillary and I just looked at each other. We had had a wonderful childhood in Park Ridge, but we obviously hadn't gotten the whole story."

Back at Wellesley in the fall, Hillary worked for the Democratic nominee, Senator Hubert Humphrey of Minnesota. But there was not the same passion at Wellesley that Hillary had seen on the streets of Chicago. No one there was about to be drafted. These young women did not have to worry about being sent to the jungles of Vietnam. For Hillary, political activism was more of an intellectual exercise. As president of the student government, she organized teach-ins to educate students about the Vietnam War.

"Hillary would usually run those meetings," Schechter said. "I remember that a lot of them were held in the chapel. It was never a case of people pounding their fists on tables. There was never a suggestion that we should all march downtown. Hillary and most of the other students were against the war, but everything was approached in a very pragmatic way. I'm sure people on neighboring campuses blanched at our lack of radicalism at Wellesley.''

"There were not the violent protests that were going on elsewhere,'' Sampson said. ''But there was a great deal of interest in both the antiwar movement and the civil rights movement.''

Schechter recalls the stereotype of ''Wendy Wellesley,'' the girl in pearls and a tartan skirt. To a certain extent, the stereotype fit. But the things that went on in 1968 forced students to confront their values and prejudices.

''Hillary was never what I would call a hard-core conservative,'' he said. ''When she came here, I think she identified more with the Nelson Rockefeller wing of the Republican Party than the conservative wing. She was one of those young Republican intellectuals, the type one tends to find in organizations such as the Ripon Society. But as the war escalated and the demonstrations intensified, the political environment changed and kids who earlier had considered themselves Republicans changed.''

Hillary was active in student government during her four years at Wellesley. Schechter, her college mentor, was the senior faculty adviser to the college government.

''You don't get to be student government president at a place like this based solely on popularity,'' he said. ''You have to be extremely competent. Hillary became president, in part, because of her superior organizational ability. She also was able to express her thoughts verbally better than any student I've had the opportunity to meet. In fact, the only person in public life who speaks as well as Hillary is Ronald Reagan.''

* * *

In 1968, Schechter was asked to put together programs for a group of influential alumnae who would be visiting the campus. One of the things he planned was a panel of three students to talk about how Wellesley had changed. Given the atmosphere of the times, alumnae were worried about what might be happening at their alma mater. Despite her high-profile efforts to change the traditional rules at Wellesley, Schechter chose Hillary to be one of the three students on the panel.

"She was poised, and I knew she would be able to reassure the alumnae," he said. "She didn't disappoint me."

Still, Hillary continued her efforts to change the way things were done at Wellesley. "The student government changed the rules of the institution, and Hillary played a leading role in that," Schechter said. "I remember her saying, 'Treat us like adults, and we will act like adults.' But she did not set about achieving these changes with demonstrations. She always approached things in a mature, democratic way."

Part of her efforts revolved around changing the school curriculum. For instance, students were required to study the Bible as literature for a year (the Old Testament one semester and the New Testament the next) even though Wellesley was a secular institution.

"Once enough students were saying they didn't want required Bible courses, we voted them out," Schechter said. "There also were pressures to get rid of requirements such as two years of science. We never abandoned those requirements, but we made the changes that seemed sensible. Hillary was attuned to the political realities. She knew she would never get everything she wanted and thus did not try to do too much, too soon."

For her senior thesis in 1969, Hillary prepared a comparative analysis of various community action programs for the poor, concluding that while the poor themselves should have a role in taking control of their lives, government programs were still needed for there to be a long-term effect. Schechter, one of the professors who graded the thesis, described it as progressive yet not radical.

"Her conclusion—that you want the poor to have more options but that government has to provide the resources for that to be done—represents what I would describe as liberal pragmatism," he said.

Schechter was among several professors who urged Hillary to attend Yale Law School. "She was so talented," he said. "I had attended Amherst as an undergraduate and then gone to Yale Law before dropping out to get my doctorate at Columbia. I went to Yale in part because it stressed more of a social approach to the law than Harvard."

If you wanted to make big bucks as a corporate lawyer, you went to Harvard. If, like Hillary, you wanted to be a social activist, you went to Yale.

Of course, she could have gone anywhere," Schechter said. "But she had already determined that she would reject the corporate world and use her talents to help children."

In his letter of recommendation to Yale, Schechter wrote, "Hillary Rodham is by far the most outstanding young woman I have taught in the seven years I have been on the Wellesley College faculty. I have high hopes for Hillary and for her future. She has the intellectual ability, personality and character to make a remarkable contribution to American society."

"I ended up going to Yale," Hillary said, years later. "It was a good choice for me because it was smaller than a school like Harvard. That's where I met my husband to be, so it was a particularly good choice for me."

*   *   *

A small group of Wellesley seniors had decided that a member of their class should speak at graduation. They decided the student should be Hillary. But never before had the student been allowed to speak during the graduation ceremony, and the school's president, Ruth Adams, was not inclined to change tradition in 1969. The small group took their idea to the student body, and under intense pressure, Adams relented.

Hillary was the obvious choice. Not only was she a straight-A student, she had been active in student politics and was well-liked on campus. She was gregarious and affable, she loved to dance and—as Schechter pointed out—her verbal skills were unparalleled.

Adams insisted the speech reflect a consensus of the graduating class and that it be "appropriate." Hillary asked for suggestions from her classmates, and was deluged with ideas, poems and quotations. In the end the speech was drafted by a small committee, and when Adams demanded final review of it days before the ceremony, the speechwriters refused.

Hillary had final approval of the remarks. She looked it over and made some changes of her own.

Dorothy Rodham stayed home in Park Ridge with Hughie and Tony, but Hugh made the long drive east in the Cadillac to see his daughter graduate. He was in the crowd that watched Hillary Rodham shock alumnae, faculty and parents when she began her speech by chastising the day's main speaker—liberal Republican Senator Edward Brooke of Massachusetts for delivering "irrelevant" remarks. Speaking without notes, she said, "I find myself in a familiar position, that of reacting, something that our generation has been doing for quite a while now."

After criticizing Brooke, she moved on to her remarks, calling at one point for a "more immediate, ecstatic and penetrating mode of living":

*   *   *

"The challenge now is to practice politics as the art of making what appears to be impossible, possible. . . . There's a very strange conservative strain that goes through a lot of New Left college protests that I find very intriguing because it harkens back to a lot of the old virtues, to the fulfillment of original ideas. And it also a very unique American experience. It is such a great adventure. If the experiment in human living doesn't work in this country, in this age, it is not going to work anywhere."

Life later featured a photograph of a bell-bottomed Hillary Rodham and several paragraphs about her commencement address in a roundup of the commencement addresses that had been given at the nation's top colleges and universities that spring.

"The president's advice to Hillary before the speech was basically, don't do anything to embarrass us," Schechter said. "She had a prepared address, but the remarks she directed to Senator Brooke were off the cuff. And they were deserved. His speech was absolute pablum. It probably had been written by a staffer with an IQ much lower than Hillary's. But the off-the-cuff remarks flowed perfectly into the prepared remarks. You never knew when she made the transition.

"Graduations generally are a pain, especially when you have been through as many of them as I have. The speeches are so long and so boring. But this one stood out. That was a remarkable graduation speech, and student government leaders aren't always remarkable, even at Wellesley."

After delivering the speech, Hillary celebrated with several other seniors by going swimming in a lake on campus where swimming was forbidden. She stripped down to her bathing suit, leaving her glasses and clothes on the shore. Those items were confiscated by a campus security guard while Hillary was swimming.

"Blind as a bat, I had to feel my way back to my room," she said during a 1992 visit to the campus.

During the summer of 1969, Hillary visited Alaska, working at several jobs before beginning law school in the fall.

At Yale, Hillary entered into a world that was even more intellectually stimulating than Wellesley. During a trip back to the campus almost two decades after her graduation, she said, "There was a great amount of ferment and confusion about what was and wasn't the proper role of a law school education. We would have great arguments about whether we were selling out because we were getting a law degree, whether in fact we should be doing something else, not often defined clearly but passionately argued. . . . Those were difficult and turbulent times."

In the spring of 1970, Hillary read about Marian Wright Edelman in *Time*. She was tremendously impressed by the founder of the Children's Defense Fund. Edelman was scheduled to speak on the Yale campus several weeks later. Hillary later would describe the timing as "one of those strange twists of fate that enters all our lives if we're open to hear and to see them."

Listening to Edelman speak at Yale, Hillary knew right away that she had to go to work for her. Edelman urged the Yale students to work on behalf of the poor.

Hillary approached Edelman following the speech and told her that she would like to spend the summer working as an intern. Edelman quickly gave the idealistic twenty-two-year-old law student the bad news: There was no money for a summer intern. But Hillary was not easily deterred. She discovered that the school offered support for students who would work in the field of civil rights. Hillary applied for a grant and received it. So while other students spent the summer of 1970 interning at Boston, New York and Washington law firms, Hillary went to work for Edelman and the CDF.

The next fall, a shaggy young Arkansan named Bill Clinton turned up at Yale, fresh from having been a Rhodes scholar at Oxford University. The story of how they met has already taken on the patina of myth.

Bill tells it this way: "She walked up to me and said, 'Since you've been staring at me and I've been staring back, we might as well introduce ourselves. I'm Hillary Rodham,' and we shook hands."

Bill said he considered Hillary "immensely interesting and attractive." Hillary, meanwhile, found Bill to be a "nice, caring and intelligent person."

In her version, Hillary says the first thing she heard out of Bill's mouth was, ". . . and not only that, but we grow the biggest watermelons in the world."

"After hearing that, I knew I had to find out who he was," she said. "I asked my friend who he was, and she said Bill Clinton from Arkansas."

They had a class together in the spring of 1971. Hillary said their early dates consisted of "Cokes on the way home from the library" because they were both so busy. When they were together, they often debated political issues of the day. Each was impressed by the other's intellect. In fact, friends say, Bill was a bit intimidated by Hillary at first.

Bill shared a beach house at Milford, Connecticut, with three other law students. Hillary spent much of her time there once they began dating. Later, they shared a rented house in New Haven.

"He was always unusual in the midst of the Yale class because, of course, he'd been a Rhodes Scholar, and most of our classmates at Yale were aiming for clerking at the Supreme Court or very important jobs in New York or Washington or whatever," Hillary told Charles Allen. "Bill was always intent upon what he was going to do, which was come home to Arkansas.

And most of us, including myself when I first met him, didn't really have any idea what that meant.''

Bill went to Park Ridge for the first time in 1972 to meet the Rodhams. ''I thought he was interesting,'' Dorothy told *The Washington Post* years later. ''He was sincere and had traveled a lot. I remember asking him what he was going to do after Yale, and without blinking, he said: ''I'm going back to Arkansas to help the state.' I thought, gee, that's great for him. Least he knew what he wanted.''

Bill was worried that Hillary would not follow him to Arkansas after graduation from Yale. He was right to worry.

''I mean, we'd never been to Arkansas,'' Hillary said. ''We didn't know much about the state. Frankly, what we knew was colored by (the Central High School crisis of) 1957 and Orval Faubus, and so we just didn't have much of an idea at all.''

''I loved being with her, but I had very ambivalent feelings about getting involved with her,'' he told *Vanity Fair*. He did not know if she would want to spend her life in a poor Southern state she had never even visited.

That she had fallen for an Arkansan who sounded vaguely like Elvis surprised the normally rational Hillary. ''Suppose I had sat down and tried to map out my life,'' she said after Bill had become governor. ''Do you suppose I would have said I would be married to the governor of Arkansas and practicing law in Little Rock? There is no way. I think life presents opportunities. . . . You've got to be able to take opportunities when they come your way.''

Tony Rodham was cutting the grass when Bill first arrived at the Rodhams's house in Park Ridge. He said Bill ''climbed out of the car, came right over and started helping me cut the grass. We had a nice little chat and, of course, I had something else I wanted to do. So Bill immediately volunteered to help finish the job with the grass. I think Dad came out of the house and put a stop to it.''

By the end of the week-long visit, Bill had used his charm to win over Dorothy, Hughie, Tony and even Hugh.

Hillary was to have graduated in 1972, but she decided to stay at Yale an additional year to be with Bill. She studied child development at the Yale Child Study Center and did research for her article "Children Under the Law." The article was completed in November 1973 and published in the January 1974 issue of the *Harvard Educational Review*. It would be almost two decades before it received widespread publicity in the heat of Bill's presidential campaign. Still, at age 26, Hillary was making a name for herself as a children's rights advocate. During her final year at Yale, she spent part of her time as a legal intern at a hospital, helping set up one of the first child abuse reporting systems in the country.

During 1972, Bill and Hillary went to Texas, where Bill joined up with Taylor Branch to run George McGovern's Texas campaign. Branch later would write *Parting the Waters,* the award-winning history of the American civil rights movement.

In Texas, they met political activist Betsey Wright, who later would become Bill's gubernatorial chief of staff and, after Hillary the most important woman in his life. Initially, Wright was more impressed with Hillary than she was with Bill.

Following graduation, however, Bill and Hillary went their separate ways. Bill headed back to Arkansas. He had considered practicing law in Hot Springs, Arkansas, but decided instead to take a teaching job at the University of Arkansas at Fayetteville. In June Hillary took a job as staff attorney for the Children's Defense Fund.

''I first came to Arkansas to visit Bill in 1973 to

visit his family and his state," Hillary remembered. "I was very taken by how beautiful it was. He picked me up at the airport in Little Rock and we drove up Highway 7—it was just beautiful. And when we both graduated from Yale, he came right home to Arkansas to teach. I was, uh, very unsure about where I wanted to be."

She didn't want to go to Arkansas at that point because she was unsure the prolifically talented Bill Clinton would stick to his decision and resist the lure of a high-powered legal career on the East Coast. So she went back to work for the Children's Defense Fund in Boston. And waited.

In January 1974, Hillary received a call from John Doar, who had been hired by the House Judiciary Committee to head the impeachment investigation of President Nixon. Doar was a friend of Burke Marshall, who had worked in the Kennedy administration and who had taught both Hillary and Bill at Yale.

"He called Burke Marshall and said, 'I need about five young lawyers who don't mind working real hard, who will do the grunt work,'" Hillary said.

"That job required not just brightness but some sense of balance, some discretion, prudence and integrity," Marshall said. He gave Doar Hillary's name. The job was offered, and she immediately accepted it.

"One of the first ones I recruited was Hillary," Doar said. "Everybody was good. Everybody worked very hard. Nobody talked to the newspapers. They followed the rules, and they performed a dedicated task with real distinction."

Bill also was recommended for what he said would have been "the job of a lifetime." He decided, however, to stay in Arkansas rather than move to Washington. He was determined to run for Congress in

1974 against incumbent Republican John Paul Hammerschmidt.

"I tried to talk five or six people into running against him," Bill said. "I always knew I would run for public office, but I didn't intend to start so young. But when nobody else would do it, I got in. I just filed and started running, and everybody laughed at me."

Hillary, meanwhile, went to Washington and began working eighteen-hour days in cramped quarters. Late at night, she would call Bill in Fayetteville and tell him about her day. She remained on the staff from January until August 8, 1974, when Richard Nixon resigned.

"I barely ever saw her," Sara Ehrman, her Washington roommate whom Hillary had met during the McGovern campaign in Texas, told *The Washington Post*. "I just remember driving her at 7:00 A.M. to the Watergate committee offices in an old converted hotel. We used to laugh and laugh about the absurdity of the life she was leading."

"People just worked around the clock," Hillary said. "It was an unbelievable experience. The staff that was put together was so professional, experienced. They were some of the greatest lawyers I've ever worked with. I was just a fresh, young law school graduate, and I got to work with these people."

Hillary was one of only three women on the staff of forty-three lawyers and had the title of counsel, lowest in the hierarchy that included both Democrats and Republicans. One of the staff Republicans was William Weld, who would go on to become governor of Massachusetts.

Hillary said everyone "understood the constitutional significance of what we were doing. There was no attempt to slant the facts or weigh them. We were compiling information."

She had mixed feelings about Nixon, a man she described as one of the most enigmatic and compelling figures in history.

"There was no doubt that he was an extraordinarily able and intelligent person who understood a lot about America relations with other countries," Hillary said. "But he also is a person who is flawed. You can't place yourself above the law even if you think it is for moral and historical reasons."

She vividly remembers one particular Saturday during the investigation: "I was kind of locked in this soundproof room with these big headphones on, listening to a tape. It was Nixon taping himself listening to the tapes, making up his defenses to what he heard on the tapes. So you would hear Nixon talk and then you would hear very faintly the sound of a taped prior conversation with Nixon, Haldeman and Ehrlichman.... And you would hear him say, 'What I meant when I said that was ...' I mean it was surreal, unbelievable, but it was a real positive experience because the system worked. It was done in a very professional, careful way."

It was a historic legal debate, and Hillary was at the center of it, helping lay the legal groundwork for the impeachment of a President.

"Any lawyer in the country would have wanted to work on this," said Fred Altshuler, a colleague on the impeachment staff who later practiced law in San Francisco.

"The job sought ... you, you didn't seek the job," said another of those forty-three lawyers, Robert Sack.

Dagmar Hamilton, who went on to be a professor at the University of Texas at Austin, remembered Hillary as "a star from the beginning." Her immediate supervisor, senior associate special counsel Joe Woods, said Hillary was a "very good lawyer and very willing worker—an exceedingly pleasant person to work with."

Her primary assignment was establishing the procedural guidelines for the inquiry. She handled subpoenas, and kept track of the proper legal maneuvers attempted by both sides.

Special Counsel Doar ran the team along with the Republican minority's special counsel, Albert Jenner, Jr. The group of forty-three lawyers remained separate from the permanent staff of the House Judiciary Committee, which was chaired by Representative Peter Rodino, a Democrat from New Jersey. There was constant tension between the two groups, as both Doar's staff and the permanent committee staff wanted their share of the limelight.

The end came suddenly. Hillary said it was "both a relief and, I thought, a great credit to the President when (he) resigned."

Not only had the hours been long, the pressure had been intense for more than six months. Although Hillary could have stayed in Washington and joined a prestigious firm such as Williams and Connolly, she needed a break from "working like a crazy person." This first taste of high-stress Washington lawyering had made her hungry for Bill. She flew to Fayetteville.

"When Nixon resigned, we were all taken by surprise," she said. "And I really didn't know what I wanted to do, but I wanted to get out of Washington. I was exhausted. And when I visited Bill, I had met the dean of the law school at Fayetteville and he had said if you ever want to teach, let me know. So I picked up the phone—I called Wylie Davis who was the dean and I said, 'Well, Dean, you said this to me some months ago when I was visiting Bill at Fayetteville, are you serious?' He said, 'Well sure I am. I'll hire you right now.' And I said, 'Well, what will I teach?' And he said 'I'll let you know when you get here.' "

She would teach criminal law and trial advocacy. She would also help establish and run the school's legal-aid program, a project that sent students to the state prisons to work with prison inmates.

But she was coming to Arkansas for one reason: Bill Clinton.

"I loved him, I had to," she later said of her decision to move to Arkansas.

Her mother wasn't so sure. Dorothy told *The Washington Post* that she wondered "if Arkansas would be so great for Hillary. But you know, I've never told my children what to do. I had to rely on Hillary's judgment. There had never been any reason not to."

Hillary's friends were puzzled.

"I told her every twenty minutes that she was crazy to bury in Fayetteville," Ehrman told the *Post*. "You are crazy. You are out of your mind. You're going to this rural, remote place and wind up married to some country lawyer. She had been in the middle of everything, on the edge of everything. She was on the fast track to becoming a great legal star."

Hillary could not be dissuaded. She flew back to Washington, packed all her possessions in Sara Ehrman's Buick and began the thousand-mile trip to Arkansas. She quickly fell in love with the state.

"I didn't know why, but I just felt so much at home," she said. "The law school was fun. There was no air conditioning, and it was as hot as it could be. . . . But it was a great group of faculty people, people who became my closest friends as soon as I moved to Arkansas."

She immediately set out to bring order to Bill's chaotic congressional campaign. In the end, he shocked political observers by getting forty-eight percent of the vote against Hammerschmidt, who was thought to be invincible. That better-than-expected performance immediately made Bill the rising star of the Arkansas Democratic Party at age twenty-eight.

When the race was over, Bill Clinton owed about $40,000 and had a $26,000-a-year job. Hillary helped him retire the debt. She also made friends at the university and contemplated her future. After a year of living in Fayetteville, Bill and Hillary decided it was time to get married. They were tired of keeping separate residences—in small Southern towns, people talk—and were weary of the routine.

"I didn't see anything out there that I thought was more exciting or challenging than what I had in front of me," Hillary told *Vanity Fair*.

Her family came down from Illinois, and Hillary and her mother went to a local department store to buy Hillary a Jessica McClintock Victorian lace dress. She was ready to cast her lot with Bill Clinton and life in one of the nation's poorest states.

CHAPTER SEVEN
Favor and Disgrace

Considerably less tweedy than, say, New Haven, Fayetteville in a cozy little college town nestled among the Ozark Mountains of northwest Arkansas. It is, first of all, a remote place, too small to command a large airport and a difficult three-and-a-half hour drive from Little Rock. Most locals making the trip for University of Arkansas football games resort to a snaky path through dappled foliage that has long been known as the Pig Trail.

It was here, deep in what Mencken called the miasmic jungles of Arkansas, that Hillary Rodham married Bill Clinton on a cool day in football season. On October 11, 1975, the two exchanged heirloom rings in a Methodist service performed by the Reverend Victor Nixon.

It was not an elaborate ceremony. Only a few family members and friends attended the wedding, which was held at the house Hillary and Bill had been sharing in Fayetteville. Roger, Bill's younger brother drove up from Hot Springs to serve as best man.

Afterward, however, the wedding party repaired to a much larger function, a reception at the home of friends, state Senator Morriss Henry and his wife, Ann. While the wedding itself was more reflective of Hillary's private nature, this party resembled a boisterous political rally with about two hundred friends, well wishers and political types putting in appearances. Bill, who always loved a crowd, was in his element and ecstatic at the turnout. He took advantage of the occasion to announce he would be running for office again in 1976. Encouraged by his strong showing in the congressional race against incumbent Hammerschmidt the previous year, he said he would either challenge Hammerschmidt again or run for attorney general. He told the group he already had been promised considerable support if he decided to run against Hammerschmidt.

After the wedding, the couple went to Acapulco. Hillary's parents and brothers went along. "Bill and Hillary didn't have time to take a real honeymoon, and then my mom came up with the idea of going to Mexico," Hughie Rodham told *People*. "We got a special rate, and we all went down together."

One of the first times the name Hillary Rodham—as she was then still known—appeared in a statewide newspaper was on March 4, 1976, when she urged a coalition of women and prosecuting attorneys to push for state legislation requiring that a judge rule on the admissibility of "evidence of rape victims' previous sexual conduct" before such evidence was presented to a jury.

Hillary made the comments during a forum on the legal issues of rape that was part of the University of Arkansas' annual Women's Week. Under Arkansas law at the time, a jury could hear evidence about a woman's past sexual experience. It then was up to the judge to rule whether the information was admissible in an attempt to show the victim's consent or lack of consent. Obviously, such information could remain in jurors' minds and color their perceptions ever after a judge admonished them not to consider it.

But despite this blip on the radar screen of public consciousness, much of Hillary's time was spent behind the scenes, as she helped her new husband campaign for state attorney general. After weighing his options, Bill decided to make the statewide race soon after his marriage. However, he did not make public his decision immediately. He was accepting several speaking engagements per week—with Hillary often in tow—at high school graduation ceremonies, civic club meetings and the like. He also had hired a part-time secretary to answer letters and take care of congressional-type casework.

In addition to his *sub rosa* campaigning and teaching duties at the university, Bill was also building—with Hillary's help—a small private practice. When Clinton friend and former legislator Jack Yates, an attorney in the small town of Ozark, died, many of his clients—victims of black lung, the coal miners' malady, turned to Bill to help them pursue their government disability benefits. (Northwest Arkansas had once enjoyed a thriving coal mining industry.) Since Bill had used the black lung issue in his 1974 campaign against Hammerschmidt, he seemed the natural champion of these old miners.

Hillary also was busy helping her husband raise money to pay off the almost $40,000 debt left over from the 1974 campaign. In a way, deciding to run for attorney general instead of again trying to displace Hammerschmidt was a fiscal decision. Although Bill had come close to defeating the incumbent in 1974, *that* race had been run in the shadow of the Watergate scandal—and Hammerschmidt had supported the unpopular Nixon throughout the investigation. Clinton had campaigned tirelessly and had received strong financial support from organized labor, but he'd still lost.

Beating Hammerschmidt, the only Republican in the Arkansas congressional delegation, would be even more difficult in 1976. And the attorney general's office would be up for grabs, since the incumbent, Jim Guy Tucker of Little Rock, was planning to run for Congress. Large contributors to attorney general campaigns in Arkansas are rare, so making the statewide race didn't promise to be an overly expensive proposition. It certainly would be cheaper than taking on Hammerschmidt again, with the attendant political danger of losing a second straight race. It was widely acknowledged that Bill Clinton would be the front-runner in the attorney general's race.

As if Bill Clinton didn't have enough on his plate, he had also agreed to teach a course in "law and society" at the University of Arkansas Law School in Little Rock. This required him to make a round-trip to Little Rock every Monday, but also allowed him to make important contacts in the state capital and raise funds for a statewide campaign.

In January 1976, Bill requested a leave of absence from his teaching position to run for office. Hillary would continue to teach at Fayetteville. Two months later, Deputy Attorney General Clarence Cash, who had maintained a high profile as head of the state's consumer protection division, resigned from office to prepare for a race for attorney general.

On March 16, 1976, with Hillary by his side, Bill made the official announcement that he would run for attorney general. Cash formally announced his candidacy the same day. Clinton was 29 years old, and Cash had turned 35 that day.

At that time, the Arkansas attorney general was paid only $6,000 a year. In 1975, Tucker had said he would have to do private law work to supplement his salary. When he was asked if he would resort to practicing privately if elected attorney general, Bill turned to Hillary and said he hoped she could make enough money to keep him from having to do so.

Following the 9:30 A.M. news conference in Little

Rock, Bill and Hillary climbed aboard a private plane, which would take them first to Fort Smith in west Arkansas, then to Texarkana in southwest Arkansas, to El Dorado in south Arkansas and finally to Jonesboro in northeast Arkansas. They were off and running again.

It wasn't long before frizzy-haired young law professor Hillary Rodham was an issue in the race. In addition to her $18,000-a-year salary as a member of the University of Arkansas facility, Hillary was involved in a legal project made possible by a federal contract. Bill had to defend her against news reports that she had a potential income of $36,000 to $54,000 for the federal work. Bill claimed Hillary worked no more than two days a week on the project and that she was paid on an hourly basis. He estimated she would earn no more than $8,000 from the contact.

Of course, she was still making more than Bill. And in Arkansas in 1976, few wives made more money than their husbands. Fewer still retained their maiden names. Hillary did both, which, for the state's voters, took some getting used to.

When asked if the fact that his wife went by the name Hillary Rodham would hurt him politically, Bill, in his best aw-shucks manner said simply, "I hope not." During their courtship, he explained Hillary had "made quite a career for herself as a lawyer" and was a "nationally recognized authority on children's legal rights." Bill said it was important for her to maintain the name recognition she had built as Hillary Rodham. When asked if his wife would remain on the university faculty if he were elected attorney general, Bill said the issue had not been discussed. He added, however, that he did not "relish the possibility of her living in Fayetteville. . . . I am assuming we will both be living in Little Rock."

Soon, there was a third Democratic candidate in the race, thirty-six-year-old Secretary of State George Jernigan, who contended that he was the only candidate who had private clients and was licensed to practice before the U.S. Supreme Court. Bill, of course, answered that he had handled almost one hundred black lung claims and represented clients in fifteen counties. As someone who taught criminal and constitutional law, he said he was the only candidate who had filed papers with the Supreme Court for the state's attorney general and that being licensed to practice before the court was a "mere formality."

As it turned out, the attorney general's race was a mere formality.

Most of the state's political observers predicted the three-way race between Clinton, Jernigan and Cash would result in a runoff. When the votes came in on May 25, even Bill said he was "astonished" that he had received almost fifty-five percent of the vote. Jernigan finished second with twenty-five percent, and Cash finished third with twenty percent.

With no GOP opposition for attorney general—Arkansas has always had one of the nation's weakest Republican parties—Bill and Hillary were free to move on to other activities. They took a vacation to Spain to rest up from the campaign. While there Bill was contacted by Jimmy Carter's campaign staff. He promptly rejected their offer to coordinate Carter's Texas campaign despite the background he had gained in the state in 1972 running George McGovern's campaign. Bill's decision not to take the Texas post was based partly on the attitude of Carter's volunteer staff in Arkansas—they were upset by the tendency of the national campaign headquarters to staff state offices with out-of-state workers. With his eyes on the governor's job even before he had taken office as attorney general, Bill knew he could not afford to alienate Arkansas Democrats.

Bill explained to Carter's people that his preparations

for becoming attorney general in January and his unex-
pired teaching contract at the university would keep
him from taking on a state as large as Texas. But he
agreed to coordinate Carter's Arkansas campaign on a
part-time basis.

Hillary also would help out the Carter campaign, but
it wouldn't be in Arkansas. In August, it was announced that Hillary would go to Indiana to work for
the Democratic nominee. Her husband would work out
of Little Rock.

"I'm flattered they asked me to do it, especially
since Indiana is supposed to be such a tough state,"
Hillary said at the time. Her work on Carter's behalf
paid off when Carter defeated President Gerald Ford in
November. Had she wanted to, Hillary could have
headed to Washington to work for the first Democratic
administration since Lyndon Johnson left office in January 1969. Instead, she made the most important decision of her life up until that point—she moved from
Fayetteville to Little Rock, where she would work at
the Rose Law Firm and help guide her husband's political career.

It wasn't long before Hillary was being called on to
speak in Little Rock and throughout the state. She
spoke on everything from women's issues to legal issues, from politics to the media. Civic clubs, an important part of the social structure in a small state,
always were starved for good speakers and fresh faces.
Hillary fit the bill on both counts.

A May 1977 address to the North Little Rock Rotary
Club provided an example of Hillary's outspokenness.
In her speech, she criticized Little Rock's television
stations for not broadcasting a syndicated series of
David Frost interviews of Richard Nixon. She said one
of the biggest problems of living in Arkansas was getting the amount of information needed to make wise
decisions about government.

She mentioned her work as an attorney on the House Judiciary Committee staff during the Nixon impeachment inquiry and said she found it "incredible" that she could not watch Nixon's defense of his actions.

"We don't have much control over what we hear," Hillary said. "I don't want to sound like Spiro Agnew, but I do feel that sometimes the press does not exercise enough responsibility. Give us the facts and let us decide what is newsworthy."

She said that, since Watergate, the press had been more interested in investigations than in presenting the day's news.

"One of our problems is trying to control a press that is far out of line because of Watergate," she said.

In October 1977, Hillary was rewarded for her service to Carter's presidential campaign. She confirmed that the President was considering her for an appointment to the board of the Legal Services Corporation, an eleven-member board charged with administering funds to local entities for legal services to indigents. If she passed the perfunctory FBI background check, she would receive consulting fees for attending a dozen meetings a year until her term was up in 1980.

It seemed a perfect spot for the talented young lawyer. Hillary had established a clinic to train law students in indigent legal work while on the University of Arkansas faculty, and had also helped negotiate a contract with Legal Services Corporation for funds to operate Northwest Arkansas Legal Services, a legal aid bureau serving six counties.

On December 12, Hillary officially was announced as the board's newest—and youngest—member. She was thirty years old.

In January 1978, Hillary was named staff attorney for the Little Rock Airport Commission. It raised a few eyebrows around Little Rock, a socially conservative city where women traditionally had not been a part of the power structure, when the commission's previous attorney was asked to step down to make room for her.

"This was a chance for us to get a woman on the staff and involve women more in airport operations," commission Seth Ward explained. Ward had abstained from the voting because his son-in-law, Webb Hubbell—who fifteen years later would join the Justice Department under the Clinton administration—was a colleague of Hillary's at the Rose Law Firm.

George Munsey, the commission chairperson, said, "We felt we'd like to have the ladies involved in the overall operation of the airport."

If Hillary considered Munsey's tone somewhat condescending, she was pragmatic enough not to complain publicly. For her work with the Airport Commission she would be paid forty dollars an hour—perhaps as much as ten thousand dollars a year.

She had her supporters. The board of the Little Rock branch of the American Association of University Women immediately adopted a resolution commending the commission for its "perspicacity in appointing a woman with the outstanding qualifications of Hillary Rodham."

As she was making her own name around Little Rock, it soon became apparent that Hillary was not shy about offering advice to her husband and speaking out on his behalf. Her advice to him in early 1978 was that he should run for governor. Although Bill had given some thought to running for the U.S. Senate seat that was open due to the death of Senate Appropriations Committee Chairperson John L. McClellan, Hillary convinced him that he probably would lose the Democratic primary to then-Governor David Pryor, an immensely popular politician who badly wanted to be senator.

By February 1978, the scenario was set; Pryor would

run for the Senate against two of the state's four members of the U.S. House—Democrats Jim Guy Tucker and Ray Thornton—and Bill Clinton would run for governor. Already, the state's political analysts were predicting Bill would be unbeatable. In a job that didn't really require much, Bill had been an extremely vigorous campaigner and self-promoter. One newspaper account referred to him as "omnipresent."

With donated private funds, Bill published ten thousand copies of a glowing, eight-page "Attorney General's Report." The publication included such self-serving headlines as "Record Number of Opinions Issued by Division," "Aid Sought for Victims of Crime," "Clinton Leads Panel on Aged" and "Litigation Protects Interests of State."

As had been the case two years earlier, Hillary again would become a campaign issue. Even before Bill had formally announced his candidacy, a North Little Rock attorney named John Harmon was saying that the attorney general could be open to conflict-of-interest charges if elected governor. Harmon, who already had announced he would run for governor as a Democrat, told about 250 party leaders in Jonesboro, "The Little Rock Airport Commission recently replaced its attorney with Hillary Rodham. Don't you feel that the propriety of this arrangement deserves your closest examination? If, instead of being the attorney general's wife, Ms. Rodham were the first lady of Arkansas, would she be retained by Arkansas Power & Light for rate-increase cases, by oil companies for special favors, by the railroads for tax exemptions and by the truckers for higher weights on our highways?"

Harmon had trouble raising funds and dropped out of the race prior to the primary. On March 5, 1978, Bill and Hillary made their announcement at the same place his presidential campaign would begin and end—the historic Old State House at Little Rock. About 250 people braved a morning chill to hear Bill say, "As governor, I know I cannot be a miracle worker, but I will be a worker, and a doer, and will strive to see that our limited tax dollars are not wasted. Most important of all, I will try to bring out the best in all of us. From this day forward, I will campaign with that goal in mind.''

While his rhetorical style was not as finished and nuanced as the splendid instrument he would demonstrate fourteen years later, even then no politician in Arkansas could touch Bill Clinton on the stump. And Hillary was not your typical Arkansas politician's wife, the kind of wife who kept her mouth shut and smiled sweetly as her husband spoke.

A survey by Arkansas pollster Jim Ranchino showed that the thirty-one-year-old attorney general had the support of fifty-seven percent of those surveyed. Other Democratic candidates had less than ten percent of the vote combined.

One of those candidates, a former county judge from southwest Arkansas named Randall Mathis, assailed Bill for exploiting every official action of the attorney general's office for maximum political gain and running a slick, superficial campaign.

''Mr. Clinton, in seeking to become the youngest governor in the history of Arkansas, is relying on his great media exposure and his campaigning style to sweep him into the governor's chair,'' Mathis said. ''He began his campaign by saying that the people of Arkansas need him to be their governor. No doubt he feels safer basing his campaign on what he claims to be the need of the people rather than on his qualifications for the job.''

As the May primary drew near, the attacks became even more heated. The young gubernatorial candidate never hesitated to allow his wife to speak for him when he couldn't make it to events, and Hillary often could allay the heat. In mid-May, it was Hillary, not Bill, who went before a group of angry government workers to explain that the young attorney general had not meant to criticize state employees in a speech the previous month when a newspaper quoted Bill as saying many employees weren't "busy every day."

Hillary claimed the remark had been taken out of context and explained that Bill had meant to criticize state management practices, not employees. It worked—the more she talked, the less angry the crowd became. Two days later, it was Hillary, not Bill, who spoke at a traditional Arkansas political event at North Little Rock known as Levy Day. The rally is held in a working-class neighborhood, the kind of place where one might expect Hillary to receive a chilly reception. That night, Joe Woodward, a Clinton opponent from south Arkansas, called the attorney general "a pied piper in a pretty suit with a pretty flute" who was leading Arkansas to unknown places.

"Stand up and show your courage!" Woodward roared. Then, noting that Bill had raised almost half-a-million dollars—a huge sum for an Arkansas race in those days—he hollered, "Don't wait until you've elected someone you don't believe in. Everyone wants to buy a piece of the rock. Is it for sale? No, it's not for sale!"

Another Democratic candidate, Frank Lady, a Baptist from northeast Arkansas who emphasized his Christian credentials and drew much of his support from church groups, called Bill "the most liberal politician ever to come out of Arkansas" and charged him with "smiling and campaigning mostly at state expense."

But Hillary gave a rousing speech of her own that defused the vitriol the other candidates had directed at her husband. She held up the fact that Bill had run "an affirmative and positive campaign" as one reason Arkansans should vote for her husband.

In the final days of the campaign, Lady began to imply that the attorney general had failed to intervene

in an Arkansas Oklahoma Gas Corporation rate increase case because Hillary represented a company
owned by Little Rock's Stephens family. The politically influential Stephens family also controlled Arkansas Oklahoma Gas.

This tact finally got to the young, seemingly unflap-
pable candidate. During a May 27 rally in northeast
Arkansas, Bill exploded, claiming Lady was "parading
his religious credentials on his shoulder" while telling
"lies" about Hillary.

"His religious convictions tell him it's wrong to lie,
but he does it anyway because it's convenient," Bill
said, adding that if Lady had made a telephone call to
the Rose Law Firm, he would have learned that Hillary
was told simply to write a brief for the Stephens-owned
company in a lawsuit. He said Hillary had never had
any direct contact with the parties in the suit.

Despite the fact that most observers considered the
race Bill's for the taking, both Bill and Hillary refused
to let up, maintained grueling campaign schedules that
typically included a dozen or more appearances each
day. They would begin at six in the morning and work
until late in the evening; they raised more money than
the other four Democratic candidates combined. Bill
was endorsed by organized labor, by teachers and minority groups. The other campaigns operated largely by
using volunteers, but the Clinton campaign had fifteen
paid staff members, a rented airplane, a car with a
mobile telephone and national pollsters and media
consultants.

An *Arkansas Gazette* profile two days before the
election characterized Hillary as "an accomplished
speaker who frequently appears on Clinton's behalf and
gives detailed answers to complex policy questions.
She intends to be actively involved in policy making
if Clinton is governor."

Already, the state's reporters had Hillary pegged. She

would be more than just the state's first lady. She would be the governor's top adviser.

Early in the evening of May 30, 1978, as the votes were being counted, Bill and Hillary sat on a carpeted stairwell in the old Little Rock house that served as their campaign headquarters, cheering like kids at a ballgame as volunteers put county-by-county totals on a large toteboard.

Once the trend was obvious, they made the short trip to the downtown hotel. While a tepid rock band played, supporters cheered and Bill's eyes grew moist. Unlike Hillary, he always has worn his emotions on his sleeve.

Bill declared victory over his Democratic rivals at 10:50 P.M. at downtown Little Rock's Camelot Hotel, where more than a thousand supporters had gathered. With Hillary by his side, he began his victory statement by saying, "This victory belongs to many people—to my wife and family. . . ."

For all practical purposes, the Democrat was on his way to the governor's office. The Republican candidate he would face in November, Lynn Lowe of Texarkana, was, at best, a token opponent.

Facing an anticlimatic general election campaign, Hillary took on expanded duties in July when she was elected to a two-year term as chairperson of the Legal Services Corporation board, the federal panel to which Carter had appointed her in 1977. She was voted chair easily on a nine to two vote. Later in 1978, Hillary was elected by the Democratic National Committee to serve on the twenty-five member panel that would approve the delegate-selection process for the party's 1980 convention.

Despite the additional duties, Hillary kept up her heavy speaking schedule. In a September 1978 speech to the Officers Wives Club at Little Rock Air Force Base, she said, "I came to Arkansas the way many of you did—by association with my future husband at the time. He spoke of his home and how he planned to return there. I had no thoughts of Arkansas. I at least knew where it was, but I didn't know much more than that. After we came, I loved it. I've since become a sort of one-person chamber of commerce.''

She said the thing she liked most about the state was that "is a place where one person can really make a difference,'' in Hillary's case a difference in the area of equal rights for women and children. Out on the campaign trail, meanwhile, Republican Lynn Lowe used many of the same tactics that Bill's Democratic primary opponents had unsuccessfully employed in the spring. "Every time I run, people run the same race against me,'' Bill told Howell Raines of *The New York Times*. "They say, 'This guy is being foisted on us'— like I'm a creation of the media who has been cloned somehow with an Ivy League education and long hair.''

Bill's Yale law degree, his age, his liberal platform and the Ms. in front of Hillary's name were all used against him. Bill told Raines, "They talk about 'Clinton's wife,' and then they say, 'Ms. Hillary Rodham' in a sneering tone. That was probably the biggest mistake by my opponents—thinking they could use her against me.''

In 1978, Bill responded to the attacks by going on the offensive and promising to use Hillary as a key adviser if elected. He said the attacks on Hillary failed because Arkansas voters no longer feared change. Like most Southerners, he said, Arkansas now had hope and looked to well-educated politicians as role models for their own children.

"Our vote was a vindication of what my wife and I have done and what we hope to do for the state,'' he said.

On November 7, 1978, thirty-two-year-old Bill Clinton became the nation's youngest governor-elect, defeating Lowe by more than one hundred thousand votes. He received about sixty-five percent of the ballots cast.

"I hope we will be able to put behind us the negative things that occurred," the incoming governor said. "And I can't believe that some of the things that happened in this campaign anyone could have been proud of. . . . This election is fundamentally a tribute to the decency and judgment and hope of the people of Arkansas."

During the Christmas holidays, Bill and Hillary vacationed in England, where they visited friends Bill had made when he was a Rhodes Scholar at Oxford University. In the weeks immediately preceding her husband's inauguration, Hillary played the role of a traditional first lady. The state's newspapers featured articles on the gown she would wear to the inaugural ball. It had been designed by Little Rock's Connie Fails and was based on Hillary's wedding gown.

"It was always my favorite, and I asked Hillary to wear something for the inaugural ball," Bill said of the wedding gown.

"First lady? First woman? First person?" *Arkansas Democrat* Style Editor Betty Woods asked in a February 1979 article about the state's new first lady. It was evident Hillary was not yet famous since the article misspelled her name as "Hilary" throughout. "I'm the First Lady," Hillary answered. "Bill is the First Man. And Zeke is the First Dog."

Zeke, a cocker spaniel puppy, was a gift from one of Hillary's coworkers. Hillary said both she and Bill had "had a dog before, but this is our first together."

Despite the fact that she was using her maiden name, Hillary claimed she was an "old-fashioned girl" with "old-fashioned ideas about the work ethic."

"I believe in the golden rule—that sort of thing," she said.

Over and over again, she explained she had kept her maiden name because "I had made speeches in the name of Hillary Rodham, I had taught law under that name. I was, after all, twenty-eight when I married, and I was fairly well-established."

She said the new governor supported her decision to keep her maiden name and was just as supportive of her decision to have a law career: "We realized that being a governor's wife could be a full-time job. But I need to maintain my interest and my commitments. I need my own identity, too. I was concerned that we wouldn't have much time together when we moved into the mansion. Bill kept assuring me that we would. He said we would have help doing many of the things that ate into our time alone before—telephoning, correspondence, housekeeping, grocery shopping and cooking."

When she was asked if the couple planned a family, she quickly answered, "Oh, yes."

How many children?

"Well, one to start with. I think two or three children make a nice family."

She wouldn't say whether she would continue to work once Zeke was joined by a child: "A family can certainly curtail one's activities, but I couldn't say whether I would continue practicing law or not. These things can't be planned, just like my life as the governor's wife. You have to see what conflicts are presented and solve them as they come."

In a television interview later that month, she said the couple's dual careers "often do not provide enough time for us to lead private lives, to be with one another, to have a family life, to have time to think."

Bill also described his wife as old-fashioned, saying, "It depresses her some when she thinks it (the use of her maiden name) is hurting me, but she's a lawyer, and she doesn't want to go into the courtroom as somebody's wife. If people knew how old-fashioned she was in every conceivable way, they probably wouldn't do that. She's just a hardworking, no-nonsense, no-frills, intelligent girl who has done well, who doesn't see any sense to extramarital sex, who doesn't care much for drink, who's witty and sharp but without being a stick in the mud. She's just great.''

In one of the last gasps of '70s vulgarity, the Clinton inauguration on January 9, 1979, was themed—like some high school prom—"Diamonds and Denim." Virtually every part of the inauguration had a connection to Arkansas in one way or another. The performers were all Arkansas natives—Levon Helm, formerly of The Band; the Cate Brothers; the legendary rockabilly artist Ronnie Hawkins; Randy Goodrum and performers from the Ozark Mountains such as Jimmy Driftwood.

When Bill went into the governor's private rest room at the state capitol that day, he found two packets of headache powder and this message from his predecessor, David Pryor: "Good luck, Bill. I am leaving something that may come in handy."

Hillary was beginning her own intricate balancing act—attorney, first lady, advocate for children and families. She and her husband also would have to become used to the media spotlight that accompanied living in the Governor's Mansion. Little Rock was home to one of the nation's last great newspaper wars. Few small-state governors were subjected to the intense scrutiny that the Arkansas governor was.

In March 1979, for example, it was reported that Hillary and Bill had continued to make personal property tax assessments in Washington County in northwest Arkansas, although they had owned furniture and household goods in Pulaski County in central Arkansas since Bill became attorney general in January 1977. Also, no record of an assessment of a Fiat automobile owned by Hillary could be found in either county. State law requires that property be assessed in the county where it is located.

A testy governor told reporters at the state capitol the stories about his tax assessments had received more coverage than his 1978 gubernatorial election and that newspapers were using *"National Enquirer* tactics." But two days after the first story appeared in the *Arkansas Gazette,* the governor paid the 1977 tax and 1978 personal property taxes on Hillary's car with penalties for late payment of the 1977 tax and for late assessments in 1977 and 1978. The following month, Bill and Hillary assessed their personal property—an automobile and four rooms of furniture—in Pulaski County.

As the state's first lady, Hillary spent part of her time in the public schools speaking with young people. During a late April visit by Hillary to a Little Rock elementary school, a first-grade student named Bradley Holmes offered the prescient non sequitur, "The President's wife is going to help people paint their dolphins."

Young Bradley was quickly corrected by his teachers.

Hillary promised to visit a different school each week, saying she had "always been a volunteer in addition to working full time."

She also spoke on a regular basis to older students, telling the teenage delegates to Arkansas Girls State in May 1979 that "a lot of changes in the past few years have given women opportunities." She added that the new freedom required that women exercise more commitment and discipline.

Then, the following month, the governor appointed his wife honorary chairman of Arkansas' observance of the International Year of the Child, a United Nations project aimed at improving children's welfare worldwide. Hillary, already one of the most active first ladies in Arkansas history, said she would concentrate on ensuring that all school-age children were immunized, on expanding the state's immunization of preschool children, on establishing an accident-prevention program and on establishing a plan to assist families in spotting things that might cause their children to be handicapped. The state, Hillary said, should make the International Year of the Child more than a mere celebration, working instead to "produce a set of accomplishments."

It was in that Year of the Child that Hillary Rodham became pregnant. Hillary said she decided to make the announcement in September 1979, after hearing her unborn child's heartbeat for the first time, but she was beginning to show and though the couple had instructed friends, staffers and family to keep their secret until after the first trimester, word was beginning to leak out. Just two days before the announcement, gubernatorial press secretary Julie Baldridge had answered "not that I know of" when asked if the first lady was pregnant.

"I feel wonderful," Hillary said at the time of the announcement. "I had the usual stuff the first month—real fatigue and so on. But I'm doing fine. We're both really happy."

Hillary told friends that she didn't care whether the child was a boy or a girl and had not yet decided on names. Asked by reporters what the child's last name would be, Hillary replied, "Oh, it'll be Clinton."

She said she didn't know how becoming a mother would affect her career and was not sure how soon she would return to her law practice after the child's birth.

Despite her pregnancy, Hillary continued to take on new responsibilities. In October, Clinton named his wife chairperson of the Rural Health Advisory Committee, which was charged with the task of developing a state rural health program.

As chair of the committee, Hillary learned the state

Health Department had received a $310,000 federal grant to hire a staff and develop better health care in rural areas, with a goal to establish four clinics in the first two years. But the department's application for the grant had run into opposition from regional health agencies whose leaders believed they had not been consulted sufficiently about the program. There also was opposition from individual physicians, who feared clinics would meet only federal minimum guidelines that allowed examinations of patients without physicians being present. Doctors also resented the fact that the clinics would qualify for higher Medicaid reimbursements than private physicians.

Hillary dived into the quagmire.

Of course, she was still active in her role as chair of the state's International Year of the Child celebration and also was president of a group known as Arkansas Advocates for Children and Families, which she had helped establish in 1977. And she was lecturing at the University of Arkansas at Little Rock School of Law.

After the new year, Hillary began making preparations for something called the Governor's Conference on Families. The event was scheduled for March 7 and 8, 1990 in the southeast Arkansas city of Pine Bluff. President Carter had requested that each state hold such a conference to elect delegates to the White House Conference on Families.

"I hope it's not just a conference for professionals," Hillary said in her speeches promoting the event. "We would like to see as many different kinds of people as we possibly can draw." She also had to raise money to pay for the conference since no state or federal funds were allocated.

Hillary herself would not attend the conference. At 11:24 P.M. on February 27, 1980, Chelsea Clinton was born at Little Rock's Baptist Medical Center. The child weighed six pounds, one and three-quarter ounces. Bill and Hillary have often said she was named after folk-singer Judy Collins's "Chelsea Morning" (which actually was written and first recorded by Joni Mitchell).

Bill—who, in keeping with what local newscaster Steve Barnes once called his "goofy" schedule, was away in Washington—arrived home at 7:30 that Wednesday night, just in time to take his wife to the hospital for what turned out to be a short labor and a Cesarean birth.

By late April, Hillary again was taking part in public events, ranging from a Governor's Mansion reception for volunteers in the public schools (at which Chelsea was presented a shirt reading "Class of 1998"), to a workshop on trial advocacy techniques, to a ceremony in honor of two Arkansans being held hostage at the U.S. Embassy in Tehran, Iran.

Before long, though, Hillary was fighting two political battles. One, of course, was her husband's. The other was her own.

Hillary's renomination to the board of the Legal Services Corporation was in jeopardy, stalled in the Senate by Republicans intent on blocking Jimmy Carter's nominations until after the November elections. In the previous months, the LSC had come under attack from conservatives for representing migrant farm workers and homosexuals.

Richard Nixon had tried to kill the program in the early 1970s, and Ronald Reagan had said during his campaign that he wanted "to explore possible alternatives to the monolithic federal approach to legal problems of the poor. I believe there is room for increased activity on the part of the local governments and local bar associations."

Hillary's nomination did not clear the Senate prior to Reagan's victory in November, and she was replaced by a Republican once Reagan took office.

Although the LSC defeat was a disappointment, the political problems back home in Arkansas had grown serious. Bill was facing reelection, and although the first-term governor thought he had only token opposition, the Democratic primary showed he was vulnerable. Bill won, but a south Arkansas turkey farmer and perennial candidate named Monroe Schwarzlose—who had finished last in the five-man 1978 Democratic primary field—received thirty-one percent of the 1980 Democratic primary vote. Bill said the outcome didn't trouble him, that any incumbent "who tried to do anything will have a built-in negative vote of twenty-five percent."

Schwarzlose even carried seven of the state's seventy-five counties, attributing incumbent's problems to increases in automobile license fees, which were enacted by the Legislature in 1979, and by his handling of rioting Cuban refugees, who had been sent by the federal government to Fort Chaffee in the western part of the state.

"A lot of people tell me that Clinton is in trouble if he can't beat a seventy-seven-year-old man any worse than he beat me," Schwarzlose said. "When he can't defeat a seventy-seven-year-old man, he's either got to make some dramatic reforms in his political attitude or he can't beat nobody."

Nobody's name was Frank White.

White was a stronger candidate than the GOP could usually field in those days, a Little Rock banker, former Democrat and former head of the state's industrial development commission. White told voters that the state "desperately needs mature leadership, someone with business experience, someone who has met a payroll and who has indicated by what they've said they will stop the uncontrolled growth in state government."

And Bill Clinton had an image problem. He and Hillary were increasingly viewed by many Arkansans as arrogant. Some had never cottoned to Hillary's use of her maiden name.

It didn't help, when in late July, the governor announced that a recession had forced his administration to trim its revenue projections by 3.7 percent. He stated that across-the-board state agency cuts would be necessary. Still, an early October poll showed Bill with sixty-five percent of the vote, compared with twenty-four percent for White. By the middle of the month, Clinton had slipped to sixty and White was up to twenty-eight percent. At the end of October, a poll showed Clinton leading White fifty-six percent to thirty-eight percent—pointing to a victory of landslide proportions.

During the campaign's final weeks, Bill charged that his opponent was ''preying on people's fears, not their better judgment'' by running television ads showing rioting Cubans at Fort Chaffee. For her part, Hillary had been urging Bill for weeks to begin responding more forcefully to Republican attacks.

''Hillary keeps telling me I don't understand the modern world,'' Bill said in late October. ''I really should have been governor in the 1930s when I could have stayed in the office doing all this good work and then could have gone out to see the people and talk about it. I'm an old-fashioned politician. Oh, I can work myself up and give an effective, harding-hitting speech, but I really like to go out and talk to the people and answer their questions.''

Asked about the new tone of his campaign, Bill said, ''I wouldn't call it going on the attack. I'm just becoming more explicit, and I'm conscious of doing it in areas where my local people tell me there are serious problems or misunderstandings about certain issues.''

''He is not going to be the sweet little guy anymore,'' White said. ''He is going to attack me every way he can.''

As election day neared, Hillary herself became negative, saying at a press conference that she was ''speechless and bewildered'' when she first saw White's television commercial about rioting at Fort Chaffee. The ad claimed that Arkansas was selected as the site of a Cuban refugee relocation center because the governor wouldn't "stand up to" the Carter administration.

"When people are mad, it's a lot more of an incentive to get out and vote than when they're happy," White said. Relying on that voter anger, White had become the strongest Republican candidate for statewide office in a decade.

"I'm not a politician," he said in almost every speech. "I have never run for public office. I am a businessman, and state government is a two-billion dollar a year business. It needs to be run like a business, and I can do it."

Bill and Hillary knew the race had tightened up, but neither gave any thought to losing. Nobody in Arkansas thought Bill could lose. Nobody suspected the night of November 4, 1980, would be one of the toughest of the Clintons's lives.

CHAPTER EIGHT
The Arkansas Comeback

Watching the early results that Tuesday night at the Governor's Mansion, Bill and Hillary kept waiting for things to turn around. Things never did.

Their plans called for them to arrive at the state capitol at 9:00 P.M. to attend an election watch party. With White in the lead, the 9:00 P.M. arrival was pushed back to 9:30 P.M., then 11:00 P.M., then midnight. The Clintons never made it to the capitol.

Finally, after midnight they made their way to the election party in downtown Little Rock's Camelot Hotel. In the subdued atmosphere, with Hillary at his side, the governor made a five-minute statement. There were votes to be counted and "some waiting to do."

"I think we're going to win," Hillary said, trying to cheer supporters. Yet she already knew it was over. Bill had even betrayed as much in his short statement when he employed the past tense: "I feel good about everything I did as governor."

Neither the governor nor his wife would answer reporters' questions that night. After leaving the hotel, they went to their campaign headquarters where a private, tearful session was held with top aides. When national television networks called the election for White at about 1:00 A.M., the Clintons began hugging campaign workers and preparing to head back to the mansion. Some aides wiped tears from their eyes and others wept openly as the couple exited through a back door.

Frank White would become only the second Republican to be governor of Arkansas since Reconstruction. Because of a two-year term limit at the time, second terms were expected and traditional for Arkansas governors. A first-term Arkansas governor had not been defeated for reelection since 1954, when Orval Faubus defeated Francis Cherry in the Democratic primary.

White's victory was, without doubt, the greatest political upset in the state's history. It was a truly stunning event, as evidenced by these facts:

• Fewer than 8,200 people had voted statewide in the Republican primary when White captured his party's nomination.

• Clinton's percentage in statewide races had grown from 55.3 percent in the May 1976 primary for attorney general to 68.9 percent in the May 1980 Democratic gubernatorial primary.

• The final two statewide polls prior to election day had shown Clinton leading by margins of twelve and eighteen percent.

Clinton had carried only twenty-five of the state's seventy-five counties against White. In his earlier statewide elections (primary and general), he had led in at least sixty-nine counties each time. Veteran Associated Press political writer Bill Simmons blamed Clinton's loss on four factors—a complex mix of moods he described as the *Network* syndrome (I'm mad as hell, and I'm not going to take it anymore''); the political harm Clinton did to himself with several of his programs and policies; Clinton's inept campaign strategy against White's relentless attacks; and the underestimation of White and the GOP.

"Most of his aides were bearded young men, some from out of state," Simmons wrote. "His wife, a lawyer, kept her maiden name and always was identified as Hillary Rodham. His director of state purchasing was a woman under the age of thirty. Some saw all of that as a liability in a conservative state. . . . His party affiliation was not a handicap in Arkansas, long a Democratic state."

Still, White could never have been elected if not for thousands of Arkansans who were so sure Clinton would win reelection that they decided to use their vote as a protest. They wanted to send a message to the arrogant young Democrat and his snooty wife, not elect Frank White.

It was a watershed year in American politics. That same night, GOP nominee Ronald Reagan ousted Jimmy Carter from the White House and Republicans gained control of the Senate by upsetting several veteran Democratic senators. It was the beginning of the 1980s, of conservative hegemony. Bill Clinton and Hillary Rodham would have to adapt to a new American political ethos that did not pander to long-haired liberal kids who thought themselves smarter than everybody else. They would have to adjust or perish.

Hillary hid her teary eyes behind heavy sunglasses when Bill gave his official concession speech on the lawn of the Governor's Mansion the next day. She held baby Chelsea in her arms as her husband spoke.

"Hillary and I have shed a few tears for our loss of last evening, but we accept the will of our people with humility and with gratitude for having been given a chance to serve our state," he said.

Bill told of how he had grown up "in an ordinary working family in this state, was able to go through the public schools and become attorney general and governor to serve people in the way that I always wanted to since I was a boy. . . . I regret that I will not have two more years to serve as a governor because I have loved it. I have probably loved it as much as any person who ever had this office.''

Zeke, the Clintons's dog, played at his master's feet as Bill told the cheering audience, ''I love this state even more today than I did yesterday, and I care more about the future of this state even more than I did yesterday. I want you to hold your head high with me because we have everything to be proud of and nothing to be ashamed of.''

The loudest, longest cheer came when he said, ''I want you to be grateful that, with the grace of God, we will have the chance to serve again.''

Almost 250 supporters—including the state's Democratic attorney general, secretary of state and several Democratic legislators—were present. Many of the supporters embraced Bill and Hillary. Some of them were sobbing. Tears welled in Bill's eyes as he hugged his mother, Virginia, and his younger brother, Roger. But although Bill hinted he would run again, he declined to answer questions after the speech.

''Not today,'' he said. ''I'm not ready.''

Aides told reporters the governor would work the rest of the week and then leave town on a trip with Hillary.

Almost immediately, Bill received offers to practice and to teach law. His name was even mentioned as a possible new president at Hendrix College, a well-respected liberal arts school in the bucolic town of Conway, about thirty miles west of Little Rock.

Within a week of the election, word leaked out that Bill Clinton was being considered to chair the Democratic National Committee. DNC Chairman John White—who had met Clinton in 1972 while he running McGovern's Texas campaign—had called just after the defeat to tell the governor he probably would not seek a second four-year term as chair.

"Bill Clinton epitomizes the kind of leadership the Democrats need," said Anne Wexler, a senior Carter administration aide.

Bill and Hillary were vacationing in Puerto Vallarta, when the speculation about becoming DNC chairperson began. Bill told reporters who called that he had "given no thought to it. I have given no encouragement to it. . . . It is true that a lot of people have called me about it, and there seems to be some interest around the country."

But, although the job was apparently his for the asking, Bill and Hillary decided against the move to Washington. Hillary did not want to give up her booming legal practice at the Rose Law Firm and have to start over with another firm in Washington. And though he said nothing publicly, Bill was determined to make a political comeback in 1982. They rented a two-story, yellow-and-white frame house with three bedrooms and two gas fireplaces in one of Little Rock's better middle-class neighborhoods.

"I got sixty-one percent of the vote in that precinct," Bill said. "I checked that."

Bill did not grant his first lengthy post-election interview until almost two weeks after his loss. During that interview, he was at his most humbly soulful, telling the *Arkansas Gazette* that he had failed to "communicate to the people that I genuinely cared about them—that all I cared about was being their governor and having their support to do the things I thought were good for the state. . . . I think maybe I gave the appearance of trying to do too many things and not involving the people as I should. Consequently, the public's perception was that I was philosophically alienated from them. I have to take full responsibility for that, and have I to say that I failed on a fundamental level."

Bill said he had been "literally astonished" by the number of people who said they had voted against him "to send me a message" but really didn't expect or want him to lose.

"People thought I was too big for my britches, that I had come too far too fast and hadn't really worked for what I had," he said. "And they had the idea that I was the type of person who was going to do what I thought was best, without listening to what they thought. . . . I want to say, 'OK, I got the message. Now, let's vote again.' "

That November 1980 interview was the opening act in Bill's 1982 gubernatorial campaign. For the next two years, Hillary would call many of the shots in his political comeback, working first to pull her husband out of his doldrums and later to lay the groundwork for the campaign.

The week before Christmas 1980, Bill conducted a two-hour question-and-answer session with the Arkansas chapter of the Society of Professional Journalists. That same week, he received a standing ovation when he addressed the Democratic State Committee, saying that Republicans nationwide had run negative media campaigns that paid off.

"It will be bad for the people of Arkansas that they won, and I for one am ready to fight," he said as the crowd roared at a North Little Rock hotel. "We wish the President-elect well and we wish the governor-elect well, but we are going to fight for what we believe in—now and forever."

On the day Bill gave his farewell address to the Arkansas Legislature—January 12, 1981—his mother, Virginia, said, "This is just an intermission; just an intermission."

As Bill spoke, Hillary sat in the front row of the House chamber, holding baby Chelsea on her lap. Everything the governor did was now a family affair.

"I've always enjoyed what I've done," he said. "I prefer the political life, but I've enjoyed my private life. . . . I'll get up tomorrow and think about something else. Tomorrow's another day."

"I'm very proud of my husband," Hillary told reporters. "I'm grateful we had a chance very few people have, to have a position with such a magnitude of responsibility."

On his desk that first day as governor, Frank White found a note. It read: "Frank. Good luck. It's the best job in America. Bill."

While Bill went into near-seclusion, weeks later Hillary appeared with White at a political forum at the University of Arkansas at Little Rock. A reporter described her as being only "semigracious in defeat but entirely spunky and eloquent."

"I don't think we ever thought the campaign would be easy, but it was to our disadvantage that so many other people did," she said. "We were not as successful in energizing our supporters as we should have been."

She placed part of the blame for her husband's defeat on the media, noting that Bill had been criticized for hiring out-of-state aides but that White had avoided criticism for staffing his campaign with out-of-state staffers supplied by the Republican Party.

"If Bill Clinton had done that, it would never have gotten off the front page of the papers," she said.

Hillary said the main reason for Bill's defeat, however, was that the couple and those with whom they associated "didn't understand fully the depth of the change in voters' attitudes from 1978 to 1980. . . . It's easier to enthuse people if they think there's going to be a change instead of more of the same." (A dozen years later, after the "Candidate of Change" had become the President of the United States, those words would take on an ironic ring.)

Hillary said even though her husband was regarded by most to be a product of the media age, he actually was "much more an old-fashioned, one-on-one politician. And he wants to explain everything. When a voter would ask about car tags, Bill would explain his road program. Everybody around him kept saying, 'Don't do that.' People aren't interested in long explanations."

But it wasn't long before Bill's name was back in the news on what seemed like a daily basis. Although he wasn't named chairman of the Democratic National Committee—the job went to Los Angeles lawyer Charles Manatt—he was made chairman of the DNC's state and local election division. The non-salaried post placed him in charge of planning strategy for a Democratic Party comeback in the midterm elections of 1982. It also gave him a Washington-based staff and allowed him to travel the country while still keeping his home in Little Rock. It was a perfect compromise. Hillary could continue to practice at the Rose Law Firm, and Bill could remain involved in politics, and even broaden his base outside the state.

And he would not have to commit himself to staying in the DNC job for more than a year, leaving the door open for the 1982 gubernatorial race everyone knew he would enter. "I have agreed to serve as long as I can," he said. "I haven't talked about how long I'd serve."

Bill also joined forces with one of Washington's grande dames, Pamela Harriman, in forming a group known as Democrats for the '80s for the purpose of providing technical and financial support to moderate Democrats. He even joined the board of Intermark, an international trade management company based in Little Rock.

Bill's primary base of operations, however, was the Little Rock law firm of Wright Lindsey & Jennings. He didn't practice much law, however, joining the firm "of counsel." He described that as "a lawyer's term for a fellow attached to a firm but in a more independent way." He joked, however, that the job would help dispel criticism that all he knew how to do was "teach school and run for office."

Along with Hillary, Bill depended on the advice of Bruce Lindsey at the Wright Lindsey & Jennings firm. In June 1981, they enlisted the aide of Betsey Wright, a highly regarded veteran of liberal Democratic campaigns, to lay the groundwork for the 1982 race. Although Bill claimed that Wright, who would go on to become his gubernatorial chief of staff, was "between jobs" and had been hired to establish a computer filing system for his gubernatorial papers, everyone knew she was helping to plan Bill's campaign. After Hillary, Wright would become the most important woman in Clinton's life.

"People tell me that I can make a comeback if there's a feeling I've learned something, not only from the election, but from what people have told me about the mistakes I made," Bill said in July 1981. "If they were trying to teach me a lesson, they taught me. They whacked me between the eyes."

He said he would be "more restrained, more conservative and more cautious" than in his first term as governor.

By late 1981, Bill and Frank White were constantly sniping at each other in the press. Asked during a September radio interview if Bill Clinton had done anything good as governor, White said he couldn't think of anything. A few days later on the same station Bill said that the 1981 legislative session would have been more successful if "Frank White had devoted half the energy to working in the Legislature that he has to hitting the big special interests up for his next campaign. . . . (Legislators) have no leadership, no guidance and no support from the governor's office."

On November 14, 1981, Bill finally showed his hand. He told the Arkansas Jaycees that he would run in 1982 "if my family is one hundred percent behind it and my friends are willing to work. My friends have had to work in many campaigns in the past decade. They have to believe the stakes are sufficient to wage a battle.''

Of course his friends would wage the battle.

There were several subtle changes during 1981. Bill began attending Immanuel Baptist Church of Little Rock, which boasted many of the city's business and political leaders as members. He joined the choir and could often be seen seated behind the minister on Sunday mornings during the statewide telecast of the church's services. Hillary, a Methodist, rarely attended Immanuel Baptist with him.

The other, more significant change in the minds of many Arkansans was that Hillary began going by the last name of Clinton rather than her maiden name of Rodham.

''I don't have to change my name,'' she contended when asked about the switch. ''I've been Mrs. Bill Clinton since the day we were married.''

Hillary insisted that she would continue to practice law as Hillary Rodham but would introduce herself in ''non-professional capacities'' as Mrs. Bill Clinton. Since her husband's 1982 campaign would demand most of her attention, she said she would be ''Mrs. Bill Clinton for a while. But I signed my last legal brief as Hillary Rodham.''

Asked under which name she was registered to vote, Hillary said, ''Hillary Rodham.'' Asked if she was planning to change her voter registration, she said she was not.

Only three Arkansas statutes dealt with names, and all of them dealt with name changes. There was no state law covering the use of different names for business and social situations. Arkansas law said any person could file a petition in circuit or chancery court to have a name changed. The individual filing the petition was expected to show good cause, but as a practical matter, the courts would approve just about any request by an adult.

In 1978, the Arkansas Supreme Court had held that state statues were just a supplement to the common law. The common law, the Supreme Court ruled, says one "may ordinarily change his name at will, without any legal proceedings, merely by adopting another name."

In other words, a person was who he said he was under Arkansas law, as long as the name was not changed to perpetrate a fraud.

"You don't go to court to get your name changed when you get married," said Paul Casey, at the time an assistant professor at the University of Arkansas at Little Rock School of Law. "And there's nothing in the law that says a woman's name has to change to the husband's name."

If she wanted her name to be Hillary Clinton, it would now be Hillary Clinton.

Bill announced his candidacy through a series of thirty-second television ads that began February 8, 1982. In the ads, he apologized to Arkansas voters for occasionally having "missed the forest for the trees."

His formal announcement of candidacy came late that month on Chelsea's second birthday. He said he was finished apologizing and looking forward to a "good and hot" campaign. Hillary took a leave of absence from the Rose Law Firm so she could be more active in her husband's campaign than she had been in 1980.

To get to White, though, Bill first would have to win the Democratic primary. Many Arkansas Democrats feared that a divisive campaign between Clinton and former Congressman Jim Guy Tucker would benefit White.

There were striking similarities between the leading

Democratic contenders. Both were in their thirties. Both had been educated on the East Coast (Tucker at Harvard, Clinton at Georgetown). Both were lawyers. Both had been the state's attorney general. And both were returning from losses—Clinton to White in 1980 and Tucker in the 1978 Democratic primary for the U.S. Senate.

Primary night, May 25, held a surprise. While Clinton was easily the leading vote-getter in the five-man primary, his runoff opponent was not Tucker, but fifty-eight-year-old Joe Purcell, a soft-spoken former attorney general and lieutenant governor. Clinton had finished with forty-two percent, followed by Purcell with twenty-nine percent and Tucker with twenty-three percent.

Two weeks later on the night of the runoff, Hillary was at Bill's side as her husband picked up fifty-four percent of the vote against Purcell and carried forty-five of the state's seventy-five counties. As the returns came in, hundreds of Clinton supporters jammed into a building in downtown Little Rock began to chant, "We want Frank! We want Frank! We want Frank so we can kick his butt!"

Bill and Hillary arrived at the headquarters at about 9:15 P.M., but they went directly to a private room to watch returns with Betsey Wright and other key advisers. The couple emerged for the victory speech at about 10 P.M. It was, for a change, a relatively early election night.

Throughout the 1982 campaign Hillary maintained a higher profile than she had two years earlier. Yet still, much of her work was behind the scenes, offering advice and helping Wright plan strategy.

An October 1982 *Arkansas Gazette* profile described Hillary's role at events she attended with her husband as "the traditional one for candidates' wives—to be at her husband's side, to gaze raptly at him as he speaks, to enthusiastically greet well-wishers afterward. The fact that she has become accomplished at what is a rather passive role for a person of her background and temperament probably is a tribute to self-discipline. Her spirit shows when she speaks on her husband's behalf."

That spirit was exemplified by her performance at a North Little Rock political rally in May. She was substituting for Bill, and White was at the rally. Although the party primaries had not yet occurred, the general election campaign was already heating up.

As White mingled with the crowd and tried to ignore her, Hillary lit into him.

Hillary took the platform and cried out, "Frank White, I hope you're still out there to hear this. I wish my husband was here to reply himself, but since he's not, I'll have to do it."

"Bill Clinton is perhaps the best speaker Arkansas politics has ever produced," the *Gazette* profile said. "Mrs. Clinton is almost certainly the best speaker among politicians' wives, probably the only one who can fully engage an audience on her own merits rather than just as somebody's wife. . . . She speaks rapidly, precisely and knowledgeably about what her husband plans in the way of job training for the unemployed, low-interest financing for businesses, assistance for the elderly. She quotes statistics on how much utility rates have gone up under White—largely, she says, because White fired the people Clinton had hired to keep an eye on the utilities."

Hillary, as she would do a decade later during the presidential campaign, often spoke on behalf of her husband, allowing Team Clinton to cover twice as much territory.

"I'm not afraid to speak," she said in 1982. "But I get very nervous when I'm speaking on behalf of my husband. I fear that something I say might be misconstrued."

Hillary did not hesitate to criticize Frank White, however. She explained, "I feel very strongly that my husband is well-qualified to be governor. I want to do the best I can to help him. I think Frank White has pretty much made his career by criticizing my husband. Much of that criticism has been ill-founded and irresponsible. I don't like the negative effect it has had on the whole political atmosphere."

Like Bill, Hillary had learned from the 1980 loss to White. She had learned to let no charge go unanswered. She had learned that people tend to believe what they read in the newspapers and what they hear on television regardless of whether or not it is true. She already learned what Michael Dukakis never did—that passion trumps policy.

Two years earlier, Hillary had been busy with her law career and her new baby. Those dual responsibilities had left little time to campaign. But the 1982 campaign was different. Hillary was on the stump full time, and two-year-old Chelsea was often on the campaign trail with her.

"That minor fuss over her name brings up the aspect of her personality that might be a disadvantage politically," the *Gazette* profile said. "She is an Illinois native, perhaps a little brisker, a little more outspoken than the traditional Southern governor's lady. It is hard to imagine Mrs. White advising her husband on politics or public policy, and indeed Mrs. White says she seldom talks shop with her husband, except to relay comments from voters. In private, Mrs. Clinton is generous with her counsel—to her husband, to reporters covering the campaign and others. And her husband pays attention.

"The name change indicates that she's working at softening her image a bit. And succeeding, apparently. She has become a good handshaking campaigner in the traditional Arkansas style. Judging from her response to friendly Rotarians, she can melt winningly enough when the occasion demands.''

The lessons painfully learned in 1980 paid off handsomely for the Clintons in 1982. No one was complacent, as had been the case with many Clinton aides and supporters two years earlier. The day before the November 2 election, Bill said his supporters were ''on fire'' with enthusiasm.

Bill became the first man in Arkansas history to regain the governor's office after having lost it, winning easily with almost fifty-five percent of the vote. It had been the most expensive—the two candidates spent almost three million dollars—and probably the most negative race in the state's history.

As was their election night custom, the Clintons spent much of the evening at home before going to their headquarters after 9 P.M. Once there, they watched returns in a back room with aides for more than an hour. Chelsea remained at home with babysitters.

''I have been given something few people get in life—a second chance to serve the people,'' Bill told a wildly enthusiastic crowd at his headquarters. ''And I give you every bit of my mind and my heart to be worthy of the task. We have campaigned on the economic issues, and it's on those issues we must now proceed.'' Bill had carried fifty-six of seventy-five counties, including thirty-two White had won just two years before. Working behind the scenes, Hillary and Betsey Wright had put together an effective campaign organization manned by thousands of volunteers.

In the afterglow of victory, Bill and Hillary took their daughter on a long drive in the country. In two months, they would be moving back into the Governor's Mansion.

The January 11, 1983, inaugural was marred a bit by the fact that Hillary's father was rushed to a Little Rock hospital during the ceremonies. Hugh Rodham, seventy-one years old at the time, was suffering from chest pains, but a hospital spokesman said he had not had a heart attack. Still, Rodham underwent a triple coronary bypass less than a week after the inauguration. Four years later, at Hillary's insistence, her parents would move to Little Rock to be near their only grandchild.

The media still treated Hillary as a traditional first lady. A photo published a few days before the inaugural in the *Arkansas Democrat* showed her carrying a potted plant into the Governor's Mansion. The caption read, "While her husband was busy at his office getting ready for the upcoming legislative session and his inauguration, Mrs. Clinton supervised the move into their new home—the same one they moved out of two years ago when Clinton was defeated by Governor Frank White."

What the caption writer probably didn't know was that Hillary likely had spent an even harder day at the office than her husband before coming to the mansion to oversee the move.

A story two days later in the *Arkansas Gazette* noted that Hillary's dress for the inaugural ball would be "timeless, elegant and endlessly wearable. She'll be the belle of the ball."

On the same day, Hillary was quoted in the *Democrat* as saying, "I didn't have in mind what I wanted for the inaugural ball, but I felt I'd know it when I found it. This is just the kind of dress I love—elegant but comfortable. My husband had the final say. He liked it, so it was decided."

Those who knew Hillary doubted that Bill had the final say. But she had learned to play the game. When the fashion and society writers wanted a traditional first lady story, she could—and would—talk like a traditional first lady.

An Associated Press writer noted Hillary's press clippings were kept in several different envelopes under several different identities including Hillary Rodham, Lawyer; Wife of Governor Bill Clinton; and Lawyer and Wife of Governor Bill Clinton.

Which was she?

"I'm a lawyer," she said. "If I met somebody in an airport, I wouldn't say, 'Oh, I'm the first lady of Arkansas.'"

In countless interviews the week of her husband's second inauguration, Hillary talked about the lessons she and Bill had learned during the first term in 1979 to 1980.

"I did not fully appreciate what the role would require," she said. "This might sound naive now, but I really felt being a public official was a job like any other. He would do his job and I would do mine, and we would have our private life."

Instead, there was the constant overlapping of their public and private lives that Hillary said "really did come as a surprise to me. A person who marries a doctor isn't expected to stand by his side as he performs surgery."

Hillary said the couple would attempt to "protect Chelsea's childhood if we can. She is such a special child, she deserves a lot of our time and attention, and we'll be struggling to carve out that time when no one else is involved. Not hours spent campaigning or appearing at some public function, either, but special time just with her."

Hillary said the couple had "a better sense of priorities and how to achieve them. During the recent campaign, we were more relaxed, held a more positive attitude. As a result, we were happier, so we did a better job. That's the way we intend to keep it when we move into the mansion. We'll try to enjoy our stay there."

She claimed to be surprised that there was an adverse reaction to her use of her maiden name. "One of the things people never accepted was my using Hillary

Rodham professionally," she said. "To me, it seemed so logical. Both of us thought it would be the appropriate thing for me to do."

Hillary said that during the first term she worked hard to keep her legal career separate from Bill's political career, claiming she had "turned away people who came to me only because I'm the governor's wife."

This time, she would be using the name Hillary Rodham Clinton for both professional and political purposes "to eliminate all the confusion."

"She would like to minimize the significance of this concession," Mardi Epes wrote in the *Arkansas Democrat* the Sunday before the inauguration. "After all, what's in a name? But until last February, she had insisted on using her maiden name in her private life as well as in the legal circles she frequents as a lawyer. To many, the change foreshadows a major shift in attitude."

Hillary said she had been a lawyer, wife, mother and first lady before and could do it again. Her leave of absence from the Rose Law Firm, which had begun in March 1982, would end in February 1983.

"I know from past experience my schedule at work is flexible enough to fill each role," she said. "I think my problems are not that different from those of any other working wife and mother. We all share the same time demands."

What would be her special area of interest as first lady?

"The dust hasn't settled," she said just before the inauguration. "I've kind of decided I'll think about that next week. Right now, I need to work on getting my own life back on keel."

By early February, it was evident that Hillary's main interest as first lady would be education. In a February 2 speech to parents and public school teachers in Little Rock, she criticized the Reagan administration, saying the Republican's plan to turn more federally funded projects over to the states would have a devastating effect on public education in states such as Arkansas.

She also was one of the leaders of a campaign by the Little Rock public schools to maintain the school district's property tax rate.

On April 22, the governor of Arkansas announced he had appointed his wife to chair a fifteen-member committee to draft new standards for the state's public schools.

"This guarantees that I will have a person who is closer to me than anyone else overseeing a project that is more important to me than anything else," Bill said, foreshadowing the health-care issue to be faced by the Clintons in 1993.

Established during the 1983 session of the Arkansas Legislature, the unpaid committee had been directed to complete its work by January 1984. It also called for school districts to meet the new standards by the school year beginning in 1987 or be consolidated. The enacting legislation had specified the governor "or his designee" would serve as chair.

Bill said Hillary would be able to "provide more consistent, sustained work" than he would. He added, "I don't know if it's a politically wise move, but it's the right thing to do. My suspicion is that it will be good politics because it's good government, and good government is inevitably good politics."

(Bill would speak almost the same words a decade later when announcing that his wife had been named to head the nation's health-care task force.)

A woman who previously had concentrated more on her law career than on high-profile public policy roles was taking on the hot potato of education reform. Could she succeed? Hillary said she felt qualified for the job because "I've gone to school a large part of my life, and I've been involved in classroom activities and visiting with teachers as a volunteer. But I don't come at this job with a great deal of expertise."

Five days later, the committee received a huge boost when the National Commission on Excellence in Education released a report warning of a "rising tide of mediocrity" in the nation's schools. That landmark report attracted public attention nationwide and spurred politicians to act.

"The distressing conclusions will ultimately affect every schoolchild in the state," Hillary predicted the day the report was released. "It will help define the sort of standards we want in Arkansas in light of the national climate so we can be sure our students are competitive, and it will serve as a blueprint for how we get ourselves out of the serious state of deterioration we're currently in. This report will have a big effect around the country because you can bet that everybody else is going to be reading it."

The next step was for Hillary to travel across the state selling Arkansans on the idea of education reform— not an easy job in one of the most anti-intellectual states in the union. To build grass roots support, she spoke to civic clubs, at high school graduations, on radio talk shows, and at any and all public forums. She often would tell audiences the story of the student voted most likely to succeed from her high school class who had died four years later of a drug overdose.

"Apparently, he didn't have the same expectations we had of him," she would say. "All too often in our state, I think we don't have high enough expectations for ourselves."

She said talk of a crisis in education both frightened and exhilarated her. It frightened her because "I think it's true," and it exhilarated her because she felt the country was at a turning point.

She took controversial positions, saying, for instance, that the state should consider a merit pay system for teachers and school administrators. She said none of the young girls with whom she spoke across the state wanted to be teachers because of the low pay and lack of prestige.

"To me, an education is several things," Hillary said in a May 1983 interview. "It is a process by which a person learns to think and learns to communicate both orally and in writing. Education should challenge you, should expose you to ideas, concepts, other ways of thinking so that you can better hone in on your own abilities and improve your critical thinking skills. Education should give you a broad understanding of the major areas of learning, which are certainly based in mathematics and science and in language skills. I would include foreign language, learning about one's government, learning one's history, some exposure to philosophy and even to psychology."

Hillary said students in Arkansas and across the country could "handle a lot more than they're being given to handle. But one of the principle problems we face is that we are not expecting enough of ourselves, our schools or our students. We have an obligation to challenge our students and to set high expectations for them. Rather than setting minimum standards, we should set expectations and urge schools and districts to aim to achieve those expectations and not to be satisfied with meeting some artificial minimum."

Hillary, who nine years later would be bashed at the Republican National Convention for opposing family values, sounded a little like Pat Robertson or Pat Buchanan in that 1983 interview:

"The breakdown in shared social values that has gone on in this country among all of our institutions for the last twenty years has also affected the schools," she said. *"One of the results of that breakdown has been a pulling away of support for the schools by the parents of the students whom the schools are trying to teach. It is a rare student who can overcome either*

parental opposition or parental indifference to do well in school.

"I can remember very well when I was growing up, my father would say. 'If you get in trouble at school, you get in trouble at home.' Today it is rare that you will find parents who support the schools with that kind of single-minded loyalty because the bond between the parents and the schools has somehow broken down.

"One of the tasks that we face is winning back parental support for teachers and schools. The child has to believe that what he's doing is important to the most important people in his life, his parents, and has to believe that they want him to learn. I remember talking to a gentleman who had been a coach and a teacher and a principal for forty-five years. I asked him what are the differences that you see between students today and the students you knew ten, twenty, thirty, forty years ago. He said the good students are better than they've ever been before and the bad students are worse than they've ever been before, but that the single most significant difference is the number of students whose parents and families don't care one way or the other about them.

"He said, 'It never used to happen to me that I would call up a parent about student or send a letter home and get no response. I'd get somebody in my office within twenty-four hours. They might not agree with me, they might be mad at me, or they might be grateful to me, but they would have a response. Today, I can't even get them in my door.'"

Hillary remembered how her parents had stressed to her the value of a good education:

"They told me that it was my obligation to go to school, that I had an obligation to use my mind. They told me that an education would enable me to have a lot more opportunities in life, that if I went to school *and took it seriously and studied hard, not only would I learn things and become interested in the world around me, but I would open up all kinds of doors for myself. . . . My parents set really high expectations for me and were rarely satisfied. I would come from school with a good grade, and my father would say, 'Must have been an easy assignment.' I always felt challenged. I always felt as though there was something else out there I could reach for."*

She pledged to make Arkansas a national leader when it came to education standards. She said it would not "do us any good to come up with standards that move us from our existing 1965 standards to 1983 if Maryland, Alabama, South Carolina and California are moving from 1983 standards to 2000 standards. We have to be aware of what's going on in the other states."

Improving education was not just throwing more money at the problem, Hillary said over and over in her trips across the state. Her many speeches that year nearly always included this boilerplate:

"Our state has tremendous opportunity because we are poised on the brink of a real growth period. We have a tradition of people who know how to work, who are willing to make sacrifices, who sometimes can get more done with less than other folks can. They are people who, if given a chance to acquire a good education, will really respond. There is a real readiness out there to do something about education. People who never gave it a thought five years ago, who don't even have children in school, are really understanding the link between a good education and future quality of life. They want something done. They want to be sure that whatever is done is done effectively and that there are people within the system who can be held accountable, that the performance of students can be measured.

"There is a constituency out there that is growing for a good education system for our children. I'm really excited because I like being part of something that I believe can make a significant difference in people's lives."

She noted that there were far fewer agriculture jobs in Arkansas than in previous years and that even manufacturing jobs were requiring advanced skills. By the summer of 1983, people across Arkansas were paying more attention than ever to what Hillary Clinton had to say.

CHAPTER NINE
No More Excuses

Charlie Cole Chaffin, the only female member of the Arkansas thirty-five member state Senate, was one of the fifteen members of Hillary's committee on education reform. Day in and day out in 1983, she watched the governor's wife at work and witnessed the polarizing effect that work had on Arkansans. Folks either loved or hated the first lady.

Chaffin learned to love her.

"I have never known anyone who had more leadership ability," she said one afternoon in late March 1993 as she sat in her crowded fourth-floor office at the Arkansas capitol. Reminded that she had also worked closely with Hillary's husband, Chaffin smiled. "I stand by my statement," she said.

"Hillary bested me publicly once that year, and I'm not used to being bested," Chaffin added. "It was a subcommittee meeting and the debate concerned course offerings for students," Chaffin said. "I had the votes to get what I wanted. However, there was a word in this particular proposal that Hillary objected to. She walked into the room and stood at one end of the table. That was the first time I had ever been aware of body language at work. She had a powerful presence. Then, she began to talk. Within five minutes, the vote was

243

taken. She won, and I lost. She was good. She was really good.''

Few would argue the point. Chaffin has earned her reputation as a tough, strong-willed woman in the over-whelmingly male culture that was—and is—Arkansas politics. In 1979, at age forty, Chaffin was one of only thirteen female delegates at a hundred-member state constitutional convention. At the time, she was a high school science teacher at Bryant, a bedroom community just southwest of Little Rock, but already she was known for her energy and talent—her students posted a sign on her desk that read ''Wonder woman works here.''

A 1980 *Arkansas Democrat* profile described Chaffin as someone with ''a visible determination and personality, which leaves no question of strength.''

After she was elected to the constitutional convention—she won a runoff against a longtime state senator—Chaffin ran for the state House of Representatives in 1982, losing in a close race to a male incumbent. As part of Hillary's committee, she gained a good deal of media exposure in 1983 that helped her vault to the Senate the following year.

Chaffin believes the updated education standards would never have been enacted had Hillary not personally sold Arkansans on the need for them, just as the first lady would try a decade later to personally sell Americans on her ideas for health-care reform.

''It was Hillary's idea in 1983 to hold hearings in all seventy-five counties,'' Chaffin said. ''It also was her idea to publish the rationale for ever recommendation we made. The final step was her going before a special session of the Legislature and selling them on our proposals.''

Chaffin said Hillary's presentations—at hearings across the state, in speeches to civic organizations, in her pleas before legislative committees—''were perfect. You couldn't find a flaw. I don't care how good a lawyer you are, you're not as good as she is."

Hillary also convinced the other members of the committee to go out and lobby for the proposals, despite some very real political dangers. Many in the education establishment resented the comittee's proposals; teachers in particular were insulted by Hillary's call for teacher testing and minimum performance levels.

"She was treated terribly by teachers in 1983," Chaffin said. "She visited one school where teachers would slam their doors as she went down the hall. That must have hurt her to the bone. But outwardly, she was stoic."

In June 1983, Hillary told Arkansans she was basing her education effort on five principles. She described them

"First, and most important perhaps, the expectations for our students must be uniformly high. That sounds like a rather simple thing to say, but as anyone who has spent any time not just in the schools of our state but in the schools of our country knows, there are large numbers of children who are written off at a rather early age in terms of what is expected from them. One of the things that we are going to try to do is to create standards that will by necessity raise the expectations.

"Second, we think it is critical that the principals and superintendents of our districts be instructional leaders. We don't want people who are only concerned with making the building operate, making sure the bus runs on time and trying to be sure that the budget is balanced. Their primary task is instructional leadership. And it is possible, we believe, that principals and superintendents and administrators can improve their ability to deliver that kind of leadership. We think it is critical, if we are going to write standards about education in Arkansas and if we are going to try to raise

expectations with regard to our students, that the leadership come from the top so that there is a shared vision of what is expected.

"Third, it is important that the adults in each community share a view about the mission of education. Sometimes that is difficult to define. Some schools might see as their mission sending one hundred percent of their students to college. They're purely college-oriented, purely academically oriented. Another district sees as its objective raising literacy rates and being able to educate people to get out into the job world and compete for the kinds of jobs that are going to be available. Each mission is equally valid. But it is critical that we have some kind of shared vision of a mission in order to give impetus to the educational changes that we hope to see occur.

"Fourth, it is obviously important that there be an effective learning environment and that means there must be discipline, there must be order, there must be an opportunity for students and teachers to interact in a rational and civil way.

"Fifth, there is a great deal of research that demonstrates that the use of standardized tests as learning tools by teachers and administrators can be a very useful way to improve teaching."

In July 1983, Bill Simmons, the Associated Press Little Rock bureau chief, wrote that Hillary faced an interesting dilemma:

"As Mrs. Clinton, she bears in mind the political realities of the state her husband governs, realities which, within limits, govern him and his future. As chairperson of the Arkansas Education Standards Committee, she could help make Arkansas education better. A special legislative session could be called after the AESC makes its recommendations for school standards.

"Political realities and what's better for Arkansas

education don't always go together. If they did, the educational system would be better. Mrs. Clinton and the fifteen-member AESC may be tempted to shoot only for what, in present political realities, seems readily attainable. That, of course, would diminish the pressure on Clinton to take bold steps and shorten the measuring rod that may be used to judge him after the session. It would, in fact, be foolish of the AESC to go so far in its findings that it loses credibility. On the other hand, credibility can be lost, too, by not going far enough. Some observers will weigh the committee stopping point in light of Mrs. Clinton's presence on the committee."

Simmons noted that Hillary already had shown "flashes of boldness." She had questioned the sanctity of high school athletics and the omnipotence of high school coaches. In a state where almost all principals and school superintendents were former coaches, some viewed that as sacrilege.

"She has stopped short of putting an absolute knock on extracurricular activities, but she thinks the tail is wagging the dog when instruction stops because the football team, cheerleaders and band have gone to a game," Simmons wrote. "That is penalizing the many to provide privileges for the few. Mrs. Clinton thinks students should be required to meet a grade point standard before they may participate in the extras. Educators who exclude a prominent patron's daughter from cheerleading because the academic mark wasn't met know that this can lead to conflict with parents. But the educational system purportedly is designed to develop the mind. Football and the like are mere extras."

In her speeches across the state, Hillary warned that "too often in our society, our minimum becomes our maximum. . . . We have an opportunity that may never come again and if we don't seize it, we'll fall further behind."

In late July 1983, she received a standing ovation from the members of the state Vocational-Technical Education Advisory Council when she proposed these guidelines:

•Mandatory full-day kindergarten designed to prepare children for the first and second grades.

•Classroom size restrictions in grades one to three to allow more individual instruction.

•A competency test after the third grade with two alternatives for failing students—staying in the third grade or entering an individual instruction program.

•Another mandatory competency test after the sixth grade with retention of those not passing.

•A third mandatory test after the eighth grade to make sure students are ready for high school instruction with retention mandatory for those failing.

Hillary also received cheers when she said, "Discipline must be a policy. I don't believe we have to put up with the kinds of disruptions that I've been hearing about."

A day later, she so captivated a legislative committee that a veteran member, Representative Lloyd George of Danville, said, "I think we elected the wrong Clinton." George made his comment after Hillary had testified for ninety minutes, evoking laughter and nods of agreement.

Through much of the meeting, the governor stood outside in the hallway of the state capitol, peering at his wife through the room's glass door. Later, he came in, and without comment, took a seat next to the committee chairman. He made no public statements, choosing to let his wife run the show, as legislators flooded Hillary with questions about her committee's work, and asked for her personal opinions about the status of education in Arkansas.

She was prepared for their questions, and told the

group that teachers should be paid more, computers should be used more in the classroom, additional parental involvement should be encouraged, the school year should be extended and it should be mandated that extracurricular activities be held after school or on weekends.

"We've confused our students," she said of the amount of time spent on extracurricular activities. "When you play, you should play hard. And when you work, you should work hard. But you shouldn't confuse the two."

With the school year about to begin, Hillary addressed a thousand Little Rock teachers and administrators. She told them that in letters, phone calls and statewide hearings, she had yet to find anyone who was satisfied with the state's education system.

Listeners applauded when Hilary said students should be required to attend kindergarten before entering the first grade. There was more applause when she announced that the student-teacher ratio in each class should be lowered. There was even louder applause when she said counselors should be provided for all students in kindergarten through the twelfth grade, not just in high school. But the loudest applause of all came when she said eighth-grade students who do not pass minimum skills competency exams should not be allowed to enter the ninth grade, "no matter how good an athlete they are or who their parents might be."

This was a brave statement in a state where football and family sometimes were seen as irresistible cultural forces. If Hillary's committee succeeded, the coaches who had long controlled Arkansas schools would have to learn to operate in a markedly different scholastic environment.

But the problems were so deep and so obvious that even those who hoped Hillary would fail did so covertly. The first lady herself said she had, in her travels around the state, encountered only one person who had seen no need for improvement. She told the story of a superintendent of a small, rural school district who stood up at one of the county hearings and flatly said, "I think we're doing a good job, we're doing a fine job."

The superintendent then gestured to a former student, one of the district's prizes. "Why tell 'em, Jack," he said. "You went off to the university. Tell 'em you got a good education here."

A young man in the front row, sheepishly responded, "I sure wish I could have taken Spanish."

On the final day of August, Hillary went back before a legislative committee to declare that toughening school standards would be only part of the total education package that a special session of the Legislature would be asked to consider. That package, she said, would include pay increases for teachers and require competency testing for teachers and administrators.

Hillary spoke for two hours that day. At one point, her remarks became so earnest that they must have grated on her own ears. "I know I sound preachy, but I believe in this," she said. "We want schools to take a hard look at themselves. They may say at first, 'We can't do that,' but then say, 'We can do that if we have to.' "

When Hillary said, "We are trying to set standards that will require people to reach and stretch," one state representative responded, "You're one of the best examples I know to show that the good Lord didn't give us all the same gifts. That was an exceptional presentation."

Hillary replied, "I had a lot of people pushing me. If you talked to some of my elementary teachers when I was young, they might not have agreed with you."

The committee formally presented its proposed school accreditation standards during a September news conference. Hillary said Arkansans should stop making excuses for shortcomings in education and "accept instead the challenge of excellence. We in Arkansas have a chance, if we take it, to commit ourselves anew to . . . a crusade for excellence in public education."

With the mien of a tent evangelist, Hillary stood before the television cameras and addressed the state: "To achieve and maintain a standard of consistent high quality in our schools will not be easy. It will be difficult. All our proposals will demand hard work and self-sacrifice of everyone involved, from school board presidents and superintendents to students and parents. Some proposals will also require money. But educational reforms that do not require serious efforts of mind and will are not worth attempting."

More than 7,500 Arkansans had attended the open meetings in the state's seventy-five counties. Thousands had written and called. Those contacts, Hillary said, "convinced us that the people of Arkansas understand perfectly what is at stake. They know that Arkansas cannot afford to sit still. A rallying cry suggests itself: No more excuses."

Hillary said the purpose of competency tests was not to punish students, explaining that "where failure is almost impossible, common sense tells us and experience shows that the motivation to succeed can get lost. We in Arkansas, like other Americans, have thought of education as a means, if not the means, of social progress and individual advancement. We have sometimes forgotten that education is not diplomas, degrees, certificates and titles. Rather it is the substance of what is learned. The simple truth is that a school's function is to transmit knowledge and the ability to apply knowledge. When it fails to do that, yet passes illiterate or semiliterate students along as if they were making adequate progress, it commits educational fraud."

Hillary defended her committee's recommendation that extracurricular activities be limited during school hours and that school districts develop policies for discipline.

"The first purpose of school is to educate, not to provide entertainment or opportunities to socialize," Hillary said. "Discipline holds no mystery. When it is firm, clearly understood, fairly administered and perceived to be so, it works. When it isn't, it doesn't."

Although she anticipated widespread debate on the proposed standards, Hillary said the public would not respond favorably if the Legislature attempted to water them down.

"We only ask that each of us decide that the time for excuses is over and that we go forth together committed to a better education for all our children," she said. ". . . People are tired of their children going to school but not learning anything, tired of hearing about graduates who cannot fill out job applications correctly and tired of hearing stories about classes being interrupted for various reasons."

Bill Clinton stayed in his office, away from the heat and glare of the limelight, the day of the announcement. He did, however, issue a statement saying the proposed standards were ambitious but "absolutely essential if we are to move ahead in making real improvements in education. The committee has aimed high, worked hard without pay for months and done a great service for the people of Arkansas."

In a television interview the following week, Hillary said the decline of traditional expectations in education began in the '60s with the Vietnam War when "our entire social foundation" was shaken.

"People have lost a lot of confidence in themselves and in their institutions, whether it be government or churches or public schools," she said. "Now, I believe that we are coming out of that period where we are once again understanding that as a nation, we have to expect something of ourselves."

She said the state must "return to a traditional definition of education, of requiring that teachers teach and
students learn, and that schools do what they are supposed to do."

When the inevitable question of funding came up,
Hillary maintained that many of the proposals could be
instituted without additional funding. The state she said,
would have to learn to do more with less. No more
excuses.

"It costs no money to have a discipline policy that
is disseminated to parents and teachers and students,"
she said. "It costs no money to have a policy setting
in motion homework. It costs no money to limit extracurricular activities. My husband has said constantly,
and I agree with him one hundred percent, that if all
we did was to raise money to put into our existing
system, he could not justify that. . . . But if we have
some plans and proposals and programs that we think
will make a definite improvement in public education,
then we should be able to convince any taxpayer to
support that."

In mid-September, Lloyd George, the state representative, once again suggested that Hillary should be governor rather than Bill. George said he would print
bumper stickers that said, "Clinton for Governor,"
with "Hillary, That Is" printed underneath.

"There you go, getting me into trouble," Hillary told
him. "You're always getting me in trouble at home."

During the remainder of September, Hillary spoke to
groups ranging from senior citizens to teachers. "If we
lose this opportunity, I honestly do not believe we will
have it again," she said to each group.

October 6, 1983, was a remarkable day in Arkansas
politics. The Arkansas Legislature, like other Southern
legislatures, long had been a good ol' boys club.

On that day, however, a woman took the Legislature

by storm. Hillary Clinton spoke to the hundred members of the Arkansas House for nearly two hours. When she finished, legislators stood and applauded. Visitors pressed against the windows of the galleries high above to peer down at the governor's wife.

"I believe we need to clear the air, and we need to start with ... public confidence in our teachers," she said of the most controversial aspect of the program—competency tests for public school teachers. The committee had proposed that teachers and administrators be tested to determine their academic skills, and that those failing to pass the exams would be given a chance to retake the tests as many times as possible before their teaching certificates expired.

On October 26, 1983, Hillary gave an encore performance before the state Senate.

"We have to hit head-on the widespread public belief that we have a lot of incompetent teachers," she said. "I think the public should be able to have every bit of confidence in our teachers."

Hillary said that during the public hearings she had conducted the previous spring, she had learned of the public's lack of confidence in teachers. Her committee, she said, frequently hears "wild accusations" unsupported by credible evidence. But those accusations were, in themselves, reason for concern. Hillary contended school districts should develop better evaluation systems and in-service training programs to restore public confidence. But before those things could be done, she said, the state needed to take an "inventory of where our teachers are."

The Legislature ended up approving most of the Clinton package—higher standards, student competency tests, teacher competency tests and a one-cent increase in the state sales tax to increase teacher's pay.

Long after the special session of the Legislature had ended in November, though, Hillary and her husband were under attack from the state's teachers' unions.

Members of the Arkansas Education Association assailed Hillary, legislators, the media and many of the standards that were a product of the first lady's committee and the special session.

"Our conclusion, sadly and unfortunately, is that there has not been a great deal done to improve education in the state," Bill Walters, the AEA's assistant executive secretary, told about 250 teachers on November 17. Walker said the media had not done an adequate job of reporting the organization's position and, consequently, too many of Bill and Hillary's "pronouncements" about the session had gone unchallenged. Walker challenged in particular their assertion that testing teachers would restore public confidence in education.

Cora McHenry, an AEA staff member who served on the standards committee with Hillary, also chided the governor's wife, saying she had added an unauthorized preface to the committee's preliminary report. McHenry said it was Hillary, and not other members of the committee, who suggested that school had become a place for students to be entertained and that teachers had not been held accountable for the situation.

Union representatives claimed the competency tests were insulting and racist, saying minority teachers were more likely to fail such tests than their white counterparts.

Hillary, never shy, responded immediately to the criticism. She maintained a heavy speaking schedule through the remainder of the year, telling Arkansans that they should support the improvements unless they wanted to continue an "investment in ignorance."

She said the reforms eventually would help the state or prosper economically but warned that it might take up to a decade for changes to be felt. Aiming at the teacher's unions, Hillary said accountability was "the only way teachers can expect to receive improved status and pay." Other professionals, she noted, must be aware that they could be sued for malpractice if they did not do their best. Business owners, meanwhile, had to consider the bottom line. Teachers, Hillary said in speech after speech, also should be held accountable. So should students.

"It is not at all feasible to accept that our children cannot meet the new standards," she said. "If we say that, we're selling them out. We must expect them to be able to perform. Studies have shown that if we expect more, especially from children, we will get it."

On Christmas Day 1983, *Arkansas Gazette* education writer Marion Fulk reviewed the work of the standards committee: "When the Education Standards Committee began its work, its chairman, Hillary Rodham Clinton, was almost a moderator for the group. She offered some direction and participated to a certain extent in discussions but did not dominate the committee. But as the months passed, Mrs. Clinton became more and more the driving force on the committee, until it informally came to be called the Hillary Committee. Mrs. Clinton successfully wooed legislators and hostile audiences with her impassioned insistence that higher, enforceable standards were needed for Arkansas schools, and told moving accounts of students deprived of educational opportunities."

During the November meeting of the Chief State School Officers in Little Rock, a high-ranking Arkansas Education Department official said in a speech that he initially thought the Governor had made a mistake by appointing Hillary to lead reform efforts.

"It was going to take so much time," Dr. Don Roberts told the convention. "I didn't believe the first lady of the state would be willing to spend the time it would take."

Those fears quickly evaporated as Hillary devoted countless hours to the task. Roberts joked that since the committee usually met on Saturdays and Sundays, he probably spent more weekends in 1983 with Hillary than the governor.

Indeed, Hillary had made it her committee, her proposals, her crusade. And due to her remarkable powers of argument and persuasion, the majority of the Arkansas public seemed to support her. For better or worse, the 1983 education reforms always will be indentified with Hillary Rodham Clinton.

As 1984 dawned, Hillary continued her efforts on behalf of education. In particular, she battled officials of the Arkansas Education Association. In January, AEA Executive Director Kai Erickson testified before a legislative committee in opposition to some of the standards. Hillary, who had testified earlier in the day, sat in the back of the room, appeared to roll her eyes once and then left. When a reporter followed her outside to ask about the AEA testimony, she said, "Off the record? I can only answer that off the record. I don't want to pick another fight with them."

But fight she would for a second consecutive year. As she saw it, the main stumbling block to education reform was "the fear of change."

"We expect nothing but the best from our athletes," she told a Little Rock PTA group the same month. "Discipline. Teamwork. Standards. I wish we could translate the same expectations and standards we have for athletics into the classroom. I'm always struck when administrators say we can't expect students to do well academically. In athletics, it is assumed students can achieve."

Continuing her assault on the sacred area of high school athletics, she said, "I wish we could give teachers the same support and praise for teaching children to read and write as we do those who teach them to throw a ball through a hoop."

*　　*　　*

That spring, Hillary was also involved in an effort to increase property taxes to aid Little Rock's public schools. While the campaign ultimately failed in Little Rock, seventy-one percent of similar tax increase proposals on the ballot statewide passed.

"We've turned the corner on attitude," Hillary said. "We've just begun this effort to improve education. Those of us committed to keep Arkansas moving forward are going to have to be vigilant." Still, she warned that pressures to lower the new education standards would mount as the guildelines took effect.

If anyone doubted that Hillary was something more than the standard-issue political wife, a partial list of her honors and achievements could convince the most leery skeptic. These are just some of the honors Hillary received in 1984:

• She was named Young Mother of the Year by the Arkansas Association of American Mothers.
• She was named Public Citizen of the Year by the Arkansas chapter of the National Association of Social Workers.
• She was named the Arkansas Press Association's Headliner of the Year.
• She was named the *Arkansas Democrat*'s Woman of the Year.
• She was named Layman of the Year by the Little Rock chapter of Phi Delta Kappa, a professional education fraternity.

Both Bill and Hillary were among the 272 names on *Esquire* magazine's list of the best and the brightest of the new generation. Everyone listed was younger than forty. Phillip Moffitt, *Esquire*'s editor at the time, said the list "stemmed from the realization that a torch was passing between generations. The baby boom generation was approaching the full bloom of adulthood."

It took magazine officials more than two years to compile the list from the five thousand nominations that came through advertising, direct mail, the media and *Esquire*'s regional reporters. The criteria, according to Moffitt, were courage, originality, initiative, vision and selfless service.

Among those joining the Clintons on the list were basketball player Julius Erving; actresses Meryl Streep, Debra Winger and Glenn Close; director Steven Spielberg; astronaut Sally Ride; Reagan administration official David Stockman; and mayors Henry Cisneros of San Antonio and Kathy Whitmire of Houston.

Still, Arkansas journalists—and the people of the state—refused to focus on just Hillary's professional accomplishments. Despite all of her other achievements, she was expected to be somewhat of a traditional first lady—wearing the right clothes, hosting the right parties and attending the right kinds of social events.

An *Arkansas Democrat* feature writer wrote in 1984: "Well-tailored yet feminine silk suit, becoming simple hairstyle, bright and shining—Hillary Rodham Clinton looks like the successful young woman she is. . . . And she's among the very best in anything she does apparently. A recent new project for Hillary is the forming of an Arkansas Governor's Mansion Association to support the mansion and raise funds for maintenance and improvements. . . . The former first lady, who is also the present first lady, is a successful combination of the modern young American female—wife, mother, professional and civic leader."

Bill had to face another election in 1984—the state still had two-year terms—but since neither his Democratic primary nor his Republican competition was considered serious, Hillary, didn't spend as much time on the campaign trail as she had in 1982.

"I'm here at the Rose Firm almost every day on an

eight-hour schedule," she said. "All of my partners have been so considerate and cooperative. I wouldn't let them down for the world."

Bill was opposed by three Democrats in May's primary—old nemesis Monroe Schwarzlose, northwest Arkansas attorney Lonnie Turner and a certified public accountant from Southeast Arkansas, Kermit Moss. Bill carried sixty-eight of the seventy-five counties (losing seven counties to Turner in the mountains of west Arkansas). He finished with sixty-four percent of the vote.

In the Republican primary, businessman Woody Freeman from Jonesboro in northeast Arkansas defeated lawyer Erwin Davis of Fayetteville. But Freeman never could generate much money or enthusiasm between May and November. Once more, Bill won sixty-eight counties, this time with sixty-three percent of the vote.

Although Hillary did not spend as much time campaigning as she had two years earlier, she did not ignore comments made by her husband's opponents. One of the people she responded to was Turner, the lawyer from the small town of Ozark. Turner said the new school standards were designed to force consolidation of small schools and were too stringent for the average student who would not attend college.

"The purpose of the standards is to provide a quality education so that if a young person goes immediately into the world of work, or if that young person goes on to higher education, he or she will be prepared," Hillary said.

She also was outspoken in her opposition to using a state lottery and casino gambling as methods of raising money for schools.

"It is not as rosy and promising as it is being presented," she said of proposals to create a state lottery and legalize casino gambling in the resort city of Hot Springs. "I hope it goes down in flaming defeat."

During an October rally, about five hundred anti-gambling opponents gathered at the state capitol to hear Hillary say, "We're not going to gamble on our future. We are going to build our future by hard work and investment. . . . We are on the move in Arkansas. Why on earth would we want to give ourselves a burden we can't carry and an image we don't want."

In numerous speeches, Hillary warned audiences it would be difficult to budget money because the state could not successfully predict what the revenue would be from either a lottery or from legalized gambling. Her message was heard. Arkansas voters overwhelmingly rejected the expansion of gambling in the state.

Late in the year, Hillary began preparations for Bill's third inauguration. Almost forty thousand invitations were sent for the inaugural ball, and ticket costs were kept to an affordable twenty dollars so as many people as possible could attend.

"Forget pomp and circumstance, stuffy dictates and solemn traditions," the *Arkansas Democrat* reported. "First Lady Hillary Clinton has declared the main pre-requisite for guests at the 1985 Arkansas governor's inaugural ball is to come prepared to have fun."

"Wear what you feel comfortable in," Hillary said in an interview. "It's strictly optional black tie."

Bill Clinton began his third term as governor of Arkansas on January 15, 1985. Hillary said she would remain committed during that two-year term to education reform.

"I don't want to pick up another project and devote a lot of time to it until I feel like I have carried through on my responsibility to the people of Arkansas—as well as to my own daughter—to do what I can to make sure these education standards are in place," she said. "Part of what we are trying to do with our education standards work is to provide a better-educated work force in Arkansas so we can be more competitive for jobs. I think we have laid the groundwork for that, but we have a long way to go to convince ourselves, as well as people outside of Arkansas, that our citizens are educated to the point that will enable them to compete with workers around the world.''

"There will be those who will want to turn the clock back, saying that the new standards are too high, that our kids can't compete with other people's kids in California, New York, Germany or Japan,'' Hillary told a group of teachers in the southwest Arkansas town of Malvern in March 1984. "... I think that our students should make the same kind of effort in education that we see every Friday night when they perform in sports.''

In a later speech, she said the education reforms could not have been sold to the public without teacher competency tests. She said neither legislators nor the general public would pay for changes unless they could be assured of accountability from teachers.

"There were some—not many—teachers who had no business in the classroom,'' she said. "But it is a problem that sometimes assumes large proportions in the mind of the public.''

As a class, teachers are used to being underappreciated and underpaid. But politicians—and their surrogates—could usually be counted on to soothe raw feelings by noting the dedication and tireless devotion of educators struggling under difficult circumstances. To suggest that teachers might be part of the problem was nearly blasphemous, but Hillary refused to back down. She told teachers, "The tests are not to determine if you are a good teacher but to provide a check on the basic skills levels of all of our teachers. You are more important than nearly any other professional.''

Her work on the Arkansas education reforms attracted the attention of some of the country's largest corporations. In September, Hillary went to Washington to attend a meeting of a subcommittee of the Committee for Economic Development. The CED, a private organization, was funded by large corporations. One chief executive told her at that meeting, "You know how after you've learned a new word, you see it all the time. Well, I heard about Arkansas' educational improvements and now it seems I'm hearing about Arkansas all the time."

"Business executives know if we don't have a good public school system, they aren't going to have a good work force," she said.

As it would many times during the remainder of the decade, the question of whether Hillary would be interested in seeking office came up. She demurred.

"I like having a role as a private citizen making a public contribution, and I'm really lucky my husband is the kind of man and governor who wants to involve me in his work," she answered—without really answering. "I'm really pleased that I can help do what he's basically trying to do."

In addition to her heavy work load at the Rose Law Firm, Hillary traveled widely to speak about education reform in 1985. In March, for example, she went to Atlanta to speak to education writers and reporters at a conference sponsored by the Southern Newspaper Publishers Association. She told them that public support for teacher testing in Arkansas had become stronger because of continuing opposition from the Arkansas Education Association.

In July, Hillary traveled to Washington to debate the education director of the Rand Corporation on the issue of teacher testing. The debate was part of the annual convention of the American Federation of Teachers. The AFT, and AFL-CIO affiliate, was trying to organize teachers in Arkansas at the time.

Hillary blasted the AEA during the debate and said she would welcome the AFT in Arkansas if it would bring about more responsible leadership for the state's teachers. In an impassioned address, Hillary said it was "unforgivable" that the main teacher's organization in Arkansas had failed to support any of the reform efforts just because of its opposition to teacher testing. In Arkansas, she said, problems with teacher morale were "brought about by the actions of the leadership of the AEA."

Of the 1983 special legislative session, she said, "I would go in there day after day to testify for low classroom size, for kindergartens, for the sales tax ... and I would turn around and there would be no representatives (of the teachers' organization) willing to speak out on behalf of educators because they were upset about the test."

An Arkansas teacher attending the convention, Rodney McWilliams of Hot Springs, told Hillary, "I am proud to be a teacher, and I am proud to be from Arkansas, but I am not proud to be a teacher in Arkansas. I know it was not your intention to do so, but a by-product of the testing has been a lessening of teacher morale."

Although she was in the lion's den, Hillary defended competency testing strongly, telling the hundreds of teachers, "It became clear to me that whether it was fair, whether it was accurate or whether it was true, we were going to have to come to terms with the perception that existed (that incompetent teachers were in the classroom). We saw it as one element of an overall strategy to improve the status of teachers. The package included the first sales tax increase in our state in twenty-six years. There was no doubt that the legislators felt more comfortable in going home and being able to say they had passed a test as well as a tax. It was never the point to get rid of anyone. The point was to identify deficiencies and then provide opportunities to remedy those deficiencies."

Hillary noted that of the ten percent of the state's 28,000 teachers who had failed at least one part of the test, most of them had failed a section requiring them to compose a two-hundred-word paragraph. That skill, she said, should have been the most visible to their peers and communities.

"Why had they not been offered any help?" she asked.

Hillary's debate opponent, Linda Darling-Hammond, charged that the tests were nothing more than a quick-fix political measure.

"As a means for upgrading the status of the teaching profession, for improving the overall quality of the teaching force or improving the quality of education ultimately offered to students, such a test in Arkansas or elsewhere is at best shortsighted," Darling-Hammond said. "It deflects attention from the reforms that are needed."

Hillary responded, "I think that where we go from here depends in large part on the kind of leadership the educators have. I would certainly like to see more responsive and responsible leadership."

Darling-Hammond attacked Arkansas for paying teachers less than any state except Mississippi.

"We're there because we're there in income," Hillary said. "We are a poor, poor state. The only chance we have is education for our kids, particularly our poor white kids and our black kids."

Despite her pledge to remain focused on education, Hillary still found time to devote to the Children's Defense Fund. During a CDF meeting in Washington in February 1985, Hillary said that an aggressive state-wide effort to provide better care for pregnant women and newborns had moved Arkansas in less than a decade from having one of the highest infant mortality rates in the nation to one of the lowest.

At the time, Arkansas and Texas were the only states in the South with infant mortality rates below the national average. Part of that was due to Hillary's leadership on the issue. As one might expect, though, Hillary attributed the improvements in Arkansas to her husband's initiatives. Since 1979, the state had developed rural health clinics and made more prenatal care available to pregnant women. The state also had increased the number of medical professionals in the Department of Health and expanded maternal and child health programs.

In May 1985, in recognition of her work in the area of education and on behalf of children, Hillary received an honorary law doctorate from the University of Arkansas at Little Rock.

Her education was just beginning.

CHAPTER TEN
"Politicians Are People Too"

Throughout the remainer of the 1980s, Hillary Clinton would continue to be simultaneously Chelsea's mom, a high-powered attorney and the first lady of Arkansas. Rumors Bill Clinton's extramarital indiscretions began to make the rounds—and to be fair, no man who combines, as Bill Clinton does, undeniable personal charisma with the musk of power is immune to rumors—but never did the First Relationship appeared strained. In public, at least, Bill and Hillary continued to exchange rapt, attentive looks. And to take care of business.

In April 1986, the *Arkansas Gazette* ran a feature on a day in the life of the first lady. Running the caption, "On the run constantly, Hillary Clinton's tight schedule requires careful planning, sometimes difficult choices," the story fit the Clintons's agenda so perfectly it could have been part of a campaign biography.

"Lunch, purchased at a vending machine, was a can of tomato soup, a package of peanut butter crackers and a half-pint carton of milk without a straw," wrote Irene Wassell. "It's not the kind of meal one would expect for the first lady of Arkansas, but one recent day it was lunch for Hillary Rodham Clinton.

"It was part of a typical day—if there is such a

267

thing for a woman who carries the titles of wife, mother, lawyer and first lady.''

Ever the dutiful wife, Hillary told Wassell juggling her schedule with her husband's took "a lot of thought and scheduling and sometimes creates difficult choices. My daughter's life and activities are more important to me than anything else, and I will not miss important events in her life. I don't schedule too many nights out, and we try to arrange time together on weekends when Chelsea can be with us.''

"I stay up late, which sometimes makes it difficult the next day, but when (Bill) is gone a lot, it may be the only time I can see him. Sometimes, when we know we've been on double time for days, we call a halt to it. We try to find time to let off on the pressure.''

Hillary described herself as a terrible shopper who "wait(ed) to the last minute.'' "I don't have time for comparison,'' she said. "I have called on friends for help at times. But, ironically, it's relaxing for me to just get out and go shopping and see what's in the stores. I usually think I'm being anonymous and that nobody knows who I am. It doesn't bother me when people approach me, but if I'm seeking personal time, I don't invite it.''

That so-called "personal time" was another problem for the state's first lady. "My idea of a good time is to do nothing,'' Hillary said. "Chelsea and I might spend a whole day walking or going to a movie, roller skating, shopping or visiting the museum. But our social life is almost nonexistent. We love going to friends' homes for a visit, but we seldom do it. Maybe once a month, if that often.''

Indeed, neither Bill nor Hillary were known as social animals. Although Bill loved being out among people, he preferred political rallies and civic club meetings to dinner parties and outings at the lake with friends. Hillary preferred being alone with her family—one outing a month, maybe to a movie, was about typical for the couple.

Hillary claimed she had no interest in running for public office herself. "I'll let Bill do that. I value being a private person too much." Still, many people in Arkansas thought she was planning on one day succeeding her husband as governor. She certainly had her supporters.

At an April 1986 dinner in Hillary's honor, Bill said his wife was "far better organized, more in control, more intelligent and more eloquent" than himself. Jo Luck Wilson, at the time director of the Arkansas Department of Parks and Tourism, said Hillary possessed "wisdom without being uppity, humor without being silly and tenderness without being weak."

And the stamina of a long-distance runner. Rarely did she rest. During 1985, she accompanied her husband on a trade mission to Japan, Hong Kong and Taiwan; spoke in Columbia, South Carolina, to the Southern Governors' Association task force on infant mortality; attended National Governors' Association meetings in Washington, D.C., and in Idaho; attended Southern Regional Education Board meetings in Georgia and South Carolina; and attended a workshop for first ladies in Cambridge, Massachusetts.

Following her trip to the Far East, Hillary began praising the Japanese education system in her speeches, saying Japan was doing a superior job of educating its youth and preparing them to fight an economic war.

"They are intent on winning," she said. "They see competition coming from the less developed countries and know they have to do something different. . . . We don't plan for the long run. We are very short-term people. We want to make our money, and we don't want to plan ahead."

In 1986, Hillary was in Miami at a Southern Governors' Association meeting when she first read in a newspaper about an educational program that had taken root in Israeli kibbutzim—Home Instruction Program for Preschool Youngsters (HIPPY). Soon after her return to Arkansas, she began working to bring HIPPY to the attention of the state's educators. She organized a statewide conference for February 1986 on preschool programs in general and HIPPY in particular.

HIPPY had been developed in the 1960s at Hebrew University in Jerusalem. It differed from Head Start and similar programs in the United States because children were taught at home by their mothers, not at school by teachers. Home instruction was successful, according to those who developed HIPPY, because mothers learned to take responsibility for their children's education. Research showed children who began their education earlier were more likely to be successful later.

Fully funded by the Israeli government, HIPPY involved 13,000 families by 1986. Thanks to Hillary, Arkansas was one of the first places in the United States to adopt the program for children ages four and five.

At the same time she was introducing HIPPY to Arkansas, Hillary also was honorary chair of the state Mathcounts program sponsored by the Arkansas Society of Professional Engineers and the Arkansas Council of Teachers of Mathematics. The program was designed to make mathematics more interesting as a classroom subject and enhance the skills of those in the seventh and eighth grades.

Hillary also was honorary chairperson of the Adolescent Pregnancy Child Watch, a statewide project to lower teen pregnancy rates in the state. At the time, Arkansas had the second-highest teen pregnancy rate in the nation.

"The economic cost of teenaged pregnancy is astronomical," Hillary said, adding she was "shocked" to learn after talking to Arkansas physicians who treated pregnant teenagers that "a lot of these girls don't even know how they got pregnant."

In Hillary's mind, there was a connection between her efforts to reduce adolescent pregnancies and to improve education. While she was working on improved education standards, she had heard "over and over and over again" from students, teachers and parents that "one of the big problems facing the eduction system was children having children. The more I looked into it, the more I understood what I was being told."

Hillary said that even though society was "bombarding kids with sexual messages—on television, in music, everywhere they turn," families and churches were doing little to help them withstand the pressure to have sex.

"Adults are not fulfilling their responsibility to talk to young people about the future, about how they should view their lives, about self-discipline and other values they should have," Hillary said. "I don't know how we got off the track, but (educating children about sex) is not happening in the families of our kids. Adults don't feel comfortable telling their children not to do things, or they don't know how to communicate that message effectively. I'm trying to."

She said that while many people assumed teenagers were going to have sex anyway and thus simply urged them to use contraceptives, adults should urge them to abstain. "It's not birth control but self-control," she said, adding that teenagers should be told that "it's all right to say no."

Sounding quite different from the dissolute enemy of "family values" that Republicans would try to portray her as in 1992, Hillary said she thought it was wrong morally "for children to engage in sexual activity. It violates every traditional moral code, and it unleashes emotions and feelings and experiences that children are not equipped to deal with. . . . They're valuable people. They should postpone sexual activity.

They should get their education and think about the future. Parenting is a very serious and difficult responsibility that they should not willingly risk taking on."

Teenage pregnancies affected education "in two ways," she said. "Most girls who get pregnant either never finish their education or postpone it. Second, the kind of support, discipline and interaction a young child needs to prepare him or her for education requires a lot of hard work."

And those needs were less likely to be met by a teenage mother. When Hillary talked to groups of young people, she would speak bluntly, telling them they had a responsibility to themselves, to the children they would bear and to society not to become parents at a young age. If they did become parents at a young age, she would warn them that "you can resign yourself to never having control over your life."

In July 1986, when her husband was installed as chairman of the Education Commission of the States, Hillary led a session at the organization's convention in San Diego on state policies for at-risk youth—those kids unlikely to complete school because they are pregnant, have children, are drug abusers or lack the basic skills and motivation to stay in school.

Hillary could concentrate on such activities because, as had been the case two years earlier, Bill did not have serious Democratic primary competition in 1986.

Former Governor Orval Faubus, once the most imposing political figure in the South, was running, but he was not considered a serious candidate. He had served six two-year terms as Governor (from 1955 to 1966) but had lost Democratic primary battles to Dale Bumpers in 1970 and David Pryor in 1974. In this third comeback attempt, the seventy-six-year-old Faubus had little money and only a shell of an organization. Bill's other Democratic primary opponent was Dean Goldsby, the former director of the Economic Opportunity Agency of Pulaski County.

Clinton won the primary with 60.5 percent of the vote, followed by Faubus with 33.5 percent and Goldsby with six percent. Clinton carried sixty-six counties, Faubus only nine.

Once again, Clinton faced Frank White in the general election, though the 1986 race provided little of the excitement that had marked the 1980 and 1982 White-Clinton Campaigns. In fact, White ran slightly worse than either Lynn Lowe in 1978 or Woody Freeman in 1984, finishing with just thirty-six percent of the vote and carrying only seven counties, all of them in the Republican stronghold of northwest Arkansas.

As had been the case in 1984, Hillary was not compelled to spend much time campaigning for her husband, although she did fill in for Bill on a few occasions. Days before the primary election she told Young Democrats to "once and for all repudiate the past that shackles us." It was an overt reference to Faubus's actions in 1957, when, as governor, he called out the National Guard to block nine black students from attending Little Rock Central High School.

Hillary told the Young Democrats the 1957 controversy had been mentioned a few nights earlier on national television during *Resting Place*, a drama about an attempt to bury a black Vietnam War hero in a small town's all-white cemetery. In one of the scenes, an army officer asked the town's newspaper editor if he wanted the community to be known as "a Little Rock."

"We have made tremendous progress," she said. "I think it is breathtaking what the state has accomplished in the last two years. The people who are running against my husband are willing to sacrifice the future to give immediate comfort. . . . We've had that kind of leadership, and we're sick of it. If they don't like it, they can just get out of the way because we are moving forward.''

Although Bill Clinton had no trouble defeating Frank White, the campaign itself was not uneventful. Hillary was once again at the center of controversy. During the campaign, White ran radio advertisements concerning the $115,000 the state Public Service Commission had paid the Rose Law Firm during the previous fiscal year. The governor's press secretary said the PSC had requested the Rose firm represent it on several lawsuits because "it was the only law firm with the resources and experience needed. Other law firms with similar resources and experience were occupied representing other utilities or some other party in the lawsuits. Mrs. Clinton requested that special arrangements be made so that she, as a member of the firm, would not receive any payments directly or indirectly from any of the contracts.''

Later, the law firm released a statement saying the partnership had been rewritten to exclude Hillary from the profits of PSC contracts. Attorney Philip Carroll of the Rose Law Firm said Hillary received "no direct or indirect benefit from fees paid to the firm for service rendered in behalf of the Public Service Commission. All fees received from the Public Service Commission were segreated from other income and were distributed to members of the firm other than Mrs. Clinton.''

The firm chose not to release the partnership agreement itself, Hillary said, because it contained confidential information concerning other lawyers.

White concentrated in the final weeks of the campaign on conflict-of-interest charges against Hillary. Once the controvesy about the PSC died down, the former Republican governor began asserting that Hillary had benefited from state bond business done with the Rose Law Firm. The firm had been either the bond counsel or the underwriter counsel on bond issues for

the Arkansas Development Finance Authority since
1983.

This time, the governor's office didn't deny that Hillary had made money.

"She has benefited financially from the bond business the Rose firm has done with the state," Kay Williams, Clinton's campaign press secretary, confirmed.
"The firm has represented the state on bond issues
since the 1940s."

The state bonding authority later released a list that
supported the Clintons's claim that bond business had
been distributed among several firms. The Development
Finance Authority was, at the time, playing a key role
in the governor's economic development program.

"The governor has a responsibility to bend over
backwards to make sure he doesn't favor his wife's
law firm," White said. He claimed Hillary had made
$500,000 from work her firm did on the bond issues.

"Like so many things Mr. White says, that is simply
not true," Hillary said when asked about the figure.
Still, the Rose firm would not say exactly how much
Hillary had made.

"The affairs of this law firm are our own confidential
affairs and the affairs of our clients," Carroll told reporters. It was revealed that the firm had served as
counsel for six of the twenty bond issues overseen by
the state authority since 1983 and had made a total of
about $155,000.

"I don't think there is any conflict of interest there,"
Bill said. "It's not the first time (White) has attacked
Hillary. I just wish he was man enough to debate
her. . . . Frank has always had this obsession with trying
to put down Hillary. I don't understand it."

He said White would be "hard pressed to name a
first lady in the history of the state who has made a
more significant contribution than Hillary has."

Hillary later said she would disclose her earnings if
White would disclose what he made from state-related

business while employed at Stephens Incorporated, a Little Rock investment banking firm.

"I know I have received a pittance of what Frank White made from bond business with the state when he headed the bond department for Stephens," she said. "I would be willing to try to calculate what I have made indirectly through sharing in my firm's net income if White will disclose how much he has made. Bill and I offered to disclose our tax returns if Frank and Gay (White's wife) would do the same, but they refused."

Hillary said her earnings from the firm were relatively small because she had spent so much time working on education reform and other public issues.

A White spokesman fired back, saying the former governor was paid a "straight salary" at Stephens and earned no commissions. Stephens's participation in state bond issues thus did not affect White's earnings.

In September 1986, Hillary joined the list of political personalities willing—and seemingly eager—to take a drug test. Her husband already had done so. The drug tests had emerged as an issue in the Arkansas governor's race when Clinton revealed during a debate with White that he and his chief of staff, Betsey Wright, had recently taken such tests. He challenged White and his campaign manager to do the same. The test results for all four individuals were negative.

By late October, Hillary was growing weary of responding to White's various attacks. She declared she would have nothing more to say about White's charges. As luck would have it, Hillary and White appeared on the same stage at the retirement community of hot Springs Village several days later. Both were on their best behavior during a political forum sponsored by a property owners' association. White spoke first and then left. Hillary gave a more vigorous address and received a more enthusiastic response from the crowd.

Among those cheering were Hillary's parents, who were visiting from Illinois, and Bill's mother from Hot Springs.

Shortly before election day, the *Arkansas Democrat* published a feature on the wives of the two candidates. It began this way:

"There appears to be little that Gay White and Hillary Rodham Clinton have in common, other than that they are both thirty-nine and have been married eleven years to men who want to be governor of Arkansas. On March 22, 1975, Gay Daniel married businessman Frank White knowing full well that he had three children from a previous marriage, but never dreaming that he would turn into a politician. On October 11, 1975, Hillary Rodham married fellow law professor Bill Clinton knowing that he wanted a career in politics but being admittedly naive about the impact his career would have on her ability to lead a separate professional life. In 1986, as it did in 1980 and 1982 when Clinton and White previously challenged one another for governor, what each woman can bring to the role of Arkansas' first lady has become a campaign issue."

White bragged about the fact that his wife did not have a paying job when he was governor in 1981 and 1982, saying, "Gay was a full-time first lady."

Hillary responded she had "shamelessly used" her role in an attempt to improve education and health care. "I think I am a full-time first lady," Hillary said. "I have about three full-time lives."

Being a lawyer was "a big part of my sense of what I am and what I do," she said. "I think work is very important to people. I don't advocate that people work who do not choose to and have the financial option of making that choice, but for me work is important. I define work very broadly. I consider my work on behalf of education just as important as my work on behalf of my law clients. But I value both, and I appreciate the opportunity to do both.''

Hillary said she rated ''my family, my health, my sanity'' ahead of her law career. Reminded of the criticism she received in 1980 for not spending enough time on the campaign trail with her husband, Hillary said she did that for the same reason she stayed out of the courtroom that year—her infant daughter Chelsea needed her more.

Arkansas Democrat political columnist Meredith Oakley wrote in the fall of 1986 that it should be up to the first lady how she defined her role, not up to her husband, the media or campaign consultants.

''I like Hillary Clinton and Gay White,'' Oakley wrote in an October 1986 column.

''They're nice people who have made personal sacrifices for their husbands' political careers. That's why I hate to see them and their very individual styles becoming pawns in the 1986 gubernatorial campaign.

''The argument in which they are involved has to do with the role of first lady. We in Arkansas haven't had to deal with defining the role of first gentleman for we have never elected a married woman to be governor. We've had plenty of experience with first ladies, however, and before Hillary Clinton, we thought we knew what a first lady was supposed to be. A first lady:

''Should be seen and not heard except when called upon to promote a charitable or humanitarian cause.

''Should be a good hostess, devoting time not spent to rearing children to reigning over garden parties and teas for women's organization's or attending them.

''Should be a full-time housewife and companion to her husband, pursuing no interests outside the Governor's Mansion other than those activities which enhance her husband's public image.

''And God forbid that she should have a career of her own and bring home a paycheck. Individuality has

*never been part of the first lady's Code of Acceptable
Conduct. Barbara Pryor couldn't even change her
hairstyle without evoking public indignation and ridicule. In a campaign year that has seen two men who
have held the governor's office toss everything at one
another that isn't tied down, it's not surprising that the
lifestyles of their wives have been called into question."*

White's criticism of Hillary may have benefitted him
in 1980, but six years later using the same tactics backfired. Ever since Hillary had led the education standards
committee in 1983, a majority of Arkansans viewed
her as an asset rather than a detriment.

"Someone needs to tell our former governor that the
slaves have been freed, women have been given the right
to vote and the wives of politicians, just like the wives
of mere mortals, are entitled to pursue interests outside
the home," Oakley said. "Whether they bring home
paychecks or ceremonial bouquets, or try to do both,
is their own concern."

By election day, in fact, many Arkansans were saying they had voted for Bill because it was like getting
two for one. On election night, Bill thanked Hillary for
the support she had given him despite the personal
atacks she had been forced to endure during the
campaign.

"I'm proud that she made this walk with me tonight," he said. The applause that rang out at this comment surpassed that which had greeted him when he
took the stage. "I think when the history of our state
is written, probably no one will prove to have done
more to advance the cause of our children and the
future of this state than she has."

With her husband about to begin his first four-year
term—the voters had finally abolished two-year terms
with an amendment to the Arkansas Constitution—
Hillary said she was concerned that people would view
education reform as a "faddish" issue and pledged to

continue her work in that area. She also outlined the work she would do in the field of health care.

"We've come a long way, but we have a long way to go," she said. "I want to do whatever I can to keep attention on those issues so they won't be diminished. Things are not going to get better if we don't continue to work on it."

In her seventh year as first lady, Hillary promised she would work for further implementation of education standards either through "cheerleading or lobbying," attempt to improve the chances of at-risk children and try to improve educators' working conditions "so that we can both attract and retain good teachers and good administrators."

In the field of health care, she promised to raise money for Arkansas Children's Hospital, strive to improve indigent health services and continue her efforts to reduce the number of teenage pregnancies and early sexaul activity.

As 1987 dawned, Hillary was assured four more years to make her mark on Arkansas and help her husband lay out his path to the presidency.

About a week after the 1986 election, Hillary's growing influence was recognized when she was named to the board of Wal-Mart Stores, the nation's leading retailer with 962 Wal-Mart Stores and forty-four Sam's Wholesale Clubs in twenty-two states. Several weeks later, she was appointed to the William T. Grant Foundation's Commission on Work, Family and Citizenship.

Funded by a $1.2 million foundation grant, the commission's goal was to compile a study on youth and America's future; to examine how society and its institutions support young people and suggest strategies for resolving unemployment problems among the young. It also was charged with finding solutions to the problems of youth suicides, drug abuse and school dropouts.

*   *   *

By early 1987, there was speculation Bill Clinton would seek the Democratic presidential nomination the following year.

"I want him to do it if that's what he wants to do," Hillary said. "I don't have any ambition for him other than what he has for himself. If he wants to do it and he feels good about doing it, that's all I care about."

She described the decision as "a very difficult one to make and, for me, even to think about. . . . This is a big step, and it's something that has to be approached very carefully and deliberately. It has to be a Bill Clinton decision made on a Bill Clinton timetable."

While she was coy in public, behind the scenes, Hillary, Betsey Wright and others were actively planning Bill's run for the presidency. With Ronald Reagan's eight-year reign about to end, they thought 1988 would be the year for Democrats to return to the White House.

Publicly, Hillary called the decision "the kind that can only be made from very deep within yourself. It shouldn't really matter what anybody in the press or anybody in the public or even anybody personally connected with the governor as a friend or family member says. That should all be weighed, of course. But the decision is his, and I am one hundred percent supportive of his decision, whatever it might be."

She was quick to add, "Personally, I think he would be a terrific President, but that's because I think he has a lot of the personal qualities we need in our leaders." She promoted the idea that a Clinton candidacy would bring positive publicity to the state. "We have done a lot of important things in Arkansas," Hillary said. "Unfortunately, there are still a lot of people outside our state, in this country and around the world who don't even know where we are, let alone know what we are trying to accomplish."

She admitted that a presidential campaign would increase the strain on her family. "The personal cost and the absolute alteration in life as you have known it has to be the downside," Hillary said. "It is impossible even to imagine what it means. You could maybe sit here and intellectualize it, but to experience it has to be totally different."

She said their seven-year-old daughter was "aware of other people talking about it, but I don't want to bring her in now." Hillary added that if Bill "begins to feel like he's going to either do it or not do it, I'm sure he would sit down and talk to her about it."

Speculation increased that Bill would run for President when it was revealed in early July that the Clintons had bought a condominium in Little Rock for Hillary's parents. It was rumored that the Clintons wanted Hugh and Dorothy Rodham to move to Little Rock from Park Ridge, Illinois, so they could take care of Chelsea while Bill and Hillary were on the campaign trail.

"This does not have anything to do with Bill's decision," Hillary said, explaining she had been trying for six years to get her parents to move to Arkansas but had made no headway until recently. "We made the agreement in April," she said. ". . . It is totally a family matter."

On July 6, Hillary promised that her husband would announce his decision in the next two weeks, saying again that "whatever his decision is, I will support it." Eight days later, Bill stunned supporters—and many journalists—by announcing in a press release that he would not run. The Clintons had scheduled a news conference for the next day, and it had been widely believed Bill would use the event to announce the formation of an exploratory committee for his campaign. Ray Strother, a well-known Democratic consultant, was already in town planning media strategy.

Friends of the couple remained convinced that Bill was planning to run for President in 1988, and they didn't know what happened to change his mind at the last moment in July 1987. There always has been speculation that the problems encountered by Gary Hart—forced out of the race following revelations of womanizing—had something to do with the decision. Suddenly, the rules were changed and any candidate could expect to have his private life scrutinized by an emboldened press.

Hillary suspected Bill might encounter allegations similar to the Gennifer Flowers accusations that did arise four years later. She feared the questions might sink Bill's candidacy and, in the process, destroy his future political viability. Friends believe that after considering the charged atmosphere of the time, Hillary changed her mind and then convinced her husband that 1988 would be the wrong time to run.

Bill and Hillary, with tears in their eyes, told the press the next day that the main reason Bill was not making the race was his desire to watch his daughter grow up. Both talked about Chelsea with unabashed emotion during the hourlong news conference at a downtown Little Rock hotel.

Bill said the decision was a "tug-of-war" because 1988 appeared "tailor-made for my candidacy." Later he would say he "knew in his heart" it wasn't his time.

A crowd of about three hundred supporters cheered loudly when the Arkansas governor added, "For whatever it's worth, I'd still like to be President."

Bill Clinton had said earlier in the year that if he did not run for President in 1988, he might never have another chance. But during his July news conference Bill said that he no longer believed that to be the case.

"If I get another chance, I'll be 110 percent," he said.

Hillary wiped a tear from her cheek as Bill said he had promised himself "if I was ever lucky enough to have a kid, my child would never grow up wondering who her father was." She told those at the news conference that whenever she thought about the implications of her husband becoming President, her "mind shut down. I really had to work to think about it."

Of Bill's decision, she said, "I don't think we have ever been through a more difficult time, even including the loss of 1980."

There had been wild cheers that day when Bill said, "I think, very frankly, one of the reasons I would have had an excellent chance to win is Hillary."

She admitted that while she "personally did not want to do another campaign at this time," it was "difficult to walk away from the encouragement that Bill received to run."

Her husband had made thirty-four trips to twenty states in the first half of 1987. He said those trips had convinced him that "we had a chance to run well. It is certain that we would have been taken seriously, and it's entirely possible we could have won."

Bill claimed that thousands of supporters had volunteered to work in his campaign and that "total strangers" had said they would give up their jobs to help him. But the volunteers, he said, "respected my decision. They told me if there was any doubt, not to do it."

Bill said he had been through fifteen contested elections in thirteen years that had left him "aching, literally, for having a more normal personal family life."

The talk about a Clinton candidacy had increased in March 1987 when Senator Dale Bumpers of Arkansas, whom many leading Democrats were urging to run, had withdrawn from consideration. Bumpers also cited the potential "negative impact on his family."

Asked what role potential questions about his personal life played in his decision, Bill said he and Hillary had "thought about it a lot, and we debated it a lot." He said he had decided how the couple would handle questions about his personal life but declined to discuss it further "because I'm not a candidate."

"I think there are worse things than going to your grave knowing that you lived putting your child first," Bill said. ". . . I need some family time. I need some personal time. Politicians are people, too."

In later interviews, the Clintons said the turmoil they had gone through mirrored the decisions that thousands of couples in their generation were forced to make.

"The reason other people got mixed signals was because I was giving myself mixed signals," Bill said during a late July interview with *The New York Times* conducted during a Democratic Governors' Association meeting in Michigan. "I was divided against myself. Mentally, I was one hundred percent committed to the race, but emotionally I wasn't."

He told of how his father had died in an automobile accident before he was born and how his mother remarried when he was four.

"It was a fairly difficult and stormy relationship," Bill said. "And then my stepfather died when I was twenty-one. I think that makes me a little more concerned than I would otherwise be about the impact of prolonged absences. I didn't want to take a chance on Chelsea. I just didn't want her to grow up wondering if somehow she was in second place for either one of us, because I was afraid it would affect how she related to everyone else for the rest of her life."

Hillary told the *Times*, "One of the big problems right now in this country is that people are not paying enough attention to children. And it's pretty hard for us to go out selling that message and not pay attention to our own child. That's a contradiction that we weren't very comfortable with."

Bill praised Hillary in the interview, saying she "had a whole different network of friends than I have. One of the reasons I thought we had a chance to win was because of her and because of our relationship and because of what she's done and the friends she has and the kinds of constituencies she can touch and involve."

In the interview Bill again denied that the increased interest on the part of the news media in personal matters following Hart's withdrawal was the reason for his decision. But he admitted he had given a lot of thought to the incident.

"Most rational political people can deal with whatever rules they have to play by," Bill said. "But I think what most of the politicians felt was: What are the rules? What are these people doing? Are they going to print rumors? Are they going to print rumors that are ten years old or fifteen years old? Am I going to have to spend the whole campaign dealing with that, and if they don't find anything it will still be debilitating? All the politicians talked about it—every time I went to Washington."

Hillary said the Hart incident was "symptomatic of a much deeper desire, not just on the part of the press but of people in general to return to a more balanced personal-public kind of life. Although we never talked about this or thought about this, the decision we made, which was so difficult to us, forced us to say: What is really important to us right now?

"Here are the scales, and they're both overloaded, everything we care about in the public agenda and everything we care about in the personal agenda. And when it came down to it, we weighed it in favor of the personal agenda. In a funny way, that was symptomatic of what's going on generationally."

Bill took over at that point in the interview with E. J. Dionne. He said, "This is grossly oversimplifying, but basically in the 1960s, the sort of dominant mood was one of social commitments. You were for or against civil rights. You were for or against the war in Vietnam. And it was accompanied by a sort of loosening of the traditional bonds that at least publicly bound private behavior.

"In the 1970s, there was sort of a withdrawal from politics and social commitment and a kind of wide dispersal of people doing basically whatever they wanted to do in their personal lives. What Reagan reflected with all these family values and God and mother and apple pie stuff was a deeper yearning that was in almost all Americans to try to get more grounded and have more discipline and order and integrity—not goody-two-shoes integrity, but wholeness in their lives."

Bill and Hillary's decision not to run was part of their attempt to become "grounded," he said, while also admitting that it "hurt so bad to walk away from it."

In an interview the same week with the *Arkansas Gazette*, Hillary said. "Everybody knows when you're in public life, you're going to be giving up a lot of your privacy.... It is very tough talking about alleged stories. This is one thing you learn in this business: People can say anything with total impunity because there is nothing you can do about it. You're not going to sue for libel. You just hope it will not have any effect."

She spoke of people "casting about looking for models and examples. We've really lost our way."

And she said it was "very tough to lead a satisfying life these days.... I see all these stories or allegations or whatever they are as desperate attempts on the part of the press, frankly, to really figure out what's going on underneath."

But Hillary said again that her husband's decision was made "for a really old-fashioned, boring reason: You want to catch your breath, relax with your family. What's really going on is people deciding to spend more time with their children, to gain some balance. What's going on is real interesting, but no one is writing about it. Nobody understands it yet."

As part of their effort to focus more on the family, the Clintons went on an eight-day vacation to Hawaii with Chelsea in August. They also regularly attended PTA meetings during the fall at the Little Rock public school in which Chelsea attended the second grade.

But Hillary didn't appear to slow down when it came to outside activities. If anything, the pace picked up in late 1987 as Hillary managed to accomplish all these tasks:

•Accompanied her husband on a twelve-day European trade mission, saying his two-year terms as governor and reelection demands previously had "tied our hands" in their efforts to promote Arkansas internationally.

"We're ready to untie our hands and get going," she said. "The overriding objective is to promote the state and help other people recognize what can be accomplished here."

She said too many people knew Arkansas only as the site of the 1957 Little Rock school integration crisis.

"We want to give Arkansas the image it deserves," Hillary said upon the couple's departure.

The Clintons spent the first week in Italy at an economic development conference. The second week was spent visiting European companies that had invested in Arkansas to thank them and explore further investment opportunities.

•Continued her work with the Children's Defense Fund, going to Massachusetts to participate in an August workshop and bringing the organization's founder, Marian Wright Edelman, to Little Rock in October to celebrate the tenth anniversary of an organization Hillary had helped establish, Arkansas Advocates for Children and Families.

Hillary had been the Arkansas organization's first president and had helped open its first office in the fall of 1977. By 1987, Arkansas Advocates for Children and Families had a staff of seven full-time employees and a budget of $316,000. Since 1983, the organization had even assigned a full-time lobbyist to the state capitol during legislative sessions. Under Hillary's guidance, it had published reports on school dropouts, juvenile justice and child care. It also had monitored federal assistance programs and provided the state's congressional delegation with information on the effect of various programs.

•Led efforts to obtain a $7.5 million grant from the Annie E. Casey Foundation for disadvantaged young people in Little Rock. The foundation, which had been started by the founders of United Parcel Service, focused its funding efforts on programs for children and young people.

At an August news conference to announce the effort, Hillary said she would try to bring together "the educational system, the business community, state government and local government. The foundation realizes you can't address the needs of at-risk children in a vacuum."

•Continued to give speeches on the subject of education reform, saying the effort was entering its most difficult period. Hillary said it was time to determine if "the plan as it exists on paper is actually happening. We have to be in it for the long term. We're taking problems that have been building up for the past twenty-five years and saying we're ready to deal with them."

She said if Arkansas residents believed they already had done enough to improve education and that it was now up to the schools to continue the job, "then we've lost the point of the whole exercise."

•Was appointed by a federal district judge to serve on a fifteen-member citizens committee overseeing the Little Rock School District's teacher and student reassignment plans.

•Planned and presided over a regional meeting at Little Rock that dealt with how to increase the percentage of blacks in the teaching profession.

•Was one of twenty-two members of a study group headed by former Tennessee Governor Lamar Alexander that called for a sweeping overhaul of the way the country assessed the knowledge and skills of its students.

•Served on the board of the New York-based Child Care Action Campaign and brought the group's executive director, Elinor Guggenheimer, to Little Rock for a forum on day-care issues.

•Was one of nineteen members of the William T. Grant Foundation's Commission on Work, Family and Citizenship. Hillary helped put together a report on the plight of the nation's twenty-million residents ages sixteen through twenty-four who had not or would not attend college.

By early 1988, it was evident to many people that Bill Clinton already was positioning himself for a 1992 presidential campaign. Both the Arkansas governor and Hillary placed themselves at the forefront of shaping the future direction of the Democratic Party. At a January 1988 retreat of 131 House Democrats in West Virginia, family issues such as welfare reform, health care, housing, job opportunities for the young and day care were touted as the winning Democratic issues of the future.

"This is where the future of the Democratic Party lies," Bill told those in attendance at the retreat. To loud applause, he urged the members of Congress to help the party "rediscover its roots."

House Speaker Jim Wright of Texas agreed with Bill, saying, "We think this is where it's at."

* * *

During 1988 and 1989, Bill and Hillary rarely discussed foreign policy during their trips across the country. They chose instead to expound on family issues. Even after his July 14, 1987, announcement that he would not seek the Democratic nomination, Bill remained in the national spotlight. His efforts on behalf of the National Governors' Association to achieve welfare reform ensured a high profile.

Although he had given up the NGA chair the previous year, Bill received more media attention than any other governor during the February NGA meeting at Washington. He was in the spotlight again a week later during a meeting of the Democratic Leadership Council in Williamsburg, Virginia. The DLC was a group of moderate Democrats attempting to redirect the party in the wake of defeats in the 1980, 1984, and soon, the 1988 presidential elections. Impressive performances at both the NGA and DLC meetings made Bill the most famous Democrat not running for President that year and one of the early favorites for 1992.

Hillary, meanwhile, was perfectly positioned to take advantage of the party's new emphsasis on family issues. Her work with the Children's Defense Fund and other organizations gave her a forum.

In February 1988, Hillary headed the Little Rock host committee for what was billed as The Great American Family Tour. The tour, led by Representative Patricia Schroeder of Colorado, was designed to push family issues to the top of the nation's political agenda. The idea for a nationwide tour had grown out of Schroeder's exploratory bid for a presidential campaign.

The following month, Hillary was in Washington for the annual CDF conference, where she joined Edelman in attacking the Reagan administration's proposed fiscal 1989 budget.

On the state level, Bill named Hillary to a new planning body for the state, the Commission on Arkansas'

Future. The emphasis on the family also continued with Hillary heading up an event known as American Family Day in Arkansas.

"It's a shame we have to have an American Family Day or an American Family Week or an American Family Year," she said. "American families are America. . . . The needs of the American family have to be met on both the personal and the professional level. The important thing is that this event be seen as part of a long-term effort. We've made progress in our state, but we have such a long way to go."

The Arkansas event was held in conjunction with the American Family Celebration at Washington, sponsored by the Coalition of Labor Union Women. Representatives of twenty-three labor unions joined Hillary in calling for a national policy that would support family and medical job leave, child care and services for the elderly.

Later in the year, Hillary led the charge when the Arkansas Adolescent Pregnancy Child Watch Project released an eighty-page report on adolescent pregnancy. She said many of the plans for reducing teenage pregnancy rates had "absolutely nothing to do with sex, although that's all everybody wants to talk about." She claimed that adolescents were unaware of the health-care and counseling options available to them. She also said there was a "distinct link" between teenage pregnancy, education and opportunity. Young women who are behind in school have a "a far greater chance of becoming pregnant than those who are academically at par," the state's first lady said.

At the time, Arkansas ranked second in the nation in teenage births and first in teenage unmarried births. "You see the two-pound babies that are born and cost $30,000 to $40,000 to care for in the ICU, and you'll agree that if we could prevent one of these, it would be well worth the cost," Hillary said.

For too long, she said, the problem of teenage pregnancy had been "swept under the carpet. . . . Not talking about it didn't make it go away. The quality of life for too many of our young people, especially in rural areas, is deplorable."

They were strong words, and they were heard across Arkansas, a state that had become accustomed to having an outspoken first lady.

In 1988, on the education front, Hillary was a member of the National Association of State Boards of Education's Task Force on Early Childhood Education. In a fifty-five-page report, the task force recommended that school districts create separate units devoted to children between the ages of four and eight, easing undue academic pressure that school reform too often placed on young children. The panel concluded that reforms aimed at making students more accountable made sense for high school students but were doing more harm than good when applied to young pupils.

On the business front, Hillary was instrumental as a member of the Wal-Mart board in convincing the company's founder, Sam Walton, to expand the giant retailer's "Buy America" program. She had persuaded Bill to call Walton and appeal for help in preventing more textile companies from leaving Arkansas for overseas production. The "Buy America" program required Wal-Mart stories to feature made-in-America labeled goods. Company officials claimed the effort would keep more than 47,000 jobs in the United States.

"We are trying to encourage our people to exhibit the same kind of motivation and spirit that Sam Walton exhibits," Hillary said at the company's 1988 annual meeting. "That same kind of work ethic and commitment can transform a state held back too long by our heritage of poverty."

From her legal practice to politics to her service on corporate boards, Hillary was everywhere. Arkansas— or any other state for that matter—had never had a governor's wife who was so active, so widely traveled, so often quoted by the media.

Arkansas' perception of Hillary Rodham Clinton had changed. No longer just a bright lady lawyer who avoided the limelight, Hillary had become one of the state's most recognizable—and admired—figures.

CHAPTER ELEVEN
The End of Innocence

In its May 2, 1988, issue, the *National Law Journal* named the hundred most powerful lawyers in the United States. Hillary was the only Arkansan on the list, and one of only four women nationwide. She was joined by the likes of Lawrence Walsh; special prosecutor in the Iran-Contra investigation; Edward Bennett Williams, the famed Washington lawyer and owner of the Baltimore Orioles; Richard "Racehorse" Haynes, the colorful defense attorney from Houston; and Susan Estrich, who at the time was managing Michael Dukakis's presidential campaign.

On hearing the news, Hillary said she was surprised to make the list, and disappointed because the *National Law Journal* selected only four women among its top one hundred. She allowed that "a lot of women are making contributions to the legal profession" and it was a shame that, even in the 1980s, women still had to have "a little something extra" to earn recognition.

She had, of course, done the something extra. As head of an American Bar Association panel on women in the legal profession, Hillary had vowed to make the panel a catalyst for change. Though her husband was governor, Hillary said she shared many of the same problems faced by other female attorneys.

"I think any working woman has those problems," she said. "If a woman doesn't have children, she might have parents she's responsible for or other obligations. I don't think my situation is all that different from any other working woman."

Hillary said the domestic help she received from the Governor's Mansion staff was "counterbalanced by the fact that I have a lot more obligations to the state in my public life. I'm probably stretched a little further than other people."

As a result of her panel's report, delegates to the ABA's August 1988 meeting in Toronto adopted a resolution recognizing that women in the legal profession are denied the opportunity to "achieve full integration and equal participation. . . . There is no place in the profession for barriers, including practices, attitudes and discriminatory treatment."

The task force pointed out that women had to face several obstacles that men did not. For example, clients and coworkers showed less tolerance for different styles of practicing law among women than among men. Women entering the field were presumed to be incompetent, a perception which could be overcome only by a flawless performance. By comparison, men were presumed to be competent, a perception that was disproved only by numerous mistakes.

And women still had to fight discrimination against female faculty members and students in law schools, against female law school students in interviews with prospective employers, against female lawyers in the courts and against female lawyers in law offices.

"You're held to a higher degree of scrutiny," Hillary said. "You're not permitted variations in styles that men can have." She said women often were accused of being too aggressive or not aggressive enough if they "deviated from the narrow spectrum set for them by their male colleagues."

Hillary said her task force's report should be of interest to men as well as women. "We think they're quality-of-life issues, human issues," she said of the concerns expressed in the report. The task forced cited the need for parental leave, child-care facilities and part-time work arrangements. It also called attention to a bottom-line orientation that pressured lawyers to produce up to fifteen hundred billable hours per year for their firms.

The task force report noted that although more than forty percent of graduating law students were women, they comprised only twenty-five percent of associates and six percent of partners in private practice. At the time, Hillary was one of only two female partners at the Rose Law Firm, which had twenty-nine partners.

"Women just don't seem to move up in the hierarchy for a lot of different reasons," she said. Asked if law firms in Arkansas were making progress, she answered, "I do think they are progressing. Our numbers are pretty much in line with the national numbers."

George Campbell, a senior member of the Rose firm, said the expectation of women "to advance in the firms and their profession is something we are dealing with right now."

If nothing else, the task force report got the attention of male senior partners across the country.

With each such assignment, with each news conference she presided over, with each speech she gave, Hillary increased her profile, and influenced the course of public events. Dee Caperton, the wife of the man elected West Virginia's governor in 1988, said she would not be a traditional first lady. Instead, she would spend her time explaining her husband's programs to the state's residents and trying to sway lawmakers to support the new governor's agenda. She had served a two-year term in the state's House of Delegates and said she "really liked politics. Politics is people."

Her role model? Hillary Rodham Clinton. The Goldwater Girl whose mother never went to college was becoming the exemplar of the 1980s professional woman. And the awards kept on coming.

In April 1988, she and Bill were presented with the National Humanitarian Award by the Arkansas Council on Brotherhood of the National Conference of Christians and Jews for their work to improve public education and health care for children. The following month, Hillary was given one of the state's plum speaking assignments—the commencement address at the University of Arkansas at Fayetteville. She spoke of the time she had spent as a law professor at the school. She said some of her students were as fine as the best she had met at Yale. But others "could not write a paragraph."

"How do you teach those students who have been defrauded of an education?" she asked, as she detailed frustrating incidents in which she would push students, only to have them say she shouldn't expect so much of them since they had gone to school in Arkansas. If there was anything that upset Hillary Clinton, it was the habit of self-deprecation practiced by so many Southerners in general and Arkansans in particular. She simply could not accept geography as an excuse for unrealized potential.

Later in the year, Hillary spread herself even more thin when she accepted a spot on the board of Arkansas Children's Hospital at Little Rock, one of the nation's premier medical facilities for children. She also spent part of the year campaigning for the establishment of a juvenile justice system in the state.

During July's Democratic National Convention in Atlanta, Hillary helped her husband with his ill-fated nomination speech for Michael Dukakis and hosted a breakfast for Kitty Dukakis, the nominee's wife.

"I wanted to do something sort of personal for her

that her friends could go to," Hillary explained. "I like her enormously."

Hillary, however, was not overtly involved in Dukakis's run against George Bush. She kept well clear of the imploding campaign, as she spent the fall urging Arkansas legislators to allocate the money necessary to enhance the learning skills of disadvantaged preschool children.

"I believe this is one of those programs that is so critically important that no matter what our revenue situation is, we need to get started on it," she told a legislative subcommittee in November. "Without it, I don't think we would be maximizing the effort to make our educational system the best it can be."

She said the "evidence was overwhelming" that a quality preschool program had an effect on students' ability and willingness to learn once they entered elementary school. She pointed to research showing that four-year-olds who received preschool training were more likely to stay in school and avoid problems such as teenage pregnancy and welfare dependency.

Hillary envisioned an early childhood program that would target eight thousand children over two years and build upon the success of the HIPPY effort she had already initiated. "The world is not the same as it was twenty years ago," she told reluctant legislators. "We're going to have to do more to provide programs for preschool children."

At times Hillary's outspokenness put her in direct conflict with her husband's policies. In 1989, the Children's Defense Fund, with Hillary chairing the board, harshly criticized Bill and other governors for signing a letter calling on Congress and the White House to adopt a two-year freeze on the enactment of further Medicaid mandates.

The letter had been drafted during the summer meeting of the National Governors' Association. An NGA spokesman said the governors' request was a response to "the last three years of Medicaid mandates" and the effect those mandates were having on states' abilities to "properly fund education and other important services."

Bill backtracked when confronted with the CDF's opposition, saying he was "very sympathetic" to the organization's concerns and would be willing to discuss an exception to a moratorium on new mandates if it would help poor children. "If that were all we had to deal with, we would be all right," he said, adding that federal mandates in other areas had squeezed state budgets.

But Sara Rosenbaum, the policy director for the CDF, replied, "In light of the cost-effectiveness of health-care improvements for children and Arkansas' own decision to significantly expand its Medicaid program, Governor Clinton's opposition is particularly difficult to understand. . . . Children should not be made to pay for the high cost of Medicaid coverage for adults simply because they are voiceless."

More often than not, though, Bill and Hillary were singing from the same hymnbook. Both spent the late 1980s and early 1990s decrying the decade of Republican control of the White House. In May 1989, Hillary told the Arkansas Federation of Democratic Women that it was time to begin looking ahead to 1992.

"We have to be ready, and if we are, I believe George Bush will get a well-deserved retirement when he tries to run for reelection," she said. She also fired away at former President Reagan, calling him a man "for whom reality is so irrelevant. All of us let him get away with it for eight years because we didn't understand how to take him on. During the Reagan administration, a lot of Democrats held their fire and sat back to try to determine where we are going."

Hillary urged party members to maintain their commitment to education, housing and technology advancements. "If we can take on those challenges, I think the Democratic Party can take the lead," she said. "What's really reassuring is that George Bush doesn't really have a clue as to what he's doing. We've got to do something different. . . . I get awfully tired of the way the Republicans try to paint the Democrats. They always make us seem as if we're from another country. That's nobody I know."

And Hillary already was promoting her husband as the Democratic savior for 1992. "I think my husband has the right idea about the long-term challenges that are facing the country," she said. "I think he is saying what needs to be heard."

And what did Hillary want for herself?

"I just consider myself an individual, a woman, and I think I have a lot of sensitivity for and understanding of the problems women face," she told the Memphis *Commercial Appeal* in a May 1989 interview. "I also consider myself a mother, and I think I have an understanding of some of the problems children face these days growing up. Many young people, particularly young women, are reluctant to get married because they don't know if they can support a family. They are reluctant to make the commitment to have children because they don't know how that will fit into their career."

This was from a women who had not one career, but several of them.

"She carries a lot more weight with some legislators and a lot of people out there in the state than Bill does, there's no doubt about that," said state Senator Nick Wilson of Pocahontas.

A Clinton aide responded, "It would not be fair to say that he is interested in education and children's issues only because of her. But it would also be unfair to say that she has not contributed a great deal to his growth and knowledge and commitment."

*　　　*　　　*

By late 1989, the rumors Hillary would run for Congress or even for governor in 1990 if her husband decided not to seek a fifth term, were stronger than ever. Asked about the reports, Bill said Hillary would be a "wonderful," "unbelievably good" and "terrific" governor. But he wouldn't say if she would be willing to run if he chose not to seek a fifth term.

"I'm not going to speak for her," Bill said. "That's not my business." He did, however, acknowledge that if she were willing to run, "that would have a big impact on my own decision."

Hillary seemed to be everywhere during 1989 and 1990. When the Billy Graham Crusade came to Little Rock's War Memorial Stadium in September 1989, it was Hillary, not the governor, who gave the welcoming remarks during the nine-day crusade's opening service.

When the governor decided to have a series of seventy-five "town meetings" on education, Hillary conducted many of the meetings. The meetings were designed to solicit proposals on education for a special legislative session and generate ideas for the September 1989 national education summit in Charlottesville, Virginia. Hillary's message was much the same as it had been in education meetings across the state six years earlier.

"It's easier to tell when a student does well in sports than when he does well in physics," she said. "Forty percent of college freshmen show up unable to do college work. We're going to try to make it clearer what you're supposed to have when you show up for college."

Some legislators criticized the meetings.

"I thought the choir showed up, but the people who really needed to have input and tell the governor what was really happening weren't there," said state Senator Mike Kinard about a meeting in Magnolia, the south Arkansas town where he lived. "Those are the people who keep talking to me at the grocery store and cafes and service stations, and they say they don't trust the government to do what it says it will do with their money."

The forums were more a public relations campaign than anything else. They were reminiscent of what the Clintons had done in 1983 when they raised money from the private sector for television and radio ads and gave out thousands of blue ribbons meant to signify the need for a blue-ribbon education. As part of the 1989 effort, the governor's press secretary mailed eighteen-page packets to Arkansas newspapers, radio stations and television stations. The packets contained a two-page summary of what would take place at the meetings, a six-page schedule of meetings and background on the first wave of education reforms in 1983. To follow up, Hillary and Bill called radio stations to give on-air explanations of their proposals.

"Bill Clinton is always lobbying for more progress in education," Mike Gauldin, the governor's press secretary, explained when asked about the meetings and the massive public relations effort. And there was public obstinance to overcome. Bill's two hundred million dollar education package had been scuttled in the 1989 legislative session when lawmakers insisted their constitutents were opposed to tax increases.

Hillary accompanied Bill in late September to the President's education summit on the campus of the University of Virginia at Charlottesville. In fact, while other governors' wives toured Monticello and area wineries, Hillary sat in on meetings with the governors and President Bush.

Following the summit's closing news conference, media representatives were talking to Hillary in addition to interviewing the President. "I feel very good about what was accomplished here," Hillary said. "I especially am gratified that the administration has agreed to focus on the readiness to start school."

As a member of the Children's Defense Fund board,

she long had stressed the need for programs that would aid preschoolers. "I really think this summit achieved more than anyone thought it would achieve," Hillary said. "There was not just a commitment to establishing national performance goals but also a commitment to making sure that what follows this meeting is not simply rhetoric. None of the changes will come quickly. We have learned that in Arkansas."

While Hillary charmed the press, former Education Secretary William Bennett put another spin on the summit: "There was the standard Democratic and Republican pap, and something that rhymes with pap," he said. "Much of the discussion proceeded in a total absence of knowledge of what takes place in schools."

By the end of the year, Bill's longtime chief of staff, Betsey Wright, had departed the governor's office. Rumors abounded that part of the reason she left was because of differences of opinion with Hillary.

Only Wright, Bill and Hillary know what went into Wright's decision. But it was evident to observers of the Clinton administration that Hillary was calling more and more of the shots. When Wright had come aboard in 1981 to return Bill to the Governor's Mansion, she had been the chief political strategist. At the time, Hillary was concentrating on her law career and on taking care of Chelsea. But the first lady's 1983 education reform efforts had given her confidence. By 1989, there was no doubt that if there had to be one chief advisor when it came to planning Bill's political future, that person would be Hillary.

"Hillary thinks Bill ought to run for reelection, and Betsey doesn't think he ought to run for reelection," Little Rock political consultant Jerry Russell said in a November 9, 1989, speech at Hot Springs. "And so Bill is going through a very agonizing time."

By February 1990, there was increased speculation that Hillary would run for Congress if Bill did not run for governor. Former U.S. Representative Jim Guy Tucker, who was thinking about either running for Congress again or for governor, said of Hillary, "I think she would be a good member of Congress. It could be very helpful to Bill's eventual ambitions."

Tucker—and everyone else in Arkansas—knew that Bill Clinton wanted someday to be President, and that his decision whether to run for reelection as governor of Arkansas would be based on how it would fit into that ultimate ambition.

On March 1, 1990, Bill filled the rotunda of the state capitol with five hundred supporters. They came to hear whether or not he would seek a fifth term as governor. They were curious and attentive. None had a clue as to what the governor would say.

Many of those in the rotunda stood on tiptoe to see the governor. Because of bad acoustics, most of them could not hear what he was saying. One legislator, state Senator Jerry Bookout of Jonesboro, called it the best-kept political secret in Arkansas in decades.

With Hillary by his side, the Clinton began by announcing that he had grown weary of political contests, saying "I must confess that one of the reasons I have been reluctant to face this day is that the fire of an election no longer burns in me. The joy I once took at putting on an ad that answered somebody else's ad, that won some clever little argument of the moment, is long since gone."

But as a large part of the crowd, convinced Clinton would not seek another term, let out a collective sigh, the governor of Arkansas continued: "I've listened carefully to my friends and counselors around the country, but mostly just here at home—some who say, 'Leave while you're on top. Walk away from a nasty political campaign.' . . . I've listened to others who say, 'My God, you're only forty-three years old. Surely you're good for one more term.' "

Then, Bill said, "In spite of all my reservations about the personal considerations, I believe that, more than any other person who could serve as Governor, I could do the best job. . . . We know there is always the problem of arrogance of power, and we are bending over backwards to be as humble as we can in this campaign. . . . In the end, I decided that I just didn't want to stop doing the job."

As Bill Clinton announced he would seek a fifth term, Hillary Clinton bit her lip and closed her eyes.

"I don't think anyone but Hillary Clinton knew," said state Senator Lu Hardin of Russellville. Hardin had called his own news conference to announce a gubernatorial bid in the event Bill didn't run. He had to settle for telling reporters he would run for a third term in the Senate.

Many of the people who witnessed the governor's speech that day believe he changed his mind in the middle of the speech. Hillary stood beside Bill at the podium as he delivered his seventeen-minute speech without notes. Before the address, the couple hugged and talked quietly. At the end, they kissed.

If Hillary was surprised when Bill announced he would run again, she didn't show it. For the eighth time since 1974, she would be helping her husband in a political campaign.

The months leading up to that announcement were reminiscent of 1987 when Bill and Hillary had agonized over whether he should run for President. Indeed, no one but Hillary knew in advance what Bill's decision would be. Not even his mother, Virginia Kelley of Hot Springs, knew.

"I'm happy, but I would have been happy with any decision he made," Kelley said. "The last time we knew what to expect, but we didn't this time. I don't think anybody knew about it this time."

Wilma Conley, a receptionist in the governor's office, had embraced Kelley when it became evident that Clinton would run again.

"I couldn't have given you a scoop on this one," an aide to the governor told a reporter. "I found out at the same time you did. Nobody knew."

It was, of course, a gamble. What if Arkansans decided they were tired of Clinton after ten years as governor? A defeat would severely wound his presidential ambitions. Indeed, most of his close advisers had urged him not to run. They had wanted him to take over the moderate Democratic Leadership Council and travel the country garnering support for a 1992 presidential race.

"One would have assumed that if he was going to run for President in 1992, he wouldn't be seeking re-election," said Republican consultant Eddie Mahe. "I think he might chat with Michael Dukakis about trying to run for President and be a governor. Both are kind of full-time jobs. If he was serious about running for President, he should have done what Jimmy Carter did in 1974—leave office and take two years to run."

The day before the announcement, Bill's staunchest legislative supporter, state Representative David Matthews of Lowell, had said, "I think it is not in his best interest to seek another term. I think he owes it to his family, his wife and daughter to recharge his batteries and run for President later on."

But Bill and Hillary had decided to take a different route. They had decided they needed the visibility the Governor's office could give them to keep from falling into political obscurity.

The man who was expected to be Bill's toughest Democratic primary opponent—Arkansas Attorney General Steve Clark—had dropped out of the race because of ethical questions surrounding his spending practices. The next toughest opponent, Jim Guy Tucker, would drop out within weeks of Bill's entry into the race because of an inability to raise campaign funds. And what political analysts thought would be two tough

Republicans—businessman Sheffield Nelson and U.S. Representative Tommy Robinson—were carving each other up in the dirtiest GOP primary in state history.

"If you were running for governor and all your opponents were falling on their swords, it would be a little hard to resist," said Democratic consultant Jon Hutchens.

Only one of Bill's five Democratic primary opponents was considered to be a serious threat. He was Tom McRae of Little Rock, the erudite former head of the state's largest philanthropic foundation and the staff coordinator for Dale Bumpers when Bumpers was governor from 1971 to 1974.

On May 16, two weeks prior to the Democratic primary, McRae called a news conference to attack the governor on four issues—teacher's salaries, environmental contamination in a town near Little Rock, the clear-cutting of timber in national forests in Arkansas and Bill's plans to seek the presidency if elected to another term as governor.

About that time, Hillary walked up. Later, she would claim she "just happened" to be at the capitol "to pick some things up" and wanted to hear what McRae had to say.

Mcrae, never comfortable on the stump, was visibly unnerved by Hillary's appearance. The governor was not in the state that day. He was in Washington for the release of the final report of the Lower Mississippi Delta Development Commission, which he had chaired.

"Since the Governor will not debate me, we are giving our own answers," McRae said. At that moment, Hillary stepped forward and yelled out, "Do you really want an answer, Tom? Do you really want a response from Bill when you know he's in Washington doing work for the state? That sounds a bit like a stunt to me."

McRae countered that Bill had refused to debate him.

Hillary shot back, "Who's the one who didn't show up at the debate in Springdale?" McRae had missed a debate two weeks earlier in northwest Arkansas. He blamed his absence on a scheduling mix-up.

Television cameramen swung their cameras frantically from McRae to Hillary. It quickly became evident that Hillary had not just happened to be at the capitol. She pulled out a four-page prepared statement listing excerpts from reports the Winthrop Rockefeller Foundation had issued during the fourteen years McRae was its president. Many of those excerpts praised the job Bill had done.

"I went through all your reports because I've really been disappointed in you as a candidate and I've really been disappointed in you as a person, Tom," Hillary scolded.

"The issue is not whether he has done good things," McRae said after acknowledging he had approved the foundation reports. "The issue is shouldn't somebody else be given a chance to try."

McRae noted that Arkansas teachers still ranked fiftieth in pay among the states and the District of Columbia despite Bill and Hillary's efforts. "If the best he can do is last, then it's time for someone else to give it a try," McRae said.

Hillary counterattacked. She talked about the progress the state had made since 1979 when Bill first entered office. She said the percentage increase in teacher salaries was sixth nationally since 1983 and that the new standards had added 3,500 teachers to the payroll. Because student-teacher ratios had shrunk and new courses had been added, much of the money had gone to new teachers, Hillary explained.

"For goodness sakes, let Arkansas stand up and be proud," she said. "We've made more progress than any other state except South Carolina, and we're right up there with them."

McRae, appearing flustered, remained at the podium.

He mentioned a national report that said state education efforts had stagnated. "It's not that we're not making progress," he said. "It's that we're staying the same relative to other states."

Answering the charges that Bill had not been a good environmental governor, Hillary said, "Bill Clinton has never been accused of not being cautious where issues affecting people's health and the environment are concerned."

Hillary never smiled. She later admitted she was furious that McRae was displaying a caricature of her husband that showed him nude with his hands placed over his groin. The caption under the caricature read, "The emperor has no clothes."

Bill later admitted that Hillary's appearance was not entirely spontaneous—he and Hillary had discussed the possibility of her showing up at McRae's news conference. "She told me this morning (in a telephone call) she might go up there," Bill said that night. "She said, 'I just think I ought to do it.' I told her to have at it. I told her, 'If you want to do it, I just think that's fine.' I didn't really know for sure if she would go or not."

The governor said in another interview that Hillary had gone to the news conference "just to stare at him" but couldn't stand it any longer when McRae produced what Bill characterized as a "grotesque caricature of me naked."

"He has been dishing it out for six or seven months," Bill said. "All she did was show up and say it wasn't true. . . . He has been talking and talking and making wild statements about me. She pointed that out. Maybe he'll have to answer a few questions for a change. He announced that he was going to stage a debate with me at the capitol on a day when he knew I couldn't be there, a day I was legally mandated to be in Washington."

Asked afterward if Hillary had been rude, McRae said, "On one level, yes. I think . . . in a political strategy sense, it makes some sense. You send her out here, she knows the issues and she doesn't have an accountability—and she takes me on. That's fine. She's probably more popular than her husband.

"He needs to carry his own water. We're talking to him through his wife and his press secretary. It may (have been) a smoke screen to get me to participate in a personal campaign. It told me they're very concerned about the momentum I'm building."

Earlier in the day, Hillary and McRae had made remarks during a Sertoma Club luncheon in North Little Rock. McRae's comments had made Hillary angry, and she aggressively challenged her husband's opponent.

"I thought she kicked him all over the damn field," said Paul Groce, the club's president. Hillary had dominated the question-and-answer period, and "Tom didn't have an opening," Groce said. "I think he would have had to yell over everybody to get it."

Although some people questioned the wisdom of Hillary's assault, Tom McRae's campaign was all but finished.

For weeks afterward, Arkansans debated whether Hillary's appearance at McRae's news conference had been out of line.

"That's the first time I've heard of anything like that," said former Governor Orval Faubus. "And I've been around as long as anybody. I think it's going to help McRae. He has gained a front-page photograph and publicity he would otherwise not have obtained."

Tommy Robinson, the Republican congressman and gubernatorial candidate, said, "If my wife did what Hillary Clinton did, she and I would have a private discussion. She had no right interrupting his press conference. I couldn't believe my eyes when I saw it on the morning news."

The mercurial Robinson had been director of the state Department of Public Safety during Bill's first term as governor. He said Hillary's outburst wasn't surprising, because Hillary had "been the governor for the last ten years. I was in his cabinet, and I had to put up with her tirades before," he said.

"Well, folks, I guess we now know who has the real fire in the belly," Columnist Meredith Oakley wrote in the *Arkansas Democrat:*

Hillary Clinton's performance was so impressive that I don't see why hubby doesn't stay in Washington where he belongs and let her fight all his battles on the home front. . . . When (Hillary) tangled with McRae after butting into his news conference, she proved she can grandstand with the best of them. It doesn't say much for her husband, though. I don't know whether Bill sent Hill to do his work for him because he knows she's made of sterner stuff than he or whether she just got tired of all the wimping around and decided to take charge of the campaign. But it was a masterful performance by an almost-ran.

Why she sublimated her ambitions for the sake of her husband, lord only knows," Oakley said. "I suppose love could have something to do with it. She wouldn't be the first strong, capable, brilliant woman to stand aside for a weaker, less capable, less brilliant husband. In any event, she is not the candidate, and it was not her place to crash McRae's news conference and defend his opponent like a mama lion, which she did with a rudeness and a calculation heretofore unseen in her by the general public.

Don't believe that crock about her just happening by McRae's news conference to pick some things up— unless, as I suspect, what she was picking up was the four-page crib sheet, prepared by someone in the governor's office on state time, that she used in ambushing McRae. If she intended to help her husband, she misjudged the situation. She not only one-upped McRae, she one-upped Clinton, undercutting whatever com-

mand he had of the Democratic race for governor by fighting his battles for him. It was as fine a figurative castration as I've ever seen. Clinton is going to catch a lot of grief about not only lacking fire in the belly but steel in his spine. Why else would he send his wife to do his dirty work?"

Oakley went on to say "frustrated voters" could take comfort "in the notion that there is at least one Clinton ready, willing and able to do battle and earn the Democratic nomination for Governor. It's too bad that the Clinton in question isn't the one running."

Two days after the incident, Hillary told reporters, "Bill Clinton and I have a marriage that is a partnership. We work together in a lot of areas. I think my commitment goes above and beyond who I am married to. I have always been concerned about education. If you care about something as a citizen, you have a right and an obligation to speak out about it. It goes beyond my husband and running for office.

"I don't think there is a set answer on what one should or should not do on behalf of their husband. For example, I think it is perfectly appropriate for a spouse to be totally uninvolved (as Hillary herself had been in Bill's early campaigns). I also think it's appropriate for a spouse to take a very active role. Some spouses actually manage a spouse's campaign."

Bill easily won the Democratic primary, receiving about 270,000 votes, compared with 192,000 votes for McRae. The other four candidates received only 32,000 votes combined, meaning there was no runoff. In the Republican primary, millionaire businessman Sheffield Nelson upset Robinson.

In the general election campaign, Hillary was attacked, just as she had been four years earlier by White. Nelson demanded in July that the couple release their federal and state income tax returns for the previous ten years, and the Clintons complied. The returns showed that the couple had a net worth of $418,692 at the end of 1989. Their only liability was a $71,000 mortgage on the Little Rock condominium occupied by Hillary's parents.

Hillary's earnings at the Rose Law Firm ranged from a low of $46,227 in 1980 to a high of $98,089 in 1987. The Governor's only income was his $35,000 annual salary and occasional small honoraria. Nelson's financial statement showed a net worth of more than $9.3 million, which he accumulated while heading the energy company Arkla Incorporated from 1973 to 1984.

For 1981 and 1982, the two years he was away from the governor's office, Bill reported income of $55,084 and $33,792 practicing law. Hillary supplemented her earnings at the law firm with director's fees and honoraria that peaked at $26,702 in 1989.

"She's made most of the money, obviously," Bill said of his wife. "From the time I was attorney general, she has always made more because she has been a very successful private lawyer. I'm grateful that we've been able to save some money and grateful that we've had the opportunity to be in public life. If it was important to us, I think we could be millionaires because we both were fortunate enough to get a good education, we've stayed healthy and we both work real hard."

Hillary said she felt "a little bit funny" but not resentful that her personal finances had become an issue in her husband's campaign. "I've always tried to conduct my financial business and my professional involvements in a way that I wouldn't care about making public," she said. "I understand that people are curious about relationships and investments and all that. It's just part of the way the system works."

Nelson charged that the Clintons were able to acquire their wealth because they had lived for ten of the previous twelve years at the Governor's Mansion without having to pay for rent, food and utilities.

"The Clintons have done pretty well," Nelson said. "We need to remember they are costing the people of this state three-quarters of a million dollars a year to support their high style of living."

Later in the summer, Nelson stepped up his attacks, saying the Bill and Hillary had benefited from work the Rose Law Firm had done for the state. "From a practical standpoint, it's almost like a retirement benefit for the Clintons," he said. "There are certainly profits from state money that have come to the bottom line of her firm and go into her profit-sharing account."

The first lady, who reported having $80,974.85 in her profit-sharing account, reacted angrily. She said Nelson was attempting to divert attention from his own finances. "That's not true, and I resent it," she said of the Republican's accusations. "My profit-sharing account is based on the percentage of profits I share, and I don't share in any profits from the state. Sheffield Nelson is going to try as hard as he can to raise questions about our finances because of the questions about his own finances that he has been unable to answer to anybody's satisfaction. . . . Fees from state business are totally segregated. My law firm doesn't even pay for my overhead. I've bent over backward to remove any possibility of even the appearance of impropriety."

Webb Hubbell—Hillary's law partner who would go on to be associate attorney general in the Clinton presidential administration—said her work on behalf of education, children's rights and other causes actually cut into her billable hours as a lawyer.

"It's difficult in that there are so many demands on her time that she has to narrow the number and types of cases she works on," said Hubbell. "But her visibility is a tremendous asset because once people meet her, they want to hire her."

As Tom McRae had learned earlier in the year, Hillary was not shy about responding to attacks.

"If it were a man, they would probably say what a great, strong person this fellow is, how commanding he is and all the rest," Hillary said. "I'm not reluctant to say what's on my mind, and if some people interpret that one way instead of another, I can't help that."

Nelson's attacks just didn't stick. Bill outpolled the Republican nominee by more than 100,000 votes (397,000 to 292,000) and began preparations for a fifth term as governor. But more than anything—and despite Bill's promise that he would serve his entire four-year term as governor—Bill and Hillary's efforts were now directed toward preparing for a race for President.

Hillary maintained her high national profile in early 1991, again accompanying her husband to the annual winter meeting of the National Governors' Association at Washington. She played a key role in the release of a report from the Commission on the Skills of the American Workforce to the governors. The report suggested ways for employers to enhance productivity and efficiency. At the time, Hillary was a member of the board of the National Center on Education and the Economy, a nonprofit organization that operated the commission.

"They've asked me to work with them to try to come up with some state strategies," Hillary said of the governors. "There's such a link between what we're trying to do on school reform and high-performance work organization that we're trying to meld the two together. I'm convinced after looking at the education issue for a long time that if we don't have an economic incentive that links education reform to the final economic outcome, we're not going to convince the broad range of people in any state what's really at stake.

"We still have too many business people who say,

'Look, I don't care what skills kids have as long as they come to work on time and they have clean clothes on.'

"We still have too many teachers who say, 'It's not my job to prepare kids for the work force. That's somebody else's job.'

"Everybody keeps passing the buck, and the kids get all these mixed messages about what is and is not appropriate behavior for them. Nobody has a standard against which they're willing to measure because people are afraid to be measured."

Also in 1991, Hillary again was named one of the nation's hundred most influential lawyers by the *National Law Journal*. She was again the only Arkansas lawyer listed and one of only five women on the list. At age forty-three, she was the sixth-youngest lawyer named. The publication characterized Hillary as a "leading expert on the changing roles of women" and cited her contributions in the fields of education, women's rights and children's rights.

She was joined on the list by the likes of Alan Dershowitz, Ralph Nader and then-Attorney General Richard Thornburgh.

When it came to Bill's presidential ambitions, Hillary was still playing coy. In May 1991, she said, "I haven't thought about it very seriously because I don't think it's a very likely possibility."

She named the state's two Democratic senators, Dale Bumpers and David Pryor, as potential presidential candidates. Of Bumpers, who had seriously considered running for President in 1988, Hillary said, "He has a lot of the qualities that people say they are looking for. He combines common sense and compassion and has a lot of the background that would be attractive."

"I have always been one of Hillary's biggest fans," Bumpers replied. "I'm always immensely flattered whenever anyone makes the suggestion, but I'm particularly flattered in Hillary's case.''

Bumpers said he would instead seek a fourth term in the Senate in 1992. Hillary had left the door open for her husband, saying the attention Arkansas would receive from a presidential bid could put the state on the national business map and encourage foreign investment.

Bill used the same rationale with Arkansas voters. He had promised during the campaign against Nelson that he would serve the full four years as governor. ''If I did all right, I think there would be a lot of exposure given to the state,'' he said. ''A lot of people would learn a lot of things about Arkansas.''

A month later, Hillary still wasn't giving hints as to what her husband's decision might be. ''I have told him that if that's what he decides to do, I will certainly support him. That's a very personal decision he will have to make.''

Asked how much weight Bill would give her advice, she said, ''I am sure he weighs it, but that's not what's going to determine it for him. He is going to decide what is best on his own.''

Hillary said she was not thinking about a possible move to the White House: ''I just don't think about things like that. I just live where I am. I bloom where I am planted. I think you have to. I just do what happens day by day and whatever happens next I hope I am ready for it.''

That, of course, was what Hillary was saying publicly in the summer of 1991. Privately, she was busy helping Bill plan the campaign. While others were telling Bill to wait until 1996, Hillary favored a run in 1992.

In early July, Hillary was featured prominently in a lengthy *Washington Post* story on the wives of possible Democratic presidential contenders. The story described the pressures felt by high-profile political families as they tried to juggle the demands of campaigning with the competing pressures of raising children and pursuing two-career marriages.

"The professional identity and involvement of spouses are really planted deeply in a lot of marriages," Hillary said. "It makes it hard for one of the partners to say, 'You have to give up what you've been doing to pursue what I want to do these days.' "

Understanding the intense media focus that was to come, Hillary said, "I think we've made a whole lot of progress on the gubernatorial and congressional level. But apparently there's a whole different level of concern you would have to address in the presidential area, and nobody has figured that out because it is a new generation. . . . It's a hard decision to say to yourself, 'I'm going to give up not only my time with my child but also the chance that my child would have anything approaching a private life because of my personal decision.' That is a very tough decision, one my husband backed away from before and one he is still struggling with. We know more about what the costs are today—or are less willing to pay them."

The Post earlier had reported that Bill was leaning toward making the race. After talking to *The Post* reporter about some of the issues in which she and Bill believed, Hillary said, "I don't know how much longer the country can wait for those issues to be part of the national debate. I have told him that whatever he decides to do, it is his decision. . . . But I am certainly hopeful that a lot of these issues will finally break through into the public consciousness and will be given the consideration they deserve."

As the date of Bill's announcement neared, rumors about alleged affairs increased in number and intensity. Bill refused to answer questions about whether there had been extramarital affairs, saying it was nobody's business but his and Hillary's. By late summer, Hillary also was being questioned regularly about those rumors. She said they were irrelevant and diverted from the important issues of the 1992 campaign.

"I think it's a sad diversion," she said. "Everybody, including public officials, deserves some zone of privacy. This is an intrusive and irrelevant issue. Bill and I have tried to lead dignified lives. I've never put Bill on a pedestal and said he's perfect."

During one interview, Hillary became highly agitated. She pointed at a downtown Little Rock street and said, "Rumors are a dime a dozen. I could stand out here and start ten of my own. They are titillating, but the fact that they get into the mainstream media just amazes me. Who would have thought something said by Say McIntosh (a black political gadfly in Little Rock who had distributed thousands of fliers accusing Clinton of numerous affairs) would be taken seriously by anyone? It's pathetic. The press has spent more time following what Say McIntosh says than concentrating on the real issues.

"Maybe somebody will wake up and say. 'Hey, I believe in what Bill Clinton is saying and I'm going to run on that.' I might breathe a sigh of relief. I'm tired. I don't feel like running across the country."

During a five-day August vacation to the Pacific Northwest, Hillary rested. By the time they returned to Arkansas, she and Bill had made the decision to run. "I think if my husband decides, we'll all be ready," Hillary said publicly upon their return.

In mid-September, the Clintons decided to address the question of marital infidelity head-on. The event was a breakfast gathering of big-name Washington commentators and political writers. Known as the Sperling Breakfast—because its longtime sponsor was Godfrey Sperling of *The Christian Science Monitor*—the event had become a must stop for presidential hopefuls.

With Hillary sitting at his side and gazing at him, Bill acknowledged that their marriage had experienced "difficulties" but that they were committed to holding it together. Listening as they finished their breakfast were some of the nation's best-known political pundits—David Broder of *The Washington Post*, conservative columnist Robert Novak, Morton Kondracke and Fred Barnes of *The New Republic* and Howard Fineman and Eleanor Clift of *Newsweek*. Hillary and Bill knew the question would be coming. The night before, they had carefully planned the answer.

"This is the sort of thing they were interested in in Rome when they were in decline, too," Bill joked. Those in the room continued to stare at him. They wanted an answer, not a joke.

"I think the American people will have time to evaluate me and my character and my conduct just the way voters have been doing for two centuries," he said. "What you need to know about me is we have been together almost twenty years and have been married almost sixteen, and we are committed to our marriage and its obligations, to our child and to each other. We love each other very much. Like nearly anybody that's been together twenty years, our relationship has not been perfect or free of difficulties. But we feel good about where we are. We believe in our obligations. And we intend to be together thirty or forty years from now, regardless of whether I run for President or not. And I think that ought to be enough."

Hillary allowed Bill to do most of the speaking. Finally, she said that many good people would not enter public life because they knew they would have to put up with such questions. Looking at her, Bill said, "If she would run, I would gladly withdraw."

The next day, Bill denied that campaign advisers had anything to do with his decision to have Hillary appear with him at the breakfast. But it was clear Bill and Hillary hoped they had put "The Question" behind them.

"I didn't volunteer anything," Bill said. "I was asked. I didn't know for sure what they were going to ask. My staff had nothing to do with that decision. I made a decision and Hillary made a decision that we would go to that meeting because we were tired of reading media reports."

He admitted that his earlier refusal to answer have-you-ever questions about his personal life had "left too much confusion about my convictions about the obligations of marriage and family. I have had several calls from people who have been married twenty to twenty-five years saying, 'Way to go.' I have nothing else to say about this. That's not what this election would be about, and I have nothing else to say about it. It's not a very important thing. It's not important to most Americans. They haven't said anything to me about it. But I have to say it's very important to me personally, and I didn't want people to think that it wasn't important. So I said what I believed."

Two weeks later—on October 3, 1991—Bill and Hillary stepped onto a stage in front of Arkansas' Old State House to announce the presidential campaign. It was a brilliant fall day, and the couple waved at a cheering lunchtime crowd.

Bill said the nation was "headed in the wrong direction fast" and offered his solutions—investment in emerging technologies, conversion from a defense to a domestic economy, more spending on education, a national service program to pay for college, health-care reforms, welfare reform and middle-class tax relief. He used the phrase "middle class" eleven times in his announcement address.

The next day, the Arkansas governor used satellite technology to conduct interviews with television stations in twenty-five states. In what turned out to be wishful thinking, he said on NBC's *Today* show that he had said all that needed to be said about his personal life.

III

CHAPTER TWELVE
Death and Deliverance

In late March 1993, Hugh Rodham, the eighty-two-year-old conservative, Caddy-driving, former Penn State football player and father of the first lady of the United States, was felled by a massive stroke that cast him instantly into the dim reaches between life and death. Hillary Rodham Clinton's whirlwind schedule stopped as she kept a bedside vigil at Little Rock's St. Vincent Infirmary Medical Center.

Suddenly there were no meetings to attend, no appointments to keep and no telephone calls to return. She made no public appearances and was rarely seen outside the hospital. After the stroke, Hillary simply waited, spending long hours at Hugh's bedside with Dorothy, Hughie, Tony, Chelsea and even, on occasion, the President.

For two weeks Hillary watched her father's waning life ebb. It seemed cruelly ironic that Hillary, so recently charged with reforming the nation's health-care system, should have to suspend her efforts to watch a family member die. It was small comfort that Hugh Rodham's final days stilled the critics for a while, and that his death seemed to humanize a woman so many perceived as mechanical, technocratic or even chilly.

Those final, quiet, comtemplative days seemed to effect a change in Hillary. Maybe inchoate beliefs found their form in that antiseptic, shadowless hospital room—maybe Hillary Rodham Clinton found her voice. In any event, a different woman emerged from the hospital; perhaps like many who have been creased by death, Hillary shed her fear at the deathbed of her father.

Speaking by telephone from Little Rock to a meeting of the National Summit on Children and Families at Washington, Hillary said on April 2, "I'm sorry I cannot be there with you. But in my case, as in the cases of many of you in this audience, families really are the most important part of our lives, and we all need to show that commitment in every way we can."

Even though Hillary had virtually disappeared during Hugh's dying days, the media still contained stories about her. *Newsweek* reported rumors that the first lady had thrown, "take your pick—a lamp, a briefing book or a Bible at Bill." The magazine also reported that one "outlandish tale has an angry Hillary lighting a cigarette to trigger her husband's allergies—this from a woman who banned smoking in the White House."

While Eleanor Clift and Rich Thomas took pains to note that there was "no evidence to support any of the stories" and that White House Communications Director George Stephanopoulos had called them "malicious, untrue gossip," the rumors gained currency merely by being printed. They inspired syndicated columnist Charles Krauthammer to quip, on the television program *Inside Washington*, that "if (Hillary's) left-handed, the Red Sox ought to sign her."

On April 6, Hillary resurfaced in Austin, Texas, where she spoke before more than fourteen thousand people, including Texas Governor Ann Richards and former First Lady Lady Bird Johnson. Inside the insulated Elks Club that is Washington, D.C., Hillary's address has become known simply as "the Speech."

Much of the speech was written by Hillary herself, on the flight down from Little Rock. Instead of talking about health-care reform or other concrete policy issues, Hillary gave a reflective speech about what she called America's "crisis of meaning and spirituality." In it she introduced the country to a new phase, meant to embody the spirit of the Clinton administration. Hillary was talking about "the politics of meaning . . . a new ethos of individual responsibility and caring."

"The 1980s were about acquiring—acquiring wealth, power, prestige," she told the assembled crowd. "I know. I acquired more wealth, power and prestige than most. But you can acquire all you want and still feel empty. What power wouldn't I trade for a little more time with my family? What price wouldn't I pay for an evening with friends? It took a deathly illness to put me eye to eye with that truth."

America was facing graver difficulties than the ones chattered about on the evening news, she said; the crisis went beyond the merely economic and purely political problems facing the nation. The country was in the throes of a spiritual crisis that called for no less that a new vision of society based on love, she said. The political system would have to be driven by caring rather than self-interest, according to Hillary.

"Not very far from our surface are alienation, despair and hopelessness," she said. "Why is it that in a country as economically wealthy as we are, in a country with the longest surviving democracy, there is this undercurrent of discontent, that we lack at some core level meaning in our individual lives and meaning collectively?"

At one point she invoked the spirit of the late chairman of the Republican National Committee, Lee Atwater, who died of brain cancer at the age of forty. As he lay dying, Atwater—whose take-no-prisoners campaign style had been duplicated by James Carville and the Clinton team—expressed his regret at having run so hard and so recklessly against Michael Dukakis in 1988. "My illness has helped me to see what was missing in society is what was missing from me," he said. "A little heart, a lot of brotherhood."

Hillary's voice broke as she quoted Atwater: "What power wouldn't I trade for a little more time with my family? What price wouldn't I pay for an evening with friends."

"Our ancestors did not have to think about many of the issues we are now confronted with," Hillary said. "When does life start? When does life end? Who makes those decisions? How do we dare to infringe upon these areas of such delicate, difficult questions? And yet every day, in hospitals and homes and hospices all over this country, people are struggling with those very profound issues."

Hillary had plenty of time to think, to read, to pray. The answers won't be found in guidebooks, she told the crowd that spring day in Austin.

"We have to summon up what we believe is morally and ethically and spiritually correct and do the best that we can with God's guidance," she said. "How do we create a system that gets rid of the micromanagement and the regulation and the bureaucracy and substitutes instead human caring, concern and love—that is our real challenge in redefining our health-care system."

Hillary spoke of "cities that are filled with hopeless girls with babies and angry boys with guns."

"What do our governmental institutions mean?" she asked. "What do our lives in today's world mean? What does it mean in today's world to pursue not only vocations, to be part of institutions, but to be human? . . . Who will lead us out of this spiritual vacuum?

"We lack a sense that our lives are part of some greater effort, that we are connected to one another. We need a new definition of civil society . . . that fills us up again and makes us feel that we are part of something bigger than ourselves."

She concluded by saying, "Let us be willing to re-mold society by redefining what it means to be a human being in the twentieth century, moving into a new millennium."

On April 7, 1993, the day after Hillary made her speech in Austin, Hugh Rodham finally died.

The politics of meaning.

Hillary had appropriated the term from Michael Lerner, a man who by the summer of 1993 was being called Hillary's guru. Lerner's outlet was *Tikkun* magazine, a "bimonthly Jewish critique of politics, culture and society." "Tikkun" is a Hebrew word that, according to the legend line on Lerner's magazine, means "to heal, repair and transform the world." The legend goes on, noting that "all the rest is commentary," a none-too-subttle swipe at the right-wing Jewish intellectual journal founded by Norman Podhoretz. While Lerner took an obvious and understandable pride in his apparent influence on the first couple, he denied he was anybody's guru.

"I wouldn't accept such a role even if it were offered, which it hasn't been," Lerner said. "The White House wouldn't necessarily be a step up. . . . I've known enough scumbag politicians in my life and I've seen the illusions of people in power who thought they were going to change the world. Having momentary access to the White House doesn't mean anything is going to change overnight.

"My parents were involved with powerful political people. At my *bar mitzvah*, there were mayors, congressmen, police chiefs. One after another of them ended up in prison. Even at that age, I could see that the political world was full of people who speak of high ideals but live a morally insensitive life. I didn't have the language to articulate it until I found the Torah and the world of the prophets opened up to me."

Lerner's father was a judge and later director of the

New Jersey Alcoholic Beverage Control Board. His mother worked in numerous Democratic campaigns. Lerner considered becoming a rabbi but chose instead to become a writer and publisher. Bill and Hillary began reading Lerner's work when they lived in Arkansas, and the Governor sent Lerner a fan letter soon after he began publishing *Tikkun*.

When Bill Clinton became President, Lerner moved the *Tikkun* offices from the San Francisco Bay area to New York City to be closer to the center of power. He would later become a critic of the administration, claiming that Bill had moved from the politics of meaning to the politics of cynicism.

Of course, some members of the press viewed cynicism as a virtue. And their reaction to Hillary's revelations were predictable.

"In a perfect universe, calling on virtue to heal the ills of the body politic would be applauded," Joan Connell of the Newhouse News Service wrote soon after Hillary's speech in Austin. "But the suggestion that politics can rightfully have a spiritual base and an altruistic purpose has been attacked with a vehemence that speaks volumes about the nature of political discourse in this country and the hazards to any politician who stakes out moral high ground. Citizens have good reason to shudder if government wants to equip them with a new set of virtues. But it appears to be politics, not people, that the first lady wants to put on a higher moral plane. In the political piranha pool that is official Washington, her words were red meat for a feeding frenzy."

To the media, it seems hardly possible that anyone—particularly anyone in politics—could be motivated by altruistic, ethical or religious values, Lerner told Connell. "Most press people have nothing to sell but their cynicism—their ability to see through the appearance

of goodness and reveal the dirty core of self-interest,"
he said.

On May 23, 1993, *The New York Times Magazine*
featured Hillary dressed in virginal white on its cover
with the headline "Hillary Rodham Clinton and the
Politics of Virtue." Inside, *Times* White House correspondent Michael Kelly wrote a scathing piece headlined "Saint Hillary," packaged with a drawing of
Hillary as *Jeanne d'Arc*.

"Since she discovered, at the age of fourteen, that
for people less fortunate than herself the world could
be very cruel, Hillary Rodham Clinton has harbored
an ambition so large that it can scarcely be grasped,"
Kelly wrote.

*"She would like to make things right. She is forty-
five now and she knows that the earnest idealism of a
child of the 1960s may strike some people as naive or
trite or grandiose. But she holds to them without any
apparent sense of irony or inadequacy. She would like
people to live in a way that more closely follows the
Golden Rule. She would like to do good, on a grand
scale, and she would like others to do good as well.
She would like to make the world a better place—as
she defines better.*

*"While an encompassing compassion is the routine
mode of public existence for every first lady, there are
two great differences in the case of Mrs. Clinton: She
is serious and she has power. Her sense of purpose
stems from a world view rooted in the activist religion
of her youth and watered by the conviction of her generation that it was destined (and equipped) to teach
the world the errors of its ways. Together, both faiths
form the true politics of her heart, the politics of
virtue."*

Other publications came close to mocking the first
lady.

The New Republic asked, "What on earth are these people talking about?" *The Wall Street Journal* called it the politics of mumbo-jumbo. *The Washington Times* reported that Lerner had been one of the Seattle Seven, a defendant in an antiwar trial.

And, for once, Hillary seemed less than steely, almost flaky in her interview with the *Times*. When Kelly asked her to define her philosophy, she seemed to founder.

"I don't know," she answered. "I don't know. I don't have any coherent explanation. I hope one day to be able to stop long enough actually to try to write down what I do mean because it's important to me that I try to do that, because I have floated around the edges of this and talked about it for many, many years with a lot of people. But I've never regularly kept a journal or really tried to get myself organized enough to do it."

Hillary knew Hugh Rodham would have scoffed at such psychobabble.

"My father was no great talker and not very articulate and wouldn't have known Niebuhr from Bonhoeffer from Havel from Jefferson, and would have thought a conversation like this was just goofy," she admitted. "But he gave me the basic tools, and it wasn't fancy philosophical stuff. He used to say all the time, 'I will always love you, but I won't always like what you do.' And, you know, as a child I would come up with nine hundred hypotheses. It would always end with something like, 'Well, you mean, if I murdered somebody and was in jail and you came to see me, you would still love me?' And he would say, 'Absolutely. I will always love you, but I would be deeply disappointed and I would not like what you did because it would have been wrong.' "

Hillary seemed unperturbed by her critics. And, in another venue of public life, her remarks might have been embraced by the public. But with a cynical media filtering her remarks, it's no wonder she sometimes sounded goofy. Still she had defenders. "Why is the media so scared of the politics of meaning?," Lerner finally asked in an essay for *The Washington Post*. "From the moment that Hillary Clinton adopted the concept I had been developing in *Tikkun* magazine for the past seven years to describe the hunger that most Americans have for a society that supports rather than undermines loving relationships, ethical life and communities that provide a framework for transcending the individualism and me-firstism of the competitive marketplace, there has been a campaign to ridicule our ideas. . . . The attempt here is to cast us in the same mold that destroyed Jimmy Carter—elitist pretenders assuming a higher moral plane than the rest of the American people and critiquing their malaise."

"At a time when her husband's White House is in some disarray and feverishly struggling to right itself, she is grounded enough to seem a bit distant," Martha Sherrill wrote of Hillary in May 1993 in *The Washington Post*. "Hillary Rodham Clinton doesn't seem to need anything immediate from the people around her, like big smiles or nods or clapping. She has warmth, but controls it like a microwave oven. She has charm, but hesitates using such ephemeral superficial stuff. She has gravitas, far-off goals. And she is very patient. She would rather convince you of something slowly—by deed—and she would rather change your mind permanently—about the world or people or politics—than make you laugh right here and now."

But while there were those who poked fun at "the politics of meaning," compared to her husband, Hillary received rave media reviews in the spring and summer of 1993. While Bill plummeted in the polls, Hillary was, in Sherrill's words, "replacing Madonna as our leading cult figure."

Hillary granted very few interviews in those first

months of the Clinton administration, preferring to be defined by her public speeches and her actions.

"My politics are a real mixture," she told *The Post*. "An amalgam. And I get so amused when these people try to characterize me. . . . The labels are irrelevant. And yet, the political system and the reporting of it keep trying to force us back into the boxes because the boxes are so much easier to talk about. You don't have to think. You can just fall back on the old, discredited Republican versus Democrat, liberal versus conservative mindsets."

Hillary was serious about her spirituality, and she thought religion ought not to be solely the province of the religious right. "The search for meaning should cut across all kinds of religious and ideological boundaries," she said. "That's what we should be struggling with—not whether you have a corner on God."

"Faith is a wonderful gift of grace," she told the *Los Angeles Times*. "It gives you a sense of being rooted in meaning and love that goes far beyond your own life. It gives you a base of assurance as to what is really important and stands the test of time day after day, minute after minute, so that many of the pressures that come to bear from the outside world are not seen as that significant."

But what about the political implications of that faith?

"The point of the politics of meaning is not that government should dictate a particular moral or spiritual view," Lerner wrote in his explanation of the philosophy. "But we live in a time when our economy rewards the self-centered and the selfish while putting at a disadvantage those who have taken time off in order to act morally or in a caring way toward others. A progressive politics of meaning seeks to level the playing field by creating economic, political and social incentives for social and ecological responsibility—so that people can feel that choosing a moral life does not mean losing all chance for personal advancement, economic reward or social sanction.

"Why the backlash now? The simple answer is this: The politics of meaning is the Clintons's attempt to change the dominant discourse of this society from the language of selfishness to the language of caring, social responsibility and ecological sensitivity. The dominant discourse sets the framework for those specific political ideas and programs that seem plausible and those that seem outside the pale."

Publicly, Hillary expressed bemusement about the raging debate over her views.

She told David Lauter from *The Los Angeles Times*, "The thing that is, I guess, hard for me to fully appreciate is how values and views that I've held all my life and have spoken about all my life are now viewed as news because of the particular position that I'm in. . . . No matter who you are or what you're doing, people are going to nitpick around the edges. I can only be who I am."

"The most controversial and probably most powerful first lady in recent history is surrounded by polarized conflict—loved and hated, feared and admired," David Lauter wrote in *The Los Angeles Times* four months after the inauguration:

"Millions, particularly young women, tell pollsters and interviewers she is a role model and exemplar of all that a modern woman can accomplish—a latter-day Joan of Arc. At the same time, conservative opponents of the administration see her as the embodiment of American decline, a 'feminazi,' a symbol of abortion and gay rights, a 1990s version of the biblical Witch of Endor.

"The crescendo on both sides of the Hillary Clinton question has risen to a level almost certainly beyond what any one woman should reasonably be expected to

bear. But for Clinton, who revels in the influence her post brings while ruing the ceaseless attention the job entails, there is no relief in sight, no escape from the gilded cage of others' expectations. In an administration that likes to talk grandly about change, she is change incarnate.''

What *does* Hillary believe?

"I believe that personal responsibility is at the root of any kind of social structure, including the family," she told Dotson Rader in a softball interview for *Parade* magazine. "We have not done a good job in expecting people to exercise their rights responsibly and to be held accountable. There are cultural messages that undermine personal responsibility—widespread acceptance of what used to be considered inappropriate behavior, attitudes that allow people off the hook. I believe that part of the reason my husband was elected President is because, for more than ten years in Arkansas, we've been trying to figure out how you begin to reinstill responsibility where it has been undermined."

"Without addressing this and providing incentives to alter behavior and require people to be more responsible, we're not going to get ahead of the curve on the serious problems—like disintegrating families, crime and drugs—that afflict us. It's easy to place the blame at the top, but it goes all the way down. People who see their neighborhoods go to drug dealers, who see fourteen-year-old murderers, they have to take responsibility, too. they have to demand better behavior, starting with their own children."

Rader told Hillary that with all the talk about personal responsibility and discipline, she sounded almost conservative.

"But I am a conservative," she replied. "I would characterize the way I was raised and the way I still am as being conservative in the true sense of that word—not in the kind of radical, ideological, destructive way that term is often used. I was raised to be self-reliant and to be responsible but to know that I was part of a larger community to which I also have responsibilities. I'm really grateful that both my parents, in different ways, gave me the support and structure that I needed to develop a sense of personal self-worth and security.

"I've always believed, and this goes back to their teachings and my church, that because I was blessed enough to be healthy and have a strong, supportive family, I had an obligation to care for other people, to help them. It wasn't something you did as an afterthought. It was how you lived."

Reporters began interviewing those who had known Hillary through the years to interpret what she was saying. Many went to Reverend Don Jones, the former youth leader at the First United Methodist Church in Park Ridge.

"Hillary's spiritual foundation gives her some distance from all the good causes she's for," Jones said in one interview. "She is both idealistic and pragmatic. Really, she embodies that dialectic."

In another interview with *The New York Times*, Jones said, "My sense of Hillary is that she realizes absolutely the truth of the human condition, which is that you cannot depend on the basic nature of man to be good and you cannot depend entirely on moral suasion to make it good. You have to use power. And there is nothing wrong with wielding power in the pursuit of policies that will add to the human good. I think Hillary knows this. She is very much the sort of Christian who understands that the use of power to achieve social good is legitimate."

So Hillary would use her position as first lady to do what she considered right and good. That's what worried conservatives, who figured that there was a left-wing agenda hiding beneath the talk about the politics of meaning. As radio talk show phenomenon Rush

Limbaugh often said, many thought Hillary's ideas were simply reheated socialism. Limbaugh claimed Bill and Hillary Clinton were so naive as to believe that their policies could succeed where similar policies had failed because they thought they were "better people" with larger stores of compassion and empathy.

Other analyses were more trenchant, perhaps, but hardly less cynical. Michael Kelly wrote this about Hillary's politics:

They are, rather than primarily the politics of left or right, the politics of do-goodism, following directly from a powerful and continual stream that runs through American history from Harriet Beecher Stowe to Jane Addams to Carry Nation to Dorothy Day; from the social gospel of the late nineteenth century to the temperence-minded Methodism of the early twentieth century to the liberation theology of the 1960s and 1970s to the pacifistic and multiculturally correct religious left of today. The true nature of her politics makes the ambition of Hillary Rodham Clinton much larger than merely personal. She clearly wants power and has already amassed more of it than any first lady since Eleanor Roosevelt. But that ambition is merely a subcategory of the infinitely larger scope of her desires.

In the *Parade* interview, Hillary said she was "as oblivious as people in our position can be to public opinion and press opinion about how we live and who we are. Because, at the end of the day, what counts is what we feel about ourselves and each other. And we're just going to continue emphasizing that and doing it the best way we can.

"I'm sure there will be consequences and costs to pay, but people who are never in public life have consequences and costs in their lives, too, because of the things that happen to them or the decisions that they make or fail to make. You just have to do the best you can with whatever challenges life sends your way. I've believed that ever since I was a little girl, so this is not a new feeling for me. I've always believed you play the hand you're dealt, and you play it as well as you can. You take every precaution you possibly can to make sure that, at the end of the day, you are glad you lived it that way and you know that you did the best job you could do."

A week after Bill's inauguration, a *Wall Street Journal*/NBC News poll showed Hillary with a positive rating of fifty-seven percent, up from forty-six percent in December. On the subject of whether she was or was not a positive role model, seventy-four percent said she was. Only fifteen percent said she wasn't.

On the question of whether she should or should not be involved in developing policy, forty-seven percent said she should and forty-five percent said she shouldn't.

"Bill Clinton may be having trouble hitting the ground running, but there are no such fears about Hillary Rodham Clinton," *The Journal* reported in its analysis of the poll. "No sooner had she been named by her husband to head a national task force on health care than she was working the phones. . . . The people she contacted all dropped whatever they were doing to talk to a woman who gives every indication of becoming the most powerful—and perhaps the most controversial—first lady in American history. When Hillary Rodham Clinton calls, people listen. She inspires respect—even fear."

House Ways and Means Committee Chairman Dan Rostenkowski told the newspaper, "From what I hear, she's got both hands on the throttle."

Veteran *Wall Street Journal* writers James Perry and Jeffrey Birnbaum said voters seemed to sense that Hillary was "going to be a daring high-wire act, and they already are holding their collective breath as the drama begins to unfold. Democratic strategists pray she can pull it off, while Republican operatives look for signs of her losing her balance. . . . She shatters all the precedents. She goes to work in a small room . . . in the West Wing of the White House, surrounded not by social secretaries but by the largely anonymous policy experts who will lay out the new administration's domestic programs. She will be the voice most of them listen to most respectfully most of the time. . . . But Arkansas is not Washington, and education reform in that state is not health-care reform for the whole country. This is an immense challenge, and if Mrs. Clinton—for whom there are such high expectations—fails to meet it, there will be serious political consequences for her husband's administration.''

Donna Shalala, the woman Hillary apparently convinced her husband to name as secretary of Health and Human Services, said Americans had to get used to a first lady who represented "a different generational experience. . . . It's very tricky because she's on the borderline between a more traditional role and this new role for women. Twenty years from now, we won't think twice. . . . You can be sure that if I and every other Cabinet officer think she can be helpful on something specific, like trying to recruit the best person in the country, we're going to call her and say please help us recruit this person.''

If there was any doubt as to Hillary's influence in the administration, it was erased for visitors to the White House Federal Credit Union, which is in the Executive Office Building near the White House. Alongside a large color portrait of the President—presidential portraits are common in federal office buildings—hung a second portrait of equal size. It was not of the Vice-President or a member of the Cabinet. It was a portrait of Hillary.

By early May, a *Time*/CNN poll showed that sixty-three percent of Americans thought Hillary's prominent role in shaping policy was appropriate, compared with thirty-two percent who said it was not. Asked how much confidence they had in Hillary's ability to handle her role in health-care policy and other domestic issues, thirty-three percent of respondents said a lot, forty-nine percent said some and only sixteen percent said none.

Ninety-one percent of respondents described Hillary as intelligent, seventy-three percent described her as a good role model for girls, fifty-six percent said she was more liberal than her husband, fifty-two percent said they admired her and forty-one percent said she was too pushy.

"To millions of women, Hillary Clinton's career-and-family balancing act is a symbolic struggle," Margaret Carlson wrote in *Time*. "Never mind that she has plenty of help, including more top officials on her staff than Al Gore has. Hillary still has something in common with women everywhere: a day that contains only twenty-four hours and responsibilities that extend way beyond what happens in the office. Family duties fall primarily to her—from attending soccer games and helping Chelsea with her homework to shopping and organizing birthday parties. She's also looking after her mother. . . . The first lady's plea is familiar to any working woman."

"We are trying to work it out so that we have some more spare time just for ourselves," Hillary said. "The job eats up every spare minute."

Interest in the first lady was so intense that by late spring, Random House Reference and Electronic Publishing—publishers of the *Random House Webster's College Dictionary*—declared a "language watch" for new words and phrases relating to Hillary. Enid Pearsons, the dictionary's senior editor, said that because the first lady had generated so much news, she had spawned a number of new descriptions ranging from "Superconscientious" to the "feminist wife from hell."

Pearsons pointed out that every new administration had brought terms to the culture. In the 1980s, Americans added "Reaganomics," "Teflon president," "great communicator," "Bushspeak" and "Quaylisms" to their vocabularies. Teddy Roosevelt's administration gave us the term "bully pulpit." Shack communities erected during the Hoover administration came to be known as "Hooverville."

In 1993, though, most of the new words revolved around the first lady rather than the President. Because of Bill, there was an increased use of the term "Bubba." But there were far more words and terms used to describe Hillary. *Newsweek* used "New age first lady" and "First lady plus." *The New Republic* called her a "false feminist."

Terms used to describe the administration ranged from "Team Clinton," to "Billary," to the "Rodham/-Clinton" presidency. Writers even began using "FOH" for "Friends of Hillary," the counterpart to the "FOB" or "Friend of Bill." "HRC"—for "Hillary Rodham Clinton"—also gained some currency as a shorthand reference to the first lady. *The Wall Street Journal* featured a front-page story on the name "Hillary," pointing out that it means "cheerful" in Latin.

Pearsons said the reason for the many new terms was the fact that Hillary so defied tradition: "It's the dissonance between her and two hundred years or so of our image of a first lady."

"She's powerful, intelligent and creative," said Jesse Sheidlower, a Random House lexicographer. "Many people have problems with those characteristics in any woman. Certainly that is a great deal of what's blowing people's minds."

Pearsons said another reason such a large number of terms were used to describe Hillary was her complex personality. Her complexity made it difficult for pundits to characterize her. Writer Sally Quinn, for example, described Hillary as "feminine and girlish" and "serious and strident" in the same article.

"The rest of the world tries to fit her into a little box, but they don't know what to do," Pearsons said. "There are no ready labels."

In addition to the new terms, there were countless jokes.

In Arkansas, one of the most widely circulated jokes had Bill and Hillary taking a country road during a vacation from Washington. They stopped at a service station to fill up, and Hillary began talking with the guy pumping gas.

"Who was that?" Bill asked.

"Oh, that was an old boyfriend from back in high school," Hillary said.

"Just think, if you had married him, you wouldn't be married to the President of the United States right now," Bill said.

"If I had married him, Bill, you'd be pumping gas right now," Hillary replied.

They even resurrected an old Charles DeGaulle joke: Hillary is looking for a burial plot. She found one and liked it, but she was told it would cost one hundred thousand dollars.

"That's outrageous," she said. "I'm only planning to use it for three days."

There had been few Barbara Bush jokes during the preceding four years. But Barbara Bush wasn't perceived as powerful. And in 1993, a lot of Americans were still extremely uncomfortable with the thought of a powerful first lady. The fact that Hillary was controversial made her an easy target for comedians.

Columnist Mark Shields began his speeches by saying, "It's an exciting time in Washington these days. I have to confess, even as an old cynic, that it's fun to cover the new leader of the Western world . . . and her husband."

One of David Letterman's famed Top Ten lists was titled the "Top Ten Signs Hillary Is In Charge." Reason Number One? "Bill now calling her Mommy."

Even the President said at a dinner in Washington, "The opinions I will express tonight are those of my wife."

"Not everyone thinks it's funny," Nathan Cobb wrote in *The Boston Globe*. "Hillaryesque humor is seen by some people as a comment on how many Americans, from TV monologuists to watercooler wise guys, are made uncomfortable by a powerful and ambitious woman. ... Patricia Ireland is not amused. The president of the National Organization for Women points out that Hillary humor runs the gamut from the mean to the affectionate, but Ireland contends that the overall theme is one of Bill Clinton being a wuss who's being bested by his wife." "Washington passes off these comments as if they're jokes. All of this reflects the fact that people often make jokes when something makes them uncomfortable," Ireland adds. "They're trying to take a threat and their fear of it and make a joke."

Frank Marafiote who publishes *The Hillary Clinton Quarterly*, was one of the first to say that the jokes about Hillary were getting out of hand.

"Why is everyone picking on Hillary Clinton?" he asked. "The woman has a tough job to do, playing co-presidential politics in a man's world. She deserves some respect. My own theory is that Hillary reminds some people of their fifth-grade English teacher, In public, the first lady comes across as too businesslike, too severe, perhaps too self-important. The jokes are the proverbial banana peel. Nothing is funnier than watching some pompous so-and-so slip and fall."

Hillary completely overshadowed the Vice-President and members of the Cabinet during the early months of 1993. At the same time hundreds of reporters were cranking out stories on the President's first hundred days in office, journalists also were assessing Hillary's first hundred days.

She was a favorite on magazine covers worldwide.

The week after the inauguration, Hillary's photo was on the cover of *People* again, this time with a headline that read "The Real Woman Hillary Clinton."

She returned to the cover of *People* once more in the spring beside the headline "Hillary—The First Hundred Days—Sustained by family, friends and faith after the loss of her father, the new first lady is back on the job tackling health care and putting a bold stamp on the White House. And guess who's just as popular as the President?"

Hillary was on the cover of the April *Ladies' Home Journal* with the headline "Hillary Clinton—Will She Change Your Life?" *Newsweek* featured Hillary on the cover of its final issue of 1992 as one of its Women of the Year and then put her out front again in February with the headline "Hillary's Role—How Much Clout?"

Parade devoted almost an entire issue to her in April. A month later, the Sunday magazines of *The New York Times* and *The Los Angeles Times* had Hillary on the cover on the same day. There was a marketing reason for all the Hillary covers. Her face on the cover guaranteed sales—eclipsing even the drawing power of Princess Diana.

In early April, forty female journalists gathered in Washington to discuss the media's coverage of Hillary. Marian Burros of *The New York Times* said some people feared a woman "that strong, that good, that powerful. I think there's an enormous amount of jealousy among my fellow reporters, who sometimes shock me with their response to her."

"Confused about Hillary Rodham Clinton?" Roxanne Roberts wrote the next day in *The Washington*

Post. "Loving wife and mom? First hostess with the mostest? Dynamo superwoman lawyer and health czar? All of the above? Well, you must be in the media."

Betsey Wright, Bill's former gubernatorial chief of staff, was there to tell the journalists that Hillary was "operating without precedent in many ways. My guess is that life is very confusing for her also." Wright said much of the curiosity "under the guise of being about Hillary, is actually about Bill. . . . She's not only his wife and the mother of their child, but she is his most trusted, loyal adviser and the smartest person he knows."

Feminist Betty Friedan called the coverage of Hillary "fascinating because it's like a massive Rorschach test of the evolution of women in our society."

By late spring, Hillary seemed a bit weary of the burden.

"Usually, presidents are the ones who start to wear the office on their faces," Martha Sherrill wrote in *The Washington Post.* "Nixon's jowls began hitting his shoulders. Carter couldn't stop that twitchy smile. Bush looked shellshocked. In the case of the Clintons, it's Hillary who has looked more sober, more serious and seriously burdened as her deadline for a health-care reform package approaches."

But Hillary Rodham Clinton wasn't the only one under pressure.

On July 20, six months to the day after Bill Clinton's inauguration, the man who may have been Hillary's closest friend outside her family drove to Fort Marcy Park in Virginia, overlooking the Potomac River.

Vincent W. Foster, Jr., carefully removed his coat and tie and walked to a point on the bluff near a Civil War cannon. He took his 1913 Colt revolver, put the barrel in his mouth and pulled the trigger. That shot still reverberates.

Foster, who had been a colleague of Hillary's at the Rose Law Firm in Little Rock, had also been a friend of Bill Clinton's since his childhood days in Hope, Arkansas. He had certainly been Hillary's closest confidant at Rose, and had joined the White House staff as deputy legal counsel and personal attorney to the Clintons. His dramatic death sent shock waves through the community.

Sidney Blumenthal, in a piece for *The New Yorker*, quoted Hillary as saying "Of a thousand people who *might* commit suicide, I would never pick Vince." But even though the President himself seemed to plead with the media not to try and dissect Foster's decision, saying "No one can ever know why this happened. What happened was a mystery inside of him," the questions lingered.

Blumenthal touched on rumors, apparently baseless but long whispered in Arkansas, about Foster's relationship with Hillary:

In the immediate aftermath of Foster's suicide, people in Washington frantically, and predictably, searched for reasons. . . . Something dark, something other than psychological problems, must lie beneath the surface, it was speculated. There must be another story—one that makes more sense than acute depression. What was Vince Foster's real motive?

Rumors whipped through the city. The Washington Times, *it was said, had for some time been preparing a story that would explain it all. Perhaps Foster had even known of the terrible exposé that was coming and sought to preëmpt it by killing himself. Was he a closet homosexual. . . . Or would the* Washington Times *publish a story about his having had a secret affair with his former law partner Hillary Rodham Clinton? One version had it that the latter story would be published in four parts. . . . A reporter for* The New York Times *called the* Washington Times *seeking information, and wrote that a reporter for the Moonie paper "acknowl-edged he had made preliminary inquires" about Fos-ter. The next day, the* Washington Times *published an editorial headlined "THERE WAS NO VINCENT FOS-TER STORY." "The* Washington Times," *it said, "had nothing on Mr. Foster and was not in the process of developing anything. Zero."*

Although there have been many rumors about Hillary and Vince Foster, no one has ever produced any evidence that their relationship was physical. Foster and his wife Lisa were frequent dinner guests of the Clintons, and they sometimes attended performances together at the Arkansas Repertory Theatre, where Foster served as chairman of the board.

Back in Arkansas, Hillary's friends marveled at the intense focus on the woman they had known for almost two decades. Much of what they read had little to do with the Hillary they knew. They saw the toll the job and the media fascination were taking on her. Like Sherrill, they realized that Hillary was wearing the strain of the job on her face.

Yet they had seen her adjust to a new environment before—in Fayetteville in 1974. During those first years in Arkansas, one of her closest friends was Diane Blair, a professor at the University of Arkansas at Fayetteville.

"A decade before, I had come from Washington to Fayetteville," said Blair, a native of the nation's capital who married a prominent Arkansas attorney named Jim Blair, chief counsel for food-processing giant Tyson Foods. "I knew what it was like to come to a strange place and marry a native son."

"Of course, some of the articles about Hillary coming here were greatly exaggerated. Fayetteville is, after all, a college town, and college towns tend to be more cosmopolitan than other small towns. There are bookstores here. There are people who have traveled widely. It's not as if Hillary was going to some third-world backwater. But it was different. Much different.''

Blair watched as Hillary adjusted.

"Even though it was a college town, there was still that suspicion of uppity women, both in town and at the university," Blair said. "There were older men who would refer to us as 'Little Miss Diane' and 'Little Miss Hillary.' To what extend do you sweetly smile and accept that attitude; knowing those people eventually will die off? And to what extent do you come out and openly confront them? Those were the types of things we discussed.''

Blair said one thing that got Hillary through that trying time—and will get her through the trials at the White House—is her sense of humor. That sense of humor is a quality that rarely is written about.

"Her laugh comes very easy and is quite infectious," Blair said. "It's wonderful to have a friend who instantly gets your jokes and can come back with one of her own. But Hillary is so quick-witted that she has learned to suppress her wit and sense of humor in all but the most intimate gatherings. That's because the meaning of what she says can be twisted. She has taught herself to be extremely careful publicly.

"But if you were to talk with the people who traveled with her during the presidential campaign, they would tell you how much fun they had. That little plane they flew on was a ton of fun to be aboard. Hillary absolutely adored her staff, most of whom were young women. They would play music between stops. They would dance in the aisles. They would talk about movies and boyfriends, and Hillary would join in their conversations. But out in public, any gesture, any word can be misinterpreted. You simply learn not to feed the beast.''

Blair bristles, however, when people talk about Hillary having been muzzled at one point during the campaign.

"It's simply untrue," she said. "I traveled with her some during the campaign, and she was making numerous speeches each day. She would do interviews in the towns she visited. She would do satellite interviews. But most of those interviews were with the local media. The national media were with Bill. And if it's in the local press, it doesn't exist in the minds of most national reporters. So they led people to believe Hillary had been muzzled when, in fact, she was talking every day."

When the national media did report on Hillary, they often got it wrong, according to Blair. "The tea-and-cookies comment on *60 Minutes* is a good example of something that was totally misinterpreted," she said. "I have heard Hillary rebuke people for trying to put down women who choose to stay at home and work there. She's totally devoted to her family and has great respect for others who are devoted to their families."

In June 1993, Hillary called Diane Blair to tell her there was "no place the President would rather flop down" than the Blairs's home on Beaver Lake in northwest Arkansas. The President's busy schedule, however, had not allowed for a visit.

Ann Henry was another Fayetteville friend who watched from afar as Hillary tried to redefine the role of the nation's first lady.

"It takes courage to address problems that everybody knows are there but refuses to talk about," Henry said. "In 1983, Hillary saw there was not enough emphasis on basic skills in education in Arkansas. Why not talk about it? Now, there is a crisis in health care. Why not address it?

"I see a continuity in the work she has done through the years. It goes back to the trips she used to take into inner-city Chicago as a teenager. When you work in an inner city, you clearly see the dichotomy between the haves and the have nots. Hillary understands that dichotomy better than anyone I have ever met and is willing to put together proposals to start addressing it.

She has always been able to see things on a much larger scale than the rest of us. To some extent, the rest of us have blinders on.

"I was a product of the 1950s and all I ever wanted to do was teach. But Hillary wanted to do much, much more. She understood that there were thousands of kids out there who had no spokesperson. She had experiences early on that convinced her of her mission in life. She personifies the woman with a mission, the person who knows exactly what she wants her life to stand for."

And Hillary was also shaped by her Arkansas experience. Though she came to love the state, she had difficulty accepting the pathology of melancholy and self-loathing that seems to afflict so many Southerners.

"There were students who felt that just because they were from Arkansas, there shouldn't be much expected of them," Blair said. "It drove Hillary crazy to find people who were selling themselves short because they were from Arkansas or because they were women. She would do everything she could to encourage people to reach their full potential."

Ann Henry said Hillary had come out of "an extremely competitive environment in which people told her she could do anything. When she was teaching, she asked students to meet a higher standard than they were used to being asked to meet. And she was disappointed when they did not live up to what she expected of them.

"For too long, people in this part of the country have had low self-esteem. We allowed others to set low expectations for us. Students would come here not expecting to do great things. It was bred into them. But it's not what Hillary was used to. She was raised to do great things."

Diane Blair and Ann Henry, friends for almost two decades, watch from a thousand miles away as Hillary tries to do great things as first lady. They, like others who have known Hillary for years, are convinced she is up to the task.

Charlie Cole Chaffin, the only woman in Arkansas's

Senate, understands how difficult it is for Americans to get used to a strong-willed, outspoken First Lady. Chaffin was on the front lines in 1983 when Arkansans had to become accustomed to a strong-willed, outspoken first lady of their state. She's not surprised that Hillary's responded to her critics in much the same fashion she answered them in Arkansas—by pushing her agenda straight ahead. Asked to describe Hillary with a single adjective, Chaffin doesn't hesitate: "Tough."

Remembering the early days of pushing school reform in Arkansas, Chaffin recalls that it wasn't an easy time for Hillary Rodham Clinton. "Neither is this. But she'll do just fine. She always does."

Hillary Rodham Clinton is a revolutionary figure. In an America where innovative, unadulterated thinking is often considered politically unviable, she continues to offer an agenda that is baldly progressive.

Attempts by the right to demonize her as a radical enemy of the family have largely failed, and her approval ratings among the public are now consistently higher than those of the President. She is a role model for girls. She is an argument for education. She is a mother who will get up in the middle of the night to scramble a sick child's eggs. She is, if not the co-president, at least the first advisor to the most powerful leader in the world.

It is, of course, premature to assess her impact. She is still a young woman, and Bill Clinton is less than a year into his first term as president. It is possible that Americans have yet to see the best of Hillary Rodham Clinton, it is likely that her major accomplishments lie ahead.

She is not just a wife who, with the help or a staff and servants, coordinates state dinners and plans White House parties. She helps hire. She helps fire. She shapes policy. She is feared and loathed, loved and respected. She is Hillary Rodham Clinton and she is a long way from Arkansas.

INDEX

Coming Soon

BILL CLINTON
AS THEY KNOW HIM
AN ORAL BIOGRAPHY

By David Gallen
with Philip Martin

An inside look at the makings
of the man and the President

Based on more than 150 interviews

$22.95 Cloth
Gallen Publishing Group
ISBN 0-9636477-2-5